THE
PSYCHOPATH

D0491203

T.A.S.C. LIBRARY LEEDS

260438 7

"The psychopath always fascinates, and this new book rises to the challenge of its subject. The book exhaustively covers everything known about psychopathy to date. It also brings an exciting new theory, exploring the neuro-biological underpinnings of psychopaths' broken emotions. *The Psychopath* will be an engrossing read for any clinician, scientist or student who wants to understand that mysterious individual, the criminal psychopath."

Professor Terrie Moffitt, Institute of Psychiatry, London

"A gem of a contribution to the field of psychopathy, this wonderful resource provides a highly coherent and integrative review of developments in cognitive and affective neuroscience and their implications for understanding the nature of psychopathy. The authors are passionate about their research and this book presents their personal assessment of the field in a remarkably powerful, readable, and detailed manner. The book is an extraordinary accomplishment and a boon for the field."

Professor Joseph Newman, Department of Psychology, University of Wisconsin

"This timely book represents an exciting new synthesis which has taken into account emerging data on the biology of psychopathy, including its neuro-cognitive basis. The authors lucidly describe discoveries about emotional processing in psychopaths and new thinking about its psychiatric nosology. They have performed a notable service in providing this highly readable survey, which summarises objectively the strengths and weaknesses of various theoretical accounts, including their own, and the implications for forensic, adult and child psychiatry."

Trevor Robbins, Professor of Cognitive Neuroscience, University of Cambridge

"A comprehensive summary of recent research on the cognitive, emotional, and neurological correlates to psychopathy. One of the few resources to consider the manifestations of psychopathy throughout the lifespan."

Professor Paul J. Frick, Director, Applied Developmental Psychology Program, University of New Orleans

THE
PSYCHOPATH
EMOTION AND THE BRAIN

James Blair, Derek Mitchell,
and Karina Blair

Blackwell
Publishing

© 2005 by James Blair, Derek Mitchell, and Karina Blair

BLACKWELL PUBLISHING
350 Main Street, Malden, MA 02148-5020, USA
9600 Garsington Road, Oxford OX4 2DQ, UK
550 Swanston Street, Carlton, Victoria 3053, Australia

616·8582

BLA

The right of James Blair, Derek Mitchell, and Karina Blair to be identified as the Authors of this Work has been asserted in accordance with the UK Copyright, Designs, and Patents Act 1988.

All rights reserved. No part of this publication may be reproduced, stored in a retrieval system, or transmitted, in any form or by any means, electronic, mechanical, photocopying, recording or otherwise, except as permitted by the UK Copyright, Designs, and Patents Act 1988, without the prior permission of the publisher.

First published 2005 by Blackwell Publishing Ltd

2   2006

2604387

Library of Congress Cataloging-in-Publication Data

Blair, James, MD.
  The psychopath : emotion and the brain / James Blair, Derek Mitchell, and Karina Blair.
      p. cm.
  Includes bibliographical references and index.
  ISBN–13: 978–0–631–23335–0 (hard cover : alk. paper)
  ISBN–10: 0–631–23335–0 (hard cover : alk. paper)
  ISBN–13: 978–0–631–23336–7 (pbk. : alk. paper)
  ISBN–10: 0–631–23336–9 (pbk. : alk. paper)
1. Antisocial personality disorders. 2. Psychopaths. I. Mitchell, Derek Robert. II. Blair, Karina. III. Title.

RC555.B56 2005
616.85′82—dc22

                                        2005002631

A catalogue record for this title is available from the British Library.

Set in 10/12.5pt Dante
by Graphicraft Ltd, Hong Kong
Printed and bound in the United Kingdom
by TJ International Ltd, Padstow, Cornwall

The publisher's policy is to use permanent paper from mills that operate a sustainable forestry policy, and which has been manufactured from pulp processed using acid-free and elementary chlorine-free practices. Furthermore, the publisher ensures that the text paper and cover board used have met acceptable environmental accreditation standards.

For further information on
Blackwell Publishing, visit our website:
www.blackwellpublishing.com

CONTENTS

FIGURES AND TABLES

Tables

ACKNOWLEDGEMENTS

The authors and publishers gratefully acknowledge the following for permission to reproduce copyright material:

Table 1.1: from T. J. Harpur, R. D. Hare, and A. R. Hakstian (1989), Two-factor conceptualization of psychopathy: Construct validity and assessment implications, *Journal of Consulting and Clinical Psychology*, 1, 6–17. Copyright © 1989 American Psychological Association.

Table 1.2: from D. J. Cooke and C. Michie (2001), Refining the construct of psychopathy: Towards a hierarchical model, *Psychological Assessment*, 13, 171–88. Copyright © 2001 American Psychological Association.

Figure 4.1: from R. J. R. Blair, L. Jones, F. Clark, and M. Smith (1997), The psychopathic individual: A lack of responsiveness to distress cues? *Psychophysiology*, 34, 192–8. With permission from Blackwell Publishing.

Figure 4.2: from R. J. R. Blair, D. G. V. Mitchell, R. A. Richell, S. Kelly, A. Leonard, C. Newman, and S. K. Scott (2002), Turning a deaf ear to fear: Impaired recognition of vocal affect in psychopathic individuals, *Journal of Abnormal Psychology*, 111(4), 682–6. Copyright © 2002 American Psychological Association.

Figure 6.2: reprinted from *Neuroscience Letters*, 328(3), Veit, R., Flor, H., Erb, M., Hermann, C., Lotze, M., Grodd, W., & Birbaumer, N., Brain circuits involved in emotional learning in antisocial behavior and social phobia in humans, 233–6. Copyright © 2002, with permission from Elsevier.

Figure 9.1: figure 1 in Jonathan D. Cohen, Matthew Botvinick, and Cameron S. Carter, Anterior cingulated prefrontal cortex: who's in control?, *Nature Neuro-*

science, 3(5), May 2000, 421–3. Copyright © 2000 Nature Publishing Group. Reprinted by permission of the authors and Nature Publishing Group.

The publishers apologize for any errors or omissions in the above list and would be grateful to be notified of any corrections that should be incorporated in the next edition or reprint of this book.

The views expressed in this book do not necessarily represent the views of National Institutes of Health of the United States.

CHAPTER ONE
WHAT IS PSYCHOPATHY?

Humans have long been concerned by or fascinated with the concept of evil and the people thought to personify evil. Say the word psychopath and most people can easily conjure up an image of someone they believe to embody the word. Some may think of characters from the movies: Hannibal Lecter from *The Silence of the Lambs*, Mr Blonde from *Reservoir Dogs*, Norman Bates from *Psycho*, and Freddy Krueger from *A Nightmare on Elm Street*. Others may gain inspiration from the world of politics and claim that Adolf Hitler, Saddam Hussein, Margaret Thatcher, George W. Bush, or even Bill Clinton is psychopathic. Yet more may consider their current employer or ex-partner to be the ultimate psychopath. However, to help clarify the concept, we will simply describe four cases. These cases are fictionalized; they are amalgamations of individuals with whom we have worked. Only two of these cases presented with psychopathy. However, all four showed high levels of antisocial behavior.

Antisocial children

John

John is an 11-year-old boy from a middle-class family with two professional parents. He began to present with behavioral problems at an early age and was enrolled in a school for children with emotional and behavioral difficulties at the age of 5 years. John began running away from home and school at a young age. Now, he is frequently picked up by the police because he is roaming the streets of the local town late at night. He often spends time with local juvenile delinquents. He recently broke into a construction site and set fire to materials, causing $15,000 worth of damage. John is often cruel to animals. He once dangled his pet hamster over a hot stove and threatened to drop it if his parents did not give him money. He is also frequently violent towards his parents, teachers, and peers. On several occasions he has threatened to hurt his mother, and stashed knives are often retrieved from his bedroom. On one occasion he threw a kitchen knife at his mother. John does not have any genuine friends at school. Teachers often express that they have difficulty treating him kindly as they feel that nice behaviors displayed by him are not at all sincere. He is very boastful about his abilities generally, and has an inflated perception of his intelligence. John sometimes tricks people into thinking that he is simply misunderstood.

Bill

Bill is an 11-year-old boy from a troubled working-class background. His mother and father are both in jail, his father for armed robbery and his mother for drug offenses. He is cared for by his older sister. Bill often presents with oppositional behavior at home and at school. He is rude to teachers, often refusing to complete assignments, and frequently truants. He has stolen merchandise from local shops. He often fights with classmates and has on occasion used a weapon (a brick) in these fights. However, he usually apologizes if he is genuinely to blame. He enjoys playing sports with his classmates. He also often expresses love towards his sister and is comforted when she is present. Bill's emotions can be turbulent. He is often self-deprecating.

We have just described the fictionalized lives of two boys with whom we have worked. Should we consider them both in the same way? Do they both have the same difficulties? Do they both present with psychopathy? They certainly are both antisocial. But is their antisocial behavior due to the same underlying pathology?

From the fourth edition of the *Diagnostic and Statistical Manual* developed by the American Psychiatric Association, we would assume that John and Bill present with the same condition: conduct disorder (CD) (American Psychiatric Association, 1994). The diagnostic criteria associated with CD are listed in the following subsection.

Conduct disorder (CD)

According to the DSM:

> The essential feature of CD is a repetitive and persistent pattern of behavior in
> which the basic rights of others or major age-appropriate societal norms or rules

are violated . . . manifested by the presence of three (or more) of the following criteria in the past 12 months, with at least one criteria present in the past 6 months:

Aggression to people and animals:
  (1) often bullies, threatens, or intimidates others
  (2) often initiates physical fights
  (3) has used a weapon that can cause serious physical harm to others (e.g., a bat, brick, broken bottle, knife, gun).
  (4) has been physically cruel to people
  (5) has been physically cruel to animals
  (6) has stolen while confronting a victim (e.g., mugging, purse snatching, extortion, armed robbery)
  (7) has forced someone into sexual activity.
Destruction of property
  (8) has deliberately engaged in fire setting with the intention of causing serious damage
  (9) has deliberately destroyed others' property (other than by fire setting)
Deceitfulness or theft
  (10) has broken into someone else's house, building, or car
  (11) often lies to obtain goods or favors or to avoid obligations (i.e., "cons" others)
  (12) has stolen items of nontrivial value without confronting a victim (e.g., shoplifting, but without breaking and entering, forgery)
Serious violations of rules
  (13) often stays out at night despite parental prohibitions, beginning before age 13 years
  (14) has run away from home overnight at least twice while living in parental or parental surrogate home (or once without returning for a lengthy period)
  (15) is often truant from school beginning before age 13 years.
                                        (American Psychiatric Association, 1994, p. 85)

In addition, CD should result in "clinically significant impairment in social, academic, or occupational functioning." Interestingly, DSM-IV does acknowledge that individuals who meet criteria for CD are not a homogeneous population. Thus, two forms of CD are specified: childhood- and adolescent-onset types. In childhood-onset type, the onset of at least one criterion characteristic of CD must have occurred prior to 10 years of age. In adolescent-onset type there should not be any criteria characteristic of CD prior to 10 years of age.

So let us consider John and Bill again. Both have engaged in at least three of the diagnostic criteria for CD. John often engages in physical fights, has on occasion used weapons, has been cruel to animals, has engaged in fire setting and has truanted. Bill also often engages in fights, has on occasion used weapons and has truanted. Their behavioral difficulties have affected their academic functioning. Thus, both present with CD. They even present with the same type of CD, childhood-onset type; both presented with at least one of their behavioral criteria before the age of 10. But do John and Bill really have the same condition? We will argue not. We will argue that while John presents with psychopathic tendencies, Bill does not.

Antisocial adults

What about the diagnostic situation for adults? Perhaps this is better. Again, we will consider some example cases.

Ryan

Ryan is in his mid-30s and is serving a life sentence for murder. He has always had a bad temper, and this time what looked like a typical bar-fight ended up costing someone their life. In person, Ryan gives the impression of being a slightly immature, jocular, but earnest adult. Ryan is well liked by both the other inmates and the staff on the wing and does not have any adjudications recorded against him.

Ryan has approximately half a dozen offences on his record beginning at the age of 17 when he received probation for shoplifting. Although he never had any formal contact with the law before his late teens, his parents report that he started getting into trouble at home and at school at the age of 15. His parents found him difficult to manage. He broke curfew, lied frequently, vandalized property, and ran away from home. At school he frequently engaged in fights.

Ryan dropped out of school at the age of 16 and began working as a manual laborer. Although occasionally fired for failing to get along with his co-workers, Ryan maintained gainful employment. However, Ryan drank heavily, and spent his money recklessly, and so often found that he did not have enough money left over to pay his bills. In order to supplement his income, he began to sell marijuana, and occasionally stole equipment from the construction sites he worked on. These activities resulted in Ryan receiving a probation order at the age of 18.

Ryan eventually found employment and moved in with his girlfriend. Despite frequent fighting over Ryan's irresponsible financial habits, continued drug dealing and over-indulgent alcohol use, the relationship remained stable. Over the years, Ryan had two affairs, but ended both because he felt guilty and was worried his girlfriend would find out and leave him.

Ryan's drinking grew worse, and one evening he became involved in a fight at a local bar. The owner of the bar broke up the fight and Ryan was asked to leave. Although normally able to leave a fight, this time Ryan returned and hit his opponent with a bottle, which shattered and caused a fatal gash to the individual's throat. The police were called and Ryan immediately told them what had happened. In court, Ryan entered a plea of guilty.

Tyler

Tyler is in his late 30s and is serving a life sentence for murdering his traveling companion in order to steal his money. On the wing, he is a heavy drug user and dealer. He is lively and entertaining to talk to in small doses, but his conversation with staff always ends up being inappropriate and suggestive. He has had various jobs on the wing, but few have lasted more than a few weeks. He is constantly in trouble due to being unreliable and for having violent outbursts when his expectations are not met. Most of the other inmates treat him with a mixture of fear and respect, which he enjoys.

Tyler's arrest record is several pages long. His first recorded offence occurred at the age of 9 when he stole equipment from his school. Later, at age 11, he was apprehended while attempting to drown a classmate who had refused to hand over his pocket money. When asked what happened to the child, Tyler laughed as he related that the kid was bigger than him and, as a consequence, he had every intention of "finishing the job" had a teacher not intervened.

After that, Tyler's life has been spent in and out of special secure settings as a child, adolescent, and adult. His list of offences includes just about every category of crime imaginable, from shoplifting and robbery, to grievous bodily harm and hostage taking. Tyler has never had a job for more than 2 weeks. Instead, he has lived solely off friends or supported himself through crime such as drug dealing, street thefts, and pimping. He has rarely spent more than a few weeks in one place, preferring to move around frequently to settling in one place. He can appear very friendly, and had no trouble meeting people who were willing to put a roof over his head. Frequently, such arrangements ended with a serious and sometimes violent row, and Tyler would start over again.

Tyler has never been married, but has had several living-in partners. In each case, he moved in with them after "sweeping them off their feet," as he puts it. The longest relationship lasted 6 months, but each was marked by violence and instability. He speaks of countless instances where he was seeing other women while living with another. When asked whether he was ever monogamous,

Tyler says that he has always been monogamous. When this apparent inconsistency is pointed out to him, he denies any contradiction: "I've always been monogamous, because it is physically impossible for me to be in two different places at exactly the same time. Understand?"

There was overwhelming evidence that Tyler committed the crime for which he is now imprisoned; however, in court he pleaded not guilty. He still insists that he is innocent, and shows no regard for the murdered victim or his family. Despite the prospect of spending the rest of his life in prison and repeatedly being told that an appeal is futile, he is very upbeat, and speaks as though his release is imminent.

Antisocial personality disorder (ASPD)

So let us consider Ryan and Tyler. Again, do they present with the same syndrome? According to DSM-IV, they do (American Psychiatric Association, 1994). Both present with antisocial personality disorder (ASPD). The essential feature of APSD is "a pervasive pattern of disregard for, and violation of, the rights of others that begins in childhood or early adolescence and continues into adulthood". The individual must be aged at least 18, show evidence of CD before the age of 15 years, and must not present with antisocial behavior exclusively during the course of schizophrenia or a manic episode. In addition, the individual must present with at least three of the following:

(1) failure to conform to social norms with respect to lawful behaviors as indicated by repeatedly performing acts that are grounds for arrest
(2) deceitfulness, as indicated by repeated lying, use of aliases, or conning others for personal profit or pleasure
(3) impulsivity or failure to plan ahead
(4) irritability and aggressiveness, as indicated by repeated physical fights or assaults
(5) reckless disregard for safety of self or others
(6) consistent irresponsibility, as indicated by repeated failure to sustain consistent work behavior or honor financial obligations
(7) lack of remorse, as indicated by being indifferent to or rationalizing having hurt, mistreated, or stolen from another.

So let us consider Ryan and Tyler again. Both show clear indications of a failure to conform to social norms (1), both show indications of impulsivity, aggressiveness and irresponsibility (3, 4, and 6). Thus both would receive diagnoses of ASPD. However, we will again argue that they do not really have the same condition. We will argue that while Tyler presents with psychopathy, Ryan does not.

Psychopathy

The origins of the current description of the syndrome of psychopathy can be traced back to the work of Cleckley. In his book, *The Mask of Sanity*, Cleckley delineated 16 criteria for the diagnosis of psychopathy (Cleckley, 1941). These include superficial charm, lack of anxiety, lack of guilt, undependability, dishonesty, egocentricity, failure to form lasting intimate relationships, failure to learn from punishment, poverty of emotions, lack of insight into the impact of one's behavior on others, and failure to plan ahead. From these characteristics, and his own clinical impressions, Robert Hare developed the original Psychopathy Checklist (PCL) (Hare, 1980), a formalized tool for the assessment of psychopathy in adults. This has since been revised: the Psychopathy Checklist – Revised (PCL-R) (Hare, 1991). Following the development of the adult PCL-R, assessment tools for the assessment of psychopathy in childhood and adolescence have also been developed. These include the Antisocial Process Screening Device (APSD) (Frick and Hare, 2001a) and the Psychopathy Checklist: Youth Version (Forth et al., 2003; Kosson et al., 2002a). In our work, we have concentrated on using the APSD. It will therefore be the criteria from this measure that we will concentrate on below.

Both the PCL-R and the APSD consist of 20 behavioral items. The PCL-R is scored on the basis of an extensive file review and a semi-structured interview. The APSD is scored on the basis of parental/teacher review. For each behavioral item, an individual can score between 0 and 2 points. The individual's total score can therefore vary from 0 to 40 points. Adults scoring 30 or above on the PCL-R are generally considered psychopathic while those scoring less than 20 are considered non-psychopathic. There are less established criteria for considering a child to present with psychopathic tendencies. However, we have typically used a cut-off of 27 as indicating the child is presenting with psychopathic tendencies. All members of our comparison populations score less than 20 on the APSD.

Psychopathy is a disorder that consists of multiple components ranging on the emotional, interpersonal, and behavioral spectrum. Factor analysis is a means of examining how the items of a given construct hang together. For example, while the PCL-R consists of 20 items that are all thought to contribute something unique to the set of criteria, overlap will exist among items. Consequently, items that correlate with each other can be grouped together to form a cluster of traits, or a factor, that refers to a more general facet of the disorder.

In the original factor analysis of the PCL-R, Harpur and his colleagues incorporated data from six samples and hundreds of individuals to determine that the predecessor to the PCL-R, the PCL, was composed of two correlated factors

(Harpur et al., 1988): interpersonal/affective items and impulsive/antisocial life-style items. The authors argued that although highly correlated, the two factors measured separable components of the disorder and that both factors were required to yield a comprehensive assessment of psychopathy. Subsequently, the PCL-R was established and the two-factor structure was replicated in eight samples involving over 900 prison inmates and 350 forensic patients (Hare et al., 1990). Moreover, the two-factor description of psychopathy has been replicated in Belgian (Pham, 1998), Scottish (Cooke and Michie, 2001), Spanish (Molto et al., 2000), and English (Hobson and Shine, 1998) inmates. The two factors and their constituent parts are described in table 1.1. The initial factor analysis of the APSD similarly identified a two-factor structure. Moreover, these two factors can be described similarly to those obtained with the PCL-R: the first refers to a cluster of items characterized by impulsivity and conduct problems (I/CP) while the second contains items corresponding to a callous and unemo-tional interpersonal style (CU).

Recently, the traditional two-factor description of psychopathy has been ques-tioned both in terms of the persuasiveness of the results and on the statistical techniques utilized (Cooke and Michie, 2001). Instead, Cooke and Michie con-tend that a three-factor solution is more appropriate. In essence, their new description of psychopathy has separated the traditional interpersonal/affective Factor 1 into two components: an interpersonal and an abnormal affect com-ponent (see table 1.2). More recent work has similarly suggested that a three-factor solution might also provide a better fit for data obtained with the APSD (Frick and Hare, 2001b). The identified factors and their constituent items are shown in table 1.3. They are a callous/unemotional dimension (similar to the adult abnormal affect component), a narcissism dimension (overlapping with the adult interpersonal component), and an impulsivity dimension (similar to the adult antisocial behavior component).

According to many of the proponents of the concept of psychopathy, its main advantage over the psychiatric diagnoses of CD and Antisocial Personality Dis-order (ASPD) is that it not only indexes the individual's behavior but also his/her personality (Cleckley, 1941; Hare, 1991). However, this claim has also been used by its critics, who argue that the personality approach requires too much inference and is likely to have low inter-rater reliability (Moran, 1999). But these critiques are easily refuted. Low inter-rater reliability is certainly not a problem associated with PCL-R assessment (Hare, 1991). Moreover, we would argue that the difference between the DSM-IV diagnoses of CD and Antisocial Person-ality Disorder (ASPD) and psychopathy as indexed by the APSD or PCL-R is not really that psychopathy extends the DSM-IV diagnoses because it considers per-sonality, but rather that it extends these diagnoses because it considers emotion. A central argument of this book is that there are many routes to antisocial

Table 1.1 Two-factor model of psychopathy

Factor 1: Interpersonal/affective items	Factor 2: Impulsive/antisocial lifestyle items	Items that fail to load on either factor
1 Glib/superficial charm	3 Need for stimulation/proneness to boredom	11 Promiscuous sexual behavior
2 Grandiose sense of self-worth	9 Parasitic lifestyle	17 Many short-term marital affairs
4 Pathological lying	10 Poor behavioral controls	20 Criminal versatility
5 Conning/manipulative	12 Early behavioral problems	
6 Lack of remorse or guilt	13 Lack of realistic, long-term goals	
7 Shallow affect	14 Impulsivity	
8 Callous/lack of empathy	15 Irresponsibility	
16 Failure to accept responsibility for own actions	18 Juvenile delinquency	
	19 Revocation of conditional release	

Source: Harpur et al. (1989)

Table 1.2 Three-factor model of psychopathy

Arrogant and deceitful interpersonal items	Deficient affective experience	Impulsive and irresponsible items	Items not loading on any of the factors
1 Glibness/superficial charm	6 Lack of remorse or guilt	3 Need for stimulation/proneness to boredom	10 Poor behavioral controls
2 Grandiose sense of self-worth	7 Shallow affect	9 Parasitic lifestyle	11 Promiscuous sexual behavior
4 Pathological lying	8 Callous/lacks empathy	13 Lack of realistic, long-term goals	12 Early behavioral problems
5 Conning/manipulative	16 Failure to accept responsibility for own actions	14 Impulsivity	17 Many short-term marital relationships
		15 Irresponsibility	18 Juvenile delinquency
			19 Revocation of conditional release
			20 Criminal versatility

Source: (Cooke and Michie, 2001)

Table 1.3 Three-factor structure of the APSD*

Callous and unemotional items	Narcissism items	Impulsivity items
3 Concerned about schoolwork[†]	5 Emotions seem shallow	1 Blames others for mistakes
7 Keeps promises[†]	8 Brags excessively	4 Acts without thinking
12 Feels bad or guilty[†]	10 Uses or cons others	9 Gets bored easily
18 Concerned about the feelings of others[†]	11 Teases others	13 Engages in risky activities
19 Does not show emotions	14 Can be charming, but seems insincere	17 Does not plan ahead
20 Keeps the same friends[†]	15 Becomes angry when corrected	
	16 Thinks he/she is better than others	

*Note: items 2 (Engages in illegal activities) and 6 (Lies easily and skillfully) did not load on any factor.
[†]Items that are reverse-scored.

behavior. The advantage of the concept of psychopathy is that it identifies a population who share a common etiology, a dysfunction in specific forms of emotional processing. In contrast, the DSM-IV diagnoses identify the broad category of individuals who engage in antisocial behavior. As such, they identify a highly heterogeneous population who do not share a common etiology.

With respect to this issue of a single or a variety of etiologies, it is useful to consider the contrast between reactive and instrumental aggression.

Reactive and instrumental aggression

A distinction between reactive and instrumental aggression has been made for some time (Barratt et al., 1997, 1999; Berkowitz, 1993; Crick and Dodge, 1996; Linnoila et al., 1983; Vitiello and Stoff, 1997). In reactive aggression (also referred to as affective or impulsive aggression), a frustrating or threatening event triggers the aggressive act and frequently also induces anger. Importantly, the aggression is initiated without regard for any potential goal (for example, gaining the victim's possessions or increasing status within the hierarchy). In contrast, instrumental aggression (also referred to as proactive aggression) is purposeful and goal directed. The aggression is used instrumentally to achieve a specific desired goal (Berkowitz, 1993). This is not usually the pain of the victim but rather the victim's possessions or to increase status within a group hierarchy. Bullying is an example of instrumental aggression and, unsurprisingly, individuals who engage in bullying behaviors frequently engage in other forms of instrumental antisocial behavior in other contexts (Roland and Idsoe, 2001).

The distinction between reactive and instrumental aggression has been criticized because of some difficulty in characterizing the nature of specific human aggressive episodes (Bushman and Anderson, 2001). However, the discriminant validity of instrumental and reactive aggression on a factorial level has been demonstrated; while instrumental and reactive aggression are substantially correlated, a two-factor model fits the data better than a one-factor model (Poulin and Boivin, 2000). In addition, longitudinal studies have shown that while instrumental, but not reactive, aggression predicts later delinquency, high levels of reactive aggression actually weaken the relationship between instrumental aggression and later delinquency (Poulin and Boivin, 2000; Vitaro et al., 1998).

Moreover, there is considerable data suggesting that there are two relatively separable populations of aggressive individuals (Barratt et al., 1999; Connor, 2002; Crick and Dodge, 1996; Linnoila et al., 1983). First, there are individuals who present with solely reactive aggression. Such individuals are particularly indifferent to conventional rules and do not modulate their behavior according to the status of the individuals with whom they are interacting. Individuals with lesions that include orbital frontal cortex may present with elevated levels of reactive aggression (Anderson et al., 1999; Blair and Cipolotti, 2000; Grafman et al., 1996). In addition, individuals with impulsive aggressive disorder can present with elevated levels of reactive aggression (Best et al., 2002; Coccaro, 1998), as can children with bipolar disorder (Leibenluft et al., 2003). The second group of individuals present with elevated levels of both instrumental and reactive aggression. Such individuals are particularly indifferent to moral transgressions and show little indication of guilt or empathy with their victims. Individuals with psychopathy present with highly elevated levels of both instrumental and reactive aggression (Cornell et al., 1996; Williamson et al., 1987). In short, the existence of two relatively separable populations of aggressive individuals (individuals who present with mostly reactive aggression and individuals who present with reactive and instrumental aggression) is strongly supported.

It is important to distinguish between reactive and instrumental aggression because they are mediated by separable neurocognitive systems (Blair, 2001); see chapters 7 and 8. Reactive aggression is the final form of the animal's response to threat. Thus, at low levels of threat, from a distant threat, the animal will freeze. At higher levels, from a closer threat, the animal will attempt to escape the environment. At higher levels still, when the threat is very close and escape is impossible, the animal will display reactive aggression (Blanchard et al., 1977). Individuals may display elevated levels of reactive aggression either because they are, or have recently been, in a situation of considerable threat or frustration, or because of reduced regulation by executive systems of the neural circuitry mediating reactive aggression (see chapter 7).

Instrumental aggression is goal-directed motor activity; the aggression is used to achieve a particular goal such as obtaining another individual's money or increasing status within a group. Indeed, most forms of antisocial behavior (shoplifting, fraud, theft, robbery) are instrumental, goal-directed behaviors. As such, when an individual is engaged in instrumental aggression, he/she is likely to be recruiting the same neurocognitive systems that are required for any other goal-directed motor program. Thus, when considering models of the neurobiology of instrumental aggression, we should be considering whether the model explains why an individual might be particularly predisposed to engage in heightened levels of this form of instrumental behavior. Goal-directed behaviors are performed in expectation of receiving the particular desired reward and if they are not punished. While most individuals are motivated to obtain money, very few attack others to achieve this goal. Moral socialization leads the healthy individual away from antisocial behavior. To explain instrumental aggression seen in individuals with psychopathy, we need an account that explains why socialization is not achieved in this population.

Returning to our examples

So let us return and consider our examples: John, Bill, Ryan, and Tyler. We previously diagnosed John and Bill with CD and Ryan and Tyler with ASPD. However, we also said that whereas John and Tyler present with psychopathic tendencies or psychopathy, Bill and Ryan do not. Let us now consider how we reached this conclusion.

The crucial aspect of psychopathy is not the display of antisocial behavior. Instead, it is the emotional impairment. So when we consider our four examples, we need not only to assess whether they present with antisocial behavior but also whether they present with emotional impairment.

Let us first consider John and Bill. Please take a moment to consider the items on the APSD shown in table 1.3. As can be seen, John shows all the signs of the emotional impairment that is at the center of psychopathy. He does not suffer from guilt or concerns about the feelings of others. He does not keep the same friends and has no real interest in schoolwork. He also shows signs of what Frick and Hare (2001b) have referred to as narcissism. He is very boastful about his abilities and can be insincerely charming. Finally, he also presents with the impulsivity behaviors. He gets bored easily and acts without thinking. In short, John presents with psychopathic tendencies. He would comfortably score over 30 out of 40 on the APSD.

Bill, in contrast, would not. Bill, like John, shows little interest in schoolwork. But he does show guilt and is concerned about the feelings of others, particularly his sister. In short, he does not show the same level of emotional problems that John does. Moreover, with the exception that he can easily become angry, he does not show signs of narcissism. Indeed, Bill is described as self-deprecatory. The closest similarity between Bill and John concerns their impulsivity behaviors: both act without thinking and they do not plan ahead. In short, while Bill does present with serious behavioral problems, he does not present with psychopathy. His score on the APSD would be less than 20 out of 40. We have had many boys like Bill in our studies who have acted as comparison individuals for boys like John. Importantly, boys like Bill do not show the types of neurocognitive impairment that we have found in boys like John.

How about Ryan and Tyler? Taking the two-factor solution of the PCL-R (Harpur et al., 1989), we can see that both would score relatively highly on Factor 2. Both show indications of poor behavioral control, early behavioral problems, impulsivity, and irresponsibility. However, only Tyler shows indications of a need for stimulation and a parasitic lifestyle. But it is in the emotional impairment, Factor 1 behaviors that the difference between Ryan and Tyler immediately becomes apparent. Ryan really does not present with the emotional difficulties that underlie psychopathy. In contrast, Tyler clearly does. He is charming, grandiose, manipulative, and experiences little guilt, empathy, or deep emotional ties.

SUMMARY

In short, the classification of psychopathy can be considered an extension and one form of refinement of the DSM diagnoses of CD and ASPD. Specifically, psychopathy identifies one form of pathology associated with high levels of antisocial behavior; individuals who present with a particular form of emotional impairment. In contrast, the diagnoses of CD and ASPD lead to the gathering together of individuals who present with a variety of different conditions (some of which, we will argue, are not even pathological; see chapter 3). The main goal of this book will be to understand the nature of the emotional impairment shown by individuals with psychopathy.

The implications of the classification

A classification system is only as good as its usefulness. We will argue throughout the book that psychopathy is a very useful description of a particular pathology that has a specific neurocognitive basis. But does giving someone a psychopathy score provide any other form of useful information? Does it allow a more precise prediction of future behavior? The answer is that it does.

One of the major strengths of the PCL-R has been its utility in risk assessment. This is in rather striking contrast to the diagnosis of ASPD. The correlation between recidivism and psychopathy is significantly higher than that of the DSM diagnosis of ASPD (Hemphill et al., 1998).

There are now a relatively large number of studies indicating that individuals with psychopathy reoffend at higher rates than non-psychopathic individuals. For example, in an early study, the PCL-R was administered to 231 offenders prior to release from prisons (Hart et al., 1988). Within 3 years, 25 percent of non-psychopathic individuals had been re-incarcerated. In sharp contrast, 80 percent of the individuals with psychopathy had breached the terms of their release. In another study Serin and Amos (1995) followed 299 offenders, and within 3 years, 65 percent of individuals with psychopathy versus only 25 percent of the non-psychopathic individuals were convicted of a new offence. Such results have been found in European studies also. Thus, in a Swedish sample of forensic patients, Grann et al. (1999) found that individuals scoring above 25 on the PCL-R violently reoffended at a rate of 66 percent versus only 18 percent for those with a score less than 26. In Belgium, the reconviction rates of psychopathic, middle scoring, and low scoring individuals were 44 percent, 21 percent, and 11 percent, respectively (Hare et al., 2000).

An international study of 278 offenders is of particular interest. This found that 82 percent of the individuals with psychopathy but only 40 percent of non-psychopathic individuals were reconvicted of an offence (Hare et al., 2000). In the same group, 38 percent of the high psychopathy group committed a violent offence, but only 2.7 percent of those with a low PCL-R score did. Interestingly, both the individuals with psychopathy and the non-psychopathic individuals failed to show attenuated reconviction rates following treatment after controlling for age and criminal history. However, the pattern of results changes when Factor 1 scores are carefully examined. Participants with high Factor 1 scores reoffended at higher rates if they had been treated: 86 percent as opposed to 59 percent! Similarly striking results have been seen when examining participants who engage in educational and vocational training programs. Here offenders with low Factor 1 scores show an improvement in recidivism rate following the course. However, offenders with high Factor 1 scores are reconvicted at higher rates if they take part in these programs rather than if they do not.

In what is perhaps the most comprehensive review and meta-analysis to date, Hemphill and colleagues (1998) examined nine available published and unpublished prospective studies of psychopathy and recidivism. The length of follow-up for the studies reviewed ranged from 1 to 10.5 years. The authors determined that within a year of release, individuals with psychopathy are three times more likely to recidivate, and four times more likely to recidivate violently. In fact, the relative risk for reoffending (the proportion of psychopathic individuals who reoffend divided by the proportion of non-psychopathic offenders who reoffend) ranged from 1.7 to as high as 6.5 across studies. Taken together, at a 1-year follow-up, the general recidivism rate for individuals with psychopathy was three times higher than that of non-psychopathic individuals and the violent recidivism rate was three to five times higher. Psychopathy is associated with both general and violent recidivism at follow-up lengths of as little as a year, or as long as more than 10 years.

Conclusions

In this chapter, we have considered the nature of psychopathy. We have shown that the classification of psychopathy is not synonymous with the DSM diagnoses of conduct disorder and antisocial personality disorder. We will argue throughout this book that these DSM diagnoses group together a variety of pathologies associated with an increased risk of reactive aggression or antisocial behavior. In contrast, the classification of psychopathy represents a specific pathology where there is not only antisocial behavior but, more importantly, a particular form of emotional dysfunction (see chapters 4 and 8). Crucially, this emotional dysfunction puts the individual at risk for developing heightened levels of goal-directed, instrumental aggression (see chapter 8). In contrast, other pathologies associated with violence put the individual at risk for displaying reactive, frustration/threat-based aggression (see chapter 7).

In short, psychopathy is an emotional disorder, which, if it develops into its full form, puts the individual at risk of repeated displays of extreme antisocial behavior. This antisocial behavior can involve reactive aggression but it is important to note that psychopathy is unique in that it is a disorder that is also associated with elevated levels of instrumental aggression. Psychopathy is a disorder in urgent need of understanding. Without understanding, we will remain unable to efficiently treat it.

CHAPTER TWO
THE BACKGROUND FACTS

In chapter 1, we considered the nature of psychopathy and contrasted psychopathy with the DSM-IV diagnoses of conduct disorder (CD) and antisocial personality disorder (ASPD). In this chapter, we will consider the epidemiology of psychopathy. In particular, we will answer such questions as: How prevalent is psychopathy? Is there a gender imbalance? Are individuals with psychopathy highly intelligent or of lower IQ? And what is the relationship between psychopathy and socioeconomic status (SES). In addition, we will consider the degree to which psychopathy is comorbid with other psychiatric disorders such as attention deficit hyperactivity disorder (ADHD) or schizophrenia.

What is the incidence rate of psychopathy?

Upon first hearing about the behavioral and emotional correlates of psychopathy, people can often recount a story of some distant acquaintance who seems to bear a striking resemblance to the psychopathic individual. This is surprising to people who have always associated the disorder with the infamous few depicted in spectacular media accounts of serial murder and terrorism. Psychopathy is not, however, an esoteric construct that applies only to these extreme individuals. So how prevalent is psychopathy and how likely is it that individuals working outside of a forensic setting will come in contact with the disorder?

The incidence rates of CD in particular but also ASPD are high. According to DSM-IV, in community samples the rates for CD for males range from 6 percent to 16 percent and those for females range from 2 percent to 9 percent. The incidence rates from ASPD in community samples are 3 percent in males and 1 percent in females. In forensic samples, the incidence rate of ASPD is particularly high (comparable studies have not been done for CD). Thus, following a review of 62 studies including 23,000 inmates worldwide, mean incidence rates of ASPD were reported to be 47 percent for male inmates and 23 percent for female inmates (Fazel and Danesh, 2002). Within the US, the prevalence rate appears to be even higher in forensic settings; estimates suggest that between 50 percent and 80 percent of US inmates reach criteria for ASPD (Hart and Hare, 1996).

The prevalence rate of psychopathy is far lower than that of either CD or ASPD. Epidemiological studies examining the incidence of psychopathy in adults in the community have not been conducted. Categorizing individuals using the PCL-R is labor-intensive and requires extensive collateral information. However, preliminary work conducted by Paul Frick using the APSD has examined the incidence rate of psychopathic tendencies in community samples involving children. As discussed in chapter 1, we have used a score of 27 on the APSD as our cut-off point for a classification of psychopathic tendencies in many of our studies (Blair et al., 2001a, b). Using this cut-off results in a prevalence rate of psychopathic tendencies of between 1.23 percent and 3.46 percent (Frick, personal communication); i.e., approximately one quarter of the incidence rate of CD in community samples. Moreover, epidemiological studies examining the prevalence of psychopathy in forensic samples have been conducted. These reveal that while up to 80 percent of US inmates reach diagnostic criteria for ASPD, only 15–25 percent of US inmates meet criteria for psychopathy according to the criteria laid down by the PCL-R (Hare, 1996). In other words, approximately one quarter of those receiving the DSM-IV diagnosis of ASPD meet the criteria for psychopathy. Based on these findings and the 3 percent community incidence rate of ASPD suggested by the DSM-IV, the prevalence of psychopathy can be inferred. If we assume approximately 25 percent of those with a diagnosis of ASPD might meet criteria for psychopathy, we can estimate an incidence rate for psychopathy in males in the community of 0.75 percent.

Incidence and gender

Most work on psychopathy has been conducted largely or almost exclusively on males (Blair et al., 2002; Kiehl et al., 2001; Lorenz and Newman, 2002; Scerbo et al., 1990). Relatively little is known about the causes, assessment, and diagnosis of psychopathy in females (for a recent review see Cale and Lilienfeld, 2002). However, Cleckley, in his original description, considered that the condition was found in men and women; 2 of his 15 patients were female (Cleckley, 1941).

Only one published study has examined PCL-R psychopathy prevalence rates in an incarcerated female sample. Salekin et al. (1997) administered the PCL-R to 103 female inmates and found that 15 percent could be classified as being psychopathic when using a cut-off score of 29. This figure is relatively low compared with the percentages reported in male correctional samples, which range between 15 percent and 30 percent (Hare, 1991, 1996, 1998). However, unpublished data suggest that the correct figure may be higher; i.e., more in accordance with the rate for men (see Hare, 1991).

There are indications that while the callous and unemotional (Factor 1) component of psychopathy is comparable in both males and females, there may be gender differences with respect to the antisocial behavioral component (Factor 2). For example, Strachan and colleagues, in work cited in Hare (1991) reported that the internal consistency of the Factor 2 items was generally low for female offenders. Salekin and colleagues examined the factor structure of the PCL-R in females and reported that while the structure of Factor 1 was highly similar for both male and female offenders, the structure of the behavioral Factor 2 was not (Salekin et al., 1997). Moreover, whereas Factor 1 characteristics were significantly correlated with recidivism ($r = 0.26$) in females, Factor 2 items were not (Salekin et al., 1998). In other words, while the emotional dysfunction associated with psychopathy is found in females, it is not clear that the behavioral manifestation of this dysfunction is identical in both genders. Of course, this is not surprising. The behavioral manifestation of this disorder is likely to be a result of a variety of secondary influences (in addition to the primary effects of the emotional dysfunction). These might vary from social modeling to even such phenomena as physical size.

Incidence and race

Most of the work validating the PCL-R has involved Caucasian inmates. Indeed, it has been speculated that, given evidence that the overrepresentation of minority groups in the US prison system reflects social and economic inequalities, psychopathy may be a less discriminating predictor of criminality in minority groups (Kosson et al., 1990). Due to concerns about the applicability of the PCL-R to different ethnic groups, some of the earlier investigations included only Caucasian participants (Kosson and Newman, 1986; Newman and Kosson, 1986; Newman et al., 1987). More recently, some investigators have analyzed data from African American and Caucasian inmates separately.

While the psychometric properties of the PCL-R appear generally similar for Caucasian, African American and Native American male offenders (Hare, 1991, 2003), evidence exists suggesting that the individual factors may vary depending on the cultural, social, or psychiatric background of the individual. Kosson and colleagues (1990) conducted three studies aimed at examining the validity and reliability of psychopathy scores in African American inmates relative to other ethnic groups. The authors reported that 36.3 percent of African American and

21.6 percent of Caucasian offenders met criteria for psychopathy (more than 30 on the PCL-R) while 8.9 percent of African American and 21.6 percent of Caucasian individuals were classified as non-psychopathic. However, rather than reflecting anything intrinsically different about the prevalence of psychopathy by ethnicity, this inflated rate of psychopathy among the African American group may relate more to problems with assessing the disorder in non-Caucasians. The authors point out that all of the PCL-R ratings were done by Caucasian researchers. Interaction between the ethnicity of the rater and the participant has been identified as a potential source of conflict, and more research investigating this potential confound has been urged (Hare, 2003).

Kosson et al. (1990) also reported that the traditional two-factor structure identified in Caucasian inmates failed to replicate in the African American sample. This result, however, should be interpreted with caution. Thus, in a more recent study, and using more powerful factor analytic techniques, Cooke and colleagues report that the factor structure across ethnic groups was highly similar (Cooke et al., 2001). Interestingly, Cooke and colleagues (2001) also used Item Response Theory (IRT) to examine whether the "metric" or scale of the PCL-R is the same for African Americans and Caucasian Americans. IRT measures the degree to which an underlying trait is needed to be present before individual items are scored positively. The authors found that African American participants received higher ratings at lower levels of the underlying trait than Caucasian individuals in some cases, and lower ratings at higher levels of the trait in other cases. This meant that any small differences across ethnic groups tended to be averaged out. This suggests subtle influences of ethnicity on the behavioral manifestation of psychopathy that may be due to either rater effects or the influence of secondary influences.

Incidence and age

When official rates of crime are plotted against age, an explosion of antisocial behavior is seen during adolescence which peaks sharply at 17 and then rapidly declines in young adulthood (Moffitt, 1993a) (figure 2.1). While part of this explosion is due to an increase in the amount of antisocial behavior individuals express, most is a result of the actual numbers of individuals exhibiting antisocial behavior (Farrington, 1983; Wolfgang et al., 1987). The numbers engaging in antisocial behavior rapidly increase from the age of 7 to 17 (Loeber et al., 1989; Wolfgang et al., 1972). Indeed, by the middle teens so many of the peer group are engaging in some antisocial activity that it can be considered to be normative. Thus, in a community sample of youth in New Zealand, only 7 percent of males reported engaging in *no* delinquent or illegal activities, including

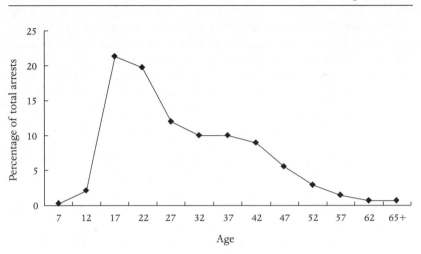

Figure 2.1   Percentage of total arrests as a function of age (figures taken from *Crime in the United States*, Federal Bureau of Investigation and Department of Justice online report, 2003).

relatively minor status offenses such as drinking alcohol and using a fake ID (Krueger et al., 1994). However, following the age of 17 the number of individuals engaging in antisocial behavior declines sharply. By their early 20s, the number of active offenders has gone down by 50 percent while by the age of 28, over 85 percent of former offenders have now desisted (Blumstein and Cohen, 1987; Farrington, 1986). Interestingly, these age-related changes in offending habits occur in most Western nations (Hirschi and Gottfredson, 1983). In line with the above data showing that the level of antisocial behavior declines rapidly with age after 20 years, there are consistent reports that the incidence of the behaviorally based diagnosis of ASPD declines with age (Samuels et al., 1994; Swanson et al., 1994).

The analysis in age-related changes in antisocial behavior prompted authors to consider that there are two forms of conduct disorder: childhood onset and adolescent limited (Hinshaw et al., 1993; Moffitt, 1993a). This subdivision has been incorporated into DSM-IV (see chapter 1) and has predictive power. Specifically, one of the best predictors of which children with severe antisocial behavior are most likely to continue to show antisocial behavior into adulthood is the onset of severe conduct problems prior to adolescence (Loeber, 1991; Robins, 1966). In addition, the children who present with childhood-onset CD display far greater levels of aggression than those who are adolescent limited (Lahey et al., 1998).

It is generally considered that there is a biological basis to childhood-onset CD. However, although Moffitt (1993a) suggested that there is one form of childhood-onset CD, it is likely that there are actually several forms with psychopathy being only one of them (Blair, 2001; Silverthorn and Frick, 1999). We will discuss other forms of childhood-onset CD in chapter 7. Adolescent-onset CD will be considered in chapter 3.

Research investigating the course of psychopathy as a function of age is primarily cross-sectional in nature. This research has revealed that while Factor 1 scores tend to be robust over time, Factor 2 scores show a reduction in time. For example, in an early study Harpur and Hare examined the relationship between PCL scores and age in 889 male prison inmates with an age range as great as 16 to 69 (Harpur and Hare, 1994). They found that the mean score and variance of Factor 1 were similar across five age cohorts. In contrast, Factor 2 scores showed a significant decrease, and the variance of these scores increased as the age of the participants increased. In the same population, this decline in Factor 2 scores was mirrored by a decline in the prevalence of ASPD.

Given that this was a cross-sectional rather than a longitudinal design, one could argue that the results might reflect differences across generations rather than any real effects of age. However, even if this were the case, the results still suggest that Factor 1 scores are more robust to cross-generational effects than Factor 2. Furthermore, an earlier study that included both cross-sectional and longitudinal data showed similar results for both analyses (Hare et al., 1988a).

Incidence and socioeconomic status

There is a considerable literature indicating a relationship between lower SES and heightened risk of presenting with antisocial behavior. However, there is rather less indication of an association between psychopathy and SES (Frick et al., 1994; Hare, 2003). Moreover, any existing relationship appears to be with the antisocial behavior component of psychopathy (Factor 2) rather than the emotional dysfunction component (Factor 1). Thus, Social Index, occupational class of inmate or father, and family background correlate with Factor 2 scores but not with Factor 1 scores (Hare, 2003), though a 7-point scale of SES ranging from unemployed to professional (Hollingshead and Redlich, 1958), used with the same sample, revealed no significant correlations with either Factor 1, Factor 2, or total scores (Hare, 2003).

Incidence and IQ

One of the urban myths regarding psychopathic individuals is that they are of above-average intellect. Indeed, given their confidence, brazen behavior, and superficial charm, they may appear so. However, empirical evidence does not support this stereotype. Thus, Hare and colleagues, using the Wechsler Adult Intelligence Scale, found little correlation between IQ and both PCL-R total scores and emotional dysfunction (Factor 1) scores. However, there was a modest negative correlation with antisocial behavior (Factor 2) scores (Hare, 1991); i.e., lower IQ was associated with higher levels of antisocial behavior. Similar findings have been reported with children with psychopathic tendencies (Frick et al., 1994). Similarly, Hare, using a battery of tests that measure over 20 mental abilities, found no correlation between cognitive functioning and Factor 1 or total PCL-R scores, but did find a significant negative correlation ($r = -0.46$) between Factor 2 and "crystallized intelligence" (Hare, 2003). Crystallized intelligence can be considered a measure of accumulated knowledge. It is highly influenced by an individual's experience (i.e., their schooling and involvement in cultural activities). Moreover, Hare, in a comprehensive review, reports a consistent, though modest, negative correlation between education and Factor 2, but not Factor 1, scores (Hare, 2003). Overall, then, there is no evidence to suggest that individuals with psychopathy have superior IQ compared to individuals with no psychopathy. However, antisocial behavior does appear to be linked with lower intelligence and lower level of schooling.

Issues of comorbidity

Little work has investigated the issue of comorbidity in psychopathy; i.e., whether individuals with the disorder present with other psychiatric conditions in addition to psychopathy more often than would be expected by chance. Part of this is because studies of comorbidity are fraught with difficulties. The most serious of these is selection bias. For example, studies that explore the diagnoses of individuals who are inpatients in a particular forensic psychiatric institution may say more about the selection of patients in the institution than the reality of the comorbidity of the disorders (Jackson et al., 1991). However, conditions which might be considered comorbid with psychopathy are schizophrenia, anxiety and mood disorders, substance abuse disorders, and ADHD. Each of these will be considered in turn.

Schizophrenia

While there is evidence that schizophrenia is associated with an increased risk of violence (Walsh et al., 2002), there appears to be little consistent evidence that schizophrenia is associated with psychopathy in particular, or even ASPD more generally. This is not surprising; schizophrenia has been associated with general cortical decline that is marked for regions of frontal cortex, particularly the dorsolateral prefrontal cortex. In contrast, there have been consistent demonstrations that psychopathy is not associated with impairment in dorsolateral prefrontal cortex (Blair et al., 2001a; Hare, 1984; LaPierre et al., 1995; Mitchell et al., 2002).

Anxiety and mood disorders

Many anxiety and mood disorders (e.g., generalized anxiety disorder, post-traumatic stress disorder (PTSD), and major depressive disorder) are all associated with an increased risk of aggression (Corruble et al., 1996; Pine et al., 2000; Robins et al., 1991; Russo and Beidel, 1993; Silva et al., 2001; Zoccolillo, 1992). For example, a recent study reported that anxiety disorders were common among a majority (61 percent) of patients with ASPD (Tomasson and Vaglum, 2000). In addition, in a recent community sample of almost 6,000 individuals, over half (54.33 percent) of the 3.3 percent of adults with ASPD had a comorbid anxiety disorder (lifetime) (Goodwin and Hamilton, 2003). Similarly, 42.31 percent of adults with a history of CD (9.4 percent) but who did not meet criteria for ASPD had a lifetime anxiety disorder. Social phobia and PTSD were associated with significantly increased odds of ASPD, after adjusting for differences in socio-demographic characteristics and other psychiatric comorbidity. However, in this study, major depressive disorder was not significantly associated with ASPD after adjusting for the presence of anxiety disorders (Goodwin and Hamilton, 2003).

In contrast to ASPD, psychopathy has traditionally been considered to be marked by reduced anxiety levels (Cleckley, 1976; Eysenck, 1964; Gray, 1987; Hare, 1970; Lykken, 1995; Patrick, 1994; Trasler, 1973); see also chapters 4 and 8. Contrary to this view, some data has been presented suggesting that both the emotional dysfunction Factor 1 and the antisocial Factor 2 dimensions of psychopathy are independent of level of anxiety (Schmitt and Newman, 1999). However, this study did not partial out the effects of the level of antisocial behavior from the effects of the emotional dysfunction. This was unfortunate given the well-documented positive correlation between anxiety and aggression in antisocial populations (Pine et al., 2000; Robins et al., 1991; Russo and Beidel, 1993; Zoccolillo, 1992). Indeed, those studies that did examine the Factor 1 and the Factor 2 dimensions of psychopathy independently reported that anxiety level is *inversely* associated with the Factor 1 dimension of psychopathy but *positively* associated with the Factor 2 dimension (Frick et al., 1999; Patrick, 1994; Verona et al., 2001). In short, increases in anxiety are associated with increases in antisocial behavior but decreases in the emotional component of psychopathy. Less work has considered the relationship between depression and anxiety. Yet here too it appears that depression is inversely associated with psychopathy (Lovelace and Gannon, 1999).

Substance abuse disorders

Two studies have directly examined the assocation between psychopathy as assessed by the PCL-R and substance abuse. In a sample of 360 male inmates, Smith and Newman examined the cooccurrence of psychopathy and lifetime prevalence of alcohol and drug disorders as defined by the DSM-IV (Smith and Newman, 1990). They found that individuals with psychopathy were significantly more likely to qualify for diagnoses of alcoholism, drug disorder, and polysubstance disorder. They also reported that while substance disorders were correlated with Factor 2 scores, they were unrelated to Factor 1 scores. These results were supported by a study and small meta-analysis conducted by Hemphill and colleagues (1994). The authors did find a correlation between DSM-IV diagnoses of drug abuse, number of drugs tried, drug-related offences, and age at first alcohol use. They also concluded that the substance abuse was more closely related to an antisocial lifestyle (Factor 2) rather than the emotional dysfunction of psychopathy (Factor 1).

Attention deficit hyperactivity disorder

ADHD is defined as "a persistent pattern of inattention and/or hyperactivity – impulsivity that is more frequent and severe than is typically observed in individuals at a comparable level of development" (American Psychiatric Association, 1994). Prevalence rates vary from 1 percent up to 20 percent (DuPaul, 1991). Considerable work has demonstrated that CD and ADHD are highly comorbid (Biederman et al., 1991; Hinshaw, 1987; Taylor et al., 1986). More recently, the issue of comorbidity between psychopathic tendencies and ADHD has been addressed also, with the suggestion being that these classifications are highly comorbid also (Babinski et al., 1999; Barry et al., 2000; Colledge and Blair, 2001; Lynam, 1996). Indeed, in our own work we find that over 75 percent of children with psychopathic tendencies also meet criteria for ADHD (Colledge and Blair, 2001). We will return to the issue of ADHD and psychopathic tendencies in chapter 9.

Conclusions

In this chapter we considered the epidemiology of psychopathy. We have reported that psychopathy is not a common disorder, being substantially less frequent than childhood CD or adult ASPD. We have estimated incidence rates of 1.23 percent to 3.46 percent for psychopathic tendencies (as opposed to 6–16 percent for CD) and an incidence rate for psychopathy in males in the community of 0.75 percent (given a 3 percent incidence rate of ASPD in male community samples and data that approximately 25 percent of those with ASPD meet criteria for psychopathy). With respect to females, the data is sparse; however, we have estimated an incidence rate for psychopathy in females in the community of 0.25 percent (given a 1 percent incidence rate of ASPD in male community samples and data that approximately 25 percent of those with ASPD meet criteria for psychopathy).

In this chapter, we also reported that age, SES, and IQ are all inversely related to antisocial behavior. The older an individual is (after the age of 20 years), the higher their SES, and the higher their IQ, the less likely they are to engage in antisocial behavior. Moreover, we also reported that all of these variables are inversely associated with the antisocial behavior (Factor 2) component of psychopathy. However, it was interesting to note that none of these variables are associated with the emotional dysfunction (Factor 1) component of psychopathy.

In the final part of this chapter, we considered disorders that might be comorbid with psychopathy. We concluded that while many disorders such as schizophrenia, generalized anxiety disorder, PTSD and major depressive disorder, substance abuse disorders, and ADHD are associated with an increased risk of antisocial behavior, only substance abuse disorders and ADHD are associated with an increased risk of psychopathy. Indeed, psychopathy is associated with decreased levels of anxiety and depression. We will consider the association between psychopathy and decreased levels of anxiety and depression in chapters 4 and 8, and the relationship between psychopathy and ADHD in chapter 9.

CHAPTER THREE

WHAT IS THE ULTIMATE CAUSE OF PSYCHOPATHY?

In chapters 1 and 2, we considered the phenomenological aspects of psychopathy: how it is defined and epidemiological findings associated with the disorder. In this chapter, we will begin to consider the cause of psychopathy. Now, there are many levels of causal explanation and any account at any single level is rarely likely to be satisfactory (Morton and Frith, 1993). For example, to say that a disorder is caused by, say, amygdala dysfunction or frontal lobe damage is not terribly useful. It does not tell us anything about what capacities this dysfunction is disrupting and therefore prevents us from adequately understanding why this dysfunction should give rise to this set of behavioral difficulties.

In this book, we will suggest that psychopathy is caused by an impairment in performing specific forms of emotional learning (see chapters 5 and 8). However, this cognitive-level impairment is symptomatic of an underlying dysfunction involving specific neural and neurotransmitter systems (chapter 8). In short, the cognitive impairment is caused by dysfunction at another level of causal explanation, the biological. Of course, while the consideration of both levels may prove more informative, it is still an incomplete account of psychopathy. Thus, even with a combined cognitive and biological account, one must consider the question: what could cause the disturbance in the functioning of the neural/neurotransmitter system? Here there are always two possibilities: a fundamental biological (i.e., genetic) contribution, or a primarily environmental one.

In this chapter, we will consider data on these two forms of ultimate cause of psychopathy. But, in addition, we will consider data on these two forms of ultimate cause with respect to the other form of antisocial behavior syndrome – pathology that is expressed as an increased risk of reactive aggression. In chapter 1, we noted that there were at least two populations of antisocial individuals: those presenting with instrumental and reactive aggression and those presenting with predominantly reactive aggression. Individuals with psychopathy are a salient example of a pathology associated with both instrumental and reactive aggression. With respect to reactive aggression alone, many conditions increase the probability of the display of this form of behavior; e.g., prior exposure to abuse (Farrington and Loeber, 2000; Widom, 1992), post-traumatic stress disorder (Cauffman et al., 1998; Silva et al., 2001; Steiner et al., 1997), depression and anxiety (Pine et al., 2000; Robins et al., 1991; Russo and Beidel, 1993; Vitaro et al., 2002; Zoccolillo, 1992), orbital frontal cortex damage (Anderson et al., 1999; Grafman et al., 1996; Pennington and Bennetto, 1993), intermittent explosive disorder/impulsive aggressive disorder (Coccaro, 1998), and childhood bipolar disorder (McClure et al., 2003). We will consider potential genetic contributions to psychopathy and disorders associated with predominantly reactive aggression. We will then consider potential social causes for these two forms of pathology.

A genetic basis to psychopathy?

Growing evidence is emerging to suggest a genetic contribution to psychopathy. Early twin, adoption, and family studies indicated the heritability of antisocial behavior (Rhee and Waldman, 2002). However, such studies are difficult to interpret. Most antisocial behavior is goal directed: the individual mugs the victim for their wallet, the individual steals the bag to obtain its contents, the individual engages in an elaborate sting operation to gain another person's money. It is extremely unlikely that there is a direct genetic contribution to these specific *behaviors,* or at least it is as likely as there is a direct genetic contribution to an individual using a light switch so that he/she can navigate a room. An individual learns to use a light switch, and under particular conditions an individual might learn to mug people for their wallets. However, where genetics *are* likely to play a role is in determining the probability that the individual will *learn* an antisocial strategy to gain money (mugging other people) as opposed to a strategy sanctioned by society (using an ATM machine at the end of the working day). Many individuals have argued that the emotional dysfunction shown by individuals with psychopathy makes them more likely to learn antisocial strategies to reach goals (Blair, 1995; Eysenck, 1964; Lykken, 1995; Trasler, 1973); see chapter 8. This suggests that there may be a genetic contribution to the emotional dysfunction *behind* the behavior, and that it is this which results in an apparent genetic contribution to antisocial behavior. Recent data suggests that there is indeed a genetic contribution to the emotional dysfunction facilitating antisocial behaviors.

Blonigen and colleagues (2003) collected data from 353 adult male twins using the self-report Psychopathic Personality Inventory (PPI) (Lilienfeld and Andrews, 1996). The PPI includes 163 items and forms a global index of psychopathy with eight subscales: "machiavellian egocentricity," "social potency," "fearlessness," "coldheartedness," "impulsive nonconformity," "blame externalization," "care-free nonplanfulness," and "stress immunity." Most of the individual subscales showed moderate heritability (h^2 = 0.29–0.56) and negligible shared environmental influence (Blonigen et al., 2003). Moreover, in a considerably larger study, examining almost 3,500 twin pairs within the Twins Early Development Study (TEDS), the callous and unemotional component of psychopathic tendencies was indexed at age 7 (Viding et al., in press). This study revealed a significant group heritability of h^2_g = 0.67 and no shared environmental influence on the callous – unemotional component; i.e., genetic factors account for two thirds of the difference between the callous – unemotional probands and the population.

SUMMARY

> In short, a strong case can be made that there is a genetic contribution to the emotional dysfunction component of psychopathy, which puts the individual at greater risk of developing the full syndrome.

The genetics of reactive aggression

A dedicated neural circuitry allows the expression of reactive aggression, and humans share this circuitry with other mammalian species (Gregg and Siegel, 2001; Panksepp, 1998); see figure 3.1. This circuitry will be discussed in detail in chapter 7. For the moment, we will just consider it as basic threat circuitry. It is the system that responds to basic threats. At low levels of stimulation, from a distant threat, it initiates freezing. At higher levels, from a closer threat, it initiates escape-related behavior. At higher levels still, when the threat is very close and escape is impossible, it initiates reactive aggression. This basic threat circuitry is regulated by executive regulatory systems, which will also be discussed in considerably greater detail in chapter 7. These regulatory systems are considered to be able to either augment or suppress the baseline level of stimulation of the basic threat circuitry. Augmentation of the baseline stimulation level will increase the risk of reactive aggression; a threat stimulus will have to activate the circuitry to significantly less of a degree in order to initiate reactive aggression. Suppression of the baseline stimulation level will decrease the risk of reactive aggression; a threat stimulus will have to activate the circuitry significantly more in order to initiate reactive aggression.

Genetic effects might be able to influence the functioning of the circuitry mediating/regulating reactive aggression in two main ways: first, by having an

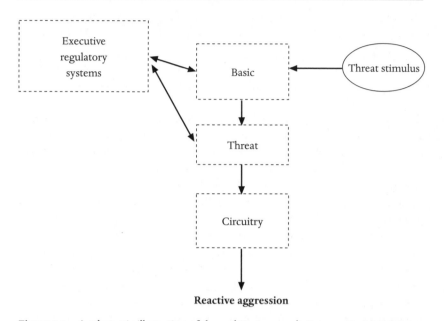

Reactive aggression

Figure 3.1 A schematic illustration of the architecture mediating reactive aggression.

effect on the average stimulation level of the basic threat circuitry, and second, by influencing the efficacy of the executive regulatory systems. We will consider these two possibilities in turn.

A genetic contribution to the average baseline stimulation level of the basic threat circuitry

It is probable that endogenous factors may predispose an individual's basic threat responsiveness to be either high or low. As noted above, an increased risk of reactive aggression is seen in children, and adults, with depression and anxiety. Importantly, recent work has shown that the relationship between depression/anxiety and aggression applies to reactive, but not instrumental, aggression (Vitaro et al., 2002). Recent positions on depression and anxiety stress the role of over-activity in the basic threat circuitry, particularly within the amygdala (Drevets, 2003; Kagan and Snidman, 1999). It is plausible that this over-activity has a genetic basis (Hettema et al., 2001; Johnson et al., 2002). We are not going to comment on the specifics of the proposal, which genes, and how they might be affecting the stimulation level of the basic threat circuitry. However, we believe that endogenous factors that predispose an individual to depression and anxiety may also increase the probability that they will express reactive aggression, especially in dangerous and criminogenic environments (Raine, 1993).

A genetic contribution to the executive regulatory systems

There are at least two psychiatric conditions that appear to be related to disruption of the executive regulatory systems: intermittent explosive disorder/impulsive aggressive disorder (Coccaro, 1998) and childhood bipolar disorder (McClure et al., 2003). Patients with both disorders express irritability and are at higher risk for reactive aggression. Data with these patients will be discussed in more detail in chapter 7. It is more than possible that the basis of these disorders is genetic; there may be genetic contributions to the efficacy of the executive regulatory systems. One way that this might occur is through a genetic contribution to serotonergic functioning. Serotonin has long been implicated in the modulation of aggression (reactive aggression in particular) and impulsivity (Brown et al., 1979; Lee and Coccaro, 2001; Swann, 2003). Generally, experimental manipulations which increase serotonin receptor activation have been found to decrease aggression, and those which decrease receptor activation have been found to increase aggression (see Bell et al., 2001; Shaikh et al., 1997).

SUMMARY

In short, there are likely potential genetic contributions to the baseline stimulation level of the basic threat circuitry as well as to the efficacy of the executive regulatory systems.

Social contributions to aggression

In the following subsections we will consider social contributions to the emergence of aggression. Specifically, in the first subsection, we will evaluate whether there could be a social basis to psychopathy (i.e., causes of heightened levels of reactive *and* instrumental aggression) or pathologies giving rise to heightened levels of reactive aggression. In addition, we will consider, in the second subsection, whether there might be social factors that might not cause the pathology *per se* but which have an influence on how the pathology is manifested.

Social bases to aggression

In this subsection, we will consider possible social bases to either psychopathy or pathologies giving rise to heightened levels of reactive aggression. Two specific potential social causes will be considered: environmental insult during gestation and the impact of environmental stressors.

Environmental insult during gestation

Birth complications such as anoxia (lack of oxygen), forceps delivery, and pre-eclampsia (hypertension leading to anoxia) are environmental factors that can give rise to brain damage. Several studies have shown that babies who suffer birth complications are more likely to develop conduct disorder (CD) and delinquency, and commit violence in adulthood, particularly when other psychosocial risk factors are present (Raine, 2002a). Raine and colleagues (1994a) prospectively assessed birth complications and maternal rejection at age 1 year in 4,269 live male births in Copenhagen, Denmark. Birth complications significantly interacted with maternal rejection of the child in predicting violent offending at age 18 years. Only 4 percent of the sample had both birth complications and maternal rejection, but this small group accounted for 18 percent of all the violent crimes committed by the entire sample (Raine et al., 1994a). Other studies have reported similar results. Thus, a prospective longitudinal study of 867 males and females from the Philadelphia Collaborative Perinatal Project found that those with both pre/perinatal disturbances and a disadvantaged familial environment were much more likely to become adult violent offenders (Piquero and Tibbetts, 1999). Moreover, pregnancy complications interacted with poor parenting in predicting adult violence in a large Swedish sample (Hodgins et al., 2001). Of course, it should be noted that there have been reports suggesting no relationship between obstetric complications and risk for antisocial behavior (Laucht et al., 2000). In addition, there has also been data suggesting that obstetric complications have a main effect on risk for antisocial behavior and do not need to interact with psychosocial risk factors (Hodgins et al., 2002).

Minor physical anomalies (MPAs) are relatively minor physical abnormalities consisting of such features as low-seated ears, adherent ear lobes, and a furrowed tongue. MPAs have been associated with disorders of pregnancy and are thought to be a marker for fetal neural maldevelopment toward the end of the first 3 months of pregnancy. MPAs can be caused by environmental factors acting on the fetus, such as anoxia, bleeding, and infection, although they can also have a genetic basis (Guy et al., 1983).

MPAs, like obstetric complications, have also been linked to the development of CD, delinquency, and violence in adulthood, again particularly when other psychosocial risk factors are present (Raine, 2002a). Thus, MPAs, assessed by an experienced pediatrician in a sample of 129 12-year-old boys, were found to be related to violent offending as assessed 9 years later when participants were aged 21 years (Mednick and Kandel, 1988). Interestingly, when participants were divided into those from unstable, non-intact homes versus those from stable homes, it was found that MPAs only predicted violence in those individuals raised in unstable home environments. Similarly, in a study of 72 male offspring of psychiatrically ill parents, those with both MPAs and family adversity had especially high rates of adult violent offending (Brennan et al., 1997). In addition, MPAs in 7-year-olds who also had environmental risk predisposed these individuals for CD at age 17 (Pine et al., 1997).

Unfortunately, the literature has not considered whether birth complications/ MPAs are a risk factor for the emergence of psychopathy or syndromes linked to heightened levels of reactive aggression. Moreover, there has been little consideration of why birth complications or problems during pregnancy, as indicated by MPAs, should interact with psychosocial behavior. There have been suggestions that "the presence of a negative psychosocial factor is required to 'trigger' the biological risk factor" (Raine, 2002a, p. 426). It is unclear, however, how a psychosocial factor could trigger the biological risk factor. Such a suggestion implies that the presence of the psychosocial factor triggers the biological risk factor to operate such that antisocial behavior is inevitable. This appears unlikely. For example, consider the dichotomy of instrumental and reactive aggression. Instrumental aggression is goal-directed behavior. It appears difficult to imagine how a particular state of a biological risk would *inevitably* result in high levels of a specific form of instrumental behavior, i.e., instrumental aggression. A similar argument can be made for reactive aggression. Reactive aggression is a response to threat or frustration. It will not occur in the absence of environmental input. But it is not that the environmental input triggers the system into a state such that reactive aggression will be regularly displayed. Rather it is that reactive aggression will not be displayed without some form of environmental stimulus (such as an imagined threat).

SUMMARY

Birth complications, or problems during pregnancy as indicated by MPAs, are risk factors for antisocial behavior, particularly violent antisocial behavior, and particularly if they occur when other psychosocial risk factors are present (Mednick and Kandel, 1988; Raine, 2002b). Unfortunately, to our knowledge, no studies have been conducted evaluating whether birth complications and MPAs are associated with an increased risk for instrumental or reactive aggression or both. An increased risk for instrumental aggression would suggest that birth complications and MPAs are associated with dysfunction in systems responsible for emotional learning. An increased risk for reactive aggression would suggest that birth complications and MPAs are associated with dysfunction in systems responsible for the regulation of the basic threat system (see figure 3.1). We believe it far more likely that birth complications and MPAs are associated with dysfunction in systems responsible for the regulation of the basic threat system (and thus an increased risk for reactive aggression). Indeed, there has been some work with animals showing that perinatal distress does indeed lead to hypofunction of systems involved in the regulation of emotional responding (Brake et al., 2000). We believe, on the basis of the current evidence, that it is unlikely that birth complications are associated with an increased risk for the instrumental aggression seen in individuals with psychopathy.

THE IMPACT OF ENVIRONMENTAL STRESSORS

It is clear that environmental stressors can affect the development of the brain. There are three ways in which this could occur. First, environmental stressors may lead, effectively, to brain damage. Thus, there are suggestions that environmental stress, such as that occurring as a consequence of abuse, may give rise to a breakdown in hippocampal function (Bremner et al., 1995). Second, environmental stressors may change the baseline activation of the neural systems that mediate an organism's basic response to threat. Third, environmental stressors may alter the level of hormonal response to threat.

Environmental stress, such as that occurring as a consequence of abuse, has been considered to give rise to a breakdown in hippocampal function (Bremner et al., 1995). This occurs because when the amygdala responds to stress/threats, it sends messages to the hypothalamus, which in turn sends messages to the pituitary gland, resulting in the release of the hormone adrenocorticotropic hormone (ACTH). ACTH passes through the bloodstream to the adrenal gland, resulting in the release of the steroid hormone cortisol. Cortisol binds to receptors in the hippocampus. These are part of a control system that helps regulate the amount of adrenal steroid hormone released (Jacobson and Sapolsky, 1991); when the hormone binds to these receptors, messages are sent to the hypothalamus and, in turn, the pituitary and adrenal glands to inhibit the release of the hormones (see also chapter 7). However, if a stressful event persists for too long, the hippocampus begins to falter in its ability to control the release of the stress hormones and to perform its routine functions (Jacobson and Sapolsky, 1991). More strikingly, stress can result in a shriveling of the dendrites of the hippocampus. This damage, if the stress is prolonged, can become irreversible (McEwen et al., 1992a, b). That is, the strong suggestion from these studies is that the neural system of the hippocampus can be damaged by environmental stressors.

If psychopathy could be considered to be due to hippocampal damage, it would then be plausible to suggest that a social cause account of psychopathy might be appropriate. However, while there have been claims that psychopathy is related to hippocampal dysfunction (Gorenstein and Newman, 1980; Newman, 1998), these claims were based on earlier ideas about the function of the hippocampus (Gray, 1971). More recent work considers the hippocampus to be involved in memory and spatial processing (Burgess et al., 2001; O'Keefe, 1991). It is unclear why impairment in either memory or spatial processing would cause psychopathy. In contrast, neural systems that do appear to be implicated in psychopathy, such as the amygdala and orbital frontal cortex (see chapter 8), have yet to be found to be damaged by environmental stressors. Indeed, recent data suggest that the same environmental stressors (e.g., chronic immobilization stress) that give rise to dendritic atrophy and debranching in CA3 pyramidal neurons of the hippocampus give rise to dendritic *arborization* in the basolateral nucleus of the amygdala (Vyas et al., 2002). In other words, stress augments rather than damages the amygdala (see also chapter 7). This would suggest, given that the amygdala is part of the basic threat circuitry depicted in figure 3.1 (see also chapter 7), that stress might selectively increase the risk for reactive aggression but would not lead to the instrumental aggression seen in individuals with psychopathy.

In addition to data suggesting that stress leads to dendritic arborization in the basolateral nucleus of the amygdala, there are other data suggesting that stress may increase the neuronal responsiveness of the basic threat circuitry depicted in figure 3.1. Thus, environmental stressors may change the baseline activation of the neural systems that mediate an organism's basic response to threat. Work with animals has shown that repetitive electrical stimulation of the superior colliculus, another component of the basic threat circuitry, can lead to a long-term (at least 3 months) increase in basic threat-related responsiveness (King, 1999). In addition, there is abundant evidence that environmental stressors may alter the level of hormonal response to threat (Bremner and Vermetten, 2001; Charney, 2003; Heim et al., 1997; Levine et al., 1993; Liu et al., 1997; Plotsky and Meaney, 1993; Stanton et al., 1988). This, again, will lead to an increase in basic threat-related responsiveness (see chapter 7 for greater details).

SUMMARY

In short, environmental stressors can lead to shrinkage of the hippocampus. However, reduced hippocampal functioning has not been empirically related to an increased risk of either instrumental or reactive aggression. Environmental stress is linked to increased dendritic arborization in the basolateral nucleus of the amygdala, increases in the neuronal responsiveness of the basic threat circuitry, and increases in the hormonal responses to threat. All three of these effects should lead to increased responsiveness of the basic threat circuitry. In short, all three of these effects would be expected to increase the risk of reactive aggression and, indeed, do so (see chapter 7). As they increase the responsiveness of the basic emotional circuitry, they would not be expected to increase the risk of psychopathy (which is associated with decreased emotional responding).

Social contributions to aggression

In the above subsection, we considered whether social factors could cause psychopathy or an increased risk of reactive aggression. We concluded that both birth trauma and environmental stressors increase the risk of reactive aggression; birth trauma by leading to dysfunction in executive regulatory systems and environmental stressors by increasing the responsiveness of the basic threat circuitry. We concluded that, in the absence of data that environmental stressors can damage areas related to the emergence of psychopathy, there are no data to support a social causal explanation of psychopathy. However, this is not to suggest that social factors do not moderate the behavioral manifestation of the disorder (or modify the probability of reactive aggression). In this section, we will consider social moderators of the expression of psychopathy and reactive aggression.

SES, CONSTRAINTS ON CHOICE, AND MOTIVATION

As discussed in chapter 1, individuals with psychopathy are notable for the degree of instrumental, goal-directed antisocial behavior. The claim will be made throughout this book that the emotional deficit present in individuals with psychopathy interferes with socialization such that individuals with the disorder do not find the prospect of goal-directed antisocial behavior aversive (see chapters 4, 5, and 8). However, such a model does not suggest that the emotional deficit associated with psychopathy in itself motivates an individual to offend.

Much antisocial behavior shown by individuals with psychopathy is instrumental in nature – it has the goal of gaining another's money, sexual favors, or "respect" (Cornell et al., 1996; Williamson et al., 1987). Individuals can attempt to achieve these goals through a variety of means. Having a higher SES (or for that matter intelligence) enables a wider choice of available routes for achieving these goals than having a lower SES (or intelligence). We suggest that a reason for the inverse relationship between SES and IQ with the antisocial behavior component of psychopathy is that lower SES/IQ limits the behavioral options available so that antisocial behavior appears a useful route to the goal. A healthy individual of limited SES/IQ may also have a narrow range of behavioral options but will exclude antisocial behavior because of aversion to this behavior formed during socialization (see chapter 8). In contrast, individuals with psychopathy may entertain the antisocial option because they do not find the required antisocial behavior aversive. SES is also likely to impact on the probability of displaying instrumental aggression by determining relative reward levels for particular actions. If someone already has $100,000, the subjective value of the $50 that could be gained if he/she mugged another person on the street is low. In contrast, if the person has only 50 cents, the subjective value of the $50 will be very high indeed (for a discussion of subjective value, see Tversky and Kahneman (1981).

In line with the influence of social factors on response choice and motivation, there have been numerous studies indicating that aggressive children regard aggressive behavior as an appropriate response choice and they evaluate aggression more positively than other children do (Crick and Dodge, 1996; Dodge, 1991; Dodge et al., 1995). Thus, they are more likely than other children to select aggressive behavior as the best and most appropriate response to peer provocations and social rejection (Garber et al., 1991). In addition, they expect more positive instrumental outcomes (Hart et al., 1990), fewer negative interpersonal outcomes (Quiggle et al., 1992), and fewer sanctional outcomes (Perry et al., 1986) to accrue for aggressing. Importantly, these tendencies are notably related to the display of instrumental aggressive behavior rather than reactive aggression (Crick and Dodge, 1996; Dodge, 1991; Dodge et al., 1995).

We have not considered the relationship between SES and the probability of reactive aggression above. Yet, it is likely that SES does play a modulatory role in the expression of reactive aggression in syndromes that are associated with this form of aggression. However, its role would be rather different than its role in instrumental aggression. It is likely that lower SES is going to put the individual at risk of experiencing/being exposed to threatening environments. The increased risk of experience of environmental stressors is likely to increase the risk of reactive aggression.

SUMMARY

In short, SES is likely to influence the probability of an individual engaging in antisocial behavior by determining the behavioral choices available to the individual and also by altering the salience of the potential rewards that might be gained from antisocial behavior. It is important to note here that SES is not seen as a cause of psychopathy but rather as an influence on the behavioral manifestation of the underlying cause. In other words, we anticipate that there are individuals of higher SES who do not present with the full psychopathic syndrome even though their emotional dysfunction is of an equivalent degree to other individuals who present with both the emotional and behavioral components of the disorder.

ATTACHMENT

Attachment theory places great emphasis on the early relationship children have with their primary caregiver as it represents their first bonding experience (Bowlby, 1982). The cornerstone of Bowlby's theory is that a child's failure to develop a healthy and secure attachment at an early age can lead to an inability to develop close relationships in adulthood. Theoretical formulations have been made relating difficulties in bonding with individuals to a more general failure to respond empathically to individuals and, hence, antisocial behavior. Recent investigations of attachment styles in offenders has revealed greatly elevated levels of disturbed attachment (Saltaris, 2002). Moreover, there have been several reports of associations between anomalous attachment styles and CD or aggression more generally (DeKlyen et al., 1998; Lyons-Ruth, 1996; Lyons-Ruth et al., 1993). Theories of attachment suggest that poor attachment contributes to psychopathy by disrupting the process that leads to the development of morality. The claim is that the mutual responsiveness characteristic of early interactions with parents provides a starting point for the development of concern and commitment toward others (Saltaris, 2002).

We do not intend to evaluate the attachment claims in depth. One problem with attachment theory is that disturbances in attachment have been associated not just with psychopathy but with a great range of other disorders, including borderline personality disorder (Fonagy, 2000) and autism (Hobson, 1993). It appears highly likely that individuals with psychopathy do have attachment difficulties. Indeed, there is reference to a lack of attachment to significant others in Hare's description of the disorder (Hare, 1991). But are these attachment difficulties causally related to the disorder? It is difficult to see how they could be. While it can be claimed that early interactions with parents are necessary for empathic responsiveness to others (Saltaris, 2002), this claim is difficult to reconcile with several strands of data. First, there are strong suggestions that the fear and sadness of others activate an automatic aversive response in observers (Vuilleumier et al., 2003). Second, and more crucially, other populations that present with pronounced attachment difficulties, e.g., individuals with autism, show indications of an aversive response to the distress of others (Blair, 1999a); i.e., appropriate attachment is not necessary for finding the distress of others aversive. Consequently, it is clear that at least some forms of empathic responding occur independently of attachment style.

We would suggest that individuals with psychopathy present with attachment difficulties as a consequence of their emotional dysfunction. Attachment is the formation of an emotional bond with another. Individuals with psychopathy show impaired emotional learning. We suggest that this impairment in emotional learning (see chapter 8) interferes with the attachment process.

With respect to syndromes associated with reactive aggression, attachment style is likely to have a modulatory role. The presence of people to whom the individual is securely attached to is likely to act as a highly reinforcing stimulus, suppressing the responsiveness of the basic threat circuitry and reducing the probability of reactive aggression. In contrast, in insecure attachments, the caregivers themselves may become a threat/frustration stimulus, thus leading to an increased probability of reactive aggression.

SUMMARY

In short, while attachment difficulties are associated with psychopathy, this association is unlikely to be causal. Instead, it is likely that the pathology giving rise to the emotional disturbance seen in psychopathy interferes with the attachment process. In contrast, it is likely with respect to reactive aggression, particularly in children, that attachment style may have a notable modulatory role on the probability of reactive aggression.

FAMILY VARIABLES AND PARENTING

Parental antisocial attitudes, inconsistent discipline, physical punishment, poor school performance, broken homes, and childhood separations have all been associated with higher psychopathy scores (Forth and Burke, 1998; Marshall and Cooke, 1999). For example, Marshall and Cooke examined two main categories of childhood experiences in psychopathic and non-psychopathic offenders. These were (1) family dynamics including parental antipathy or neglect, and (2) societal influences such as experiences and performance at school or an institution (Marshall and Cooke, 1999). The results indicated a dissociation of the two factors of the PCL-R. Although multiple regression analysis revealed that only familial dynamics were a significant predictor of Factor 1 scores, both familial dynamics and societal influences predicted Factor 2. This raises two re-emerging themes about the disorder: (1) to show the full manifestation of the disorder, at least as measured by the PCL-R, an individual not only shows an emotional dysfunction, but also tends to have been exposed to difficulties within their environment, and (2) Factor 1 and Factor 2 scores seem to be differentially sensitive to environmental influences. Another interesting finding in the study concerns the negative curvilinear nature of the relationship between familial influences and PCL-R scores. The authors found that as the score of the PCL-R increases, the effect of childhood variables decreases. Thus, medium psychopathy scores may be more heavily influenced by experiences within the family, while higher scores for psychopathy may be more heavily influence by a biological component (Marshall and Cooke, 1999).

However, the data is inconsistent, with some studies finding that psychopathic individuals report a significantly poorer family or school environment, and others reporting no significant differences (Forth and Burke, 1998). Forth and Burke (1998) assessed the impact of family factors on psychopathy scores as measured in adolescents by the PCL-YV. They found that for young offenders, the antisocial behavioral component (Factor 2), but not the emotional dysfunction component (Factor 1), was correlated with global family background. However, in the community sample, both Factor 1 and Factor 2 scores were correlated with global family dysfunction. Furthermore, while family background variables predicted PCL-YV total, Factor 1, and Factor 2 scores in the community sample, they did not predict either factor or total scores in the young offender sample. The strongest predictors of PCL-YV scores in the community were antisocial parents, inconsistent discipline, and alcoholism. However, these variables did not seem to relate to psychopathy in the young offenders.

There are various difficulties with this body of data. First, the family variables linked to psychopathy are not consistently found across samples. At best, it can be claimed that four factors are relatively consistently linked to the disorder: antisocial parents, parental alcoholism, inconsistent discipline, and a lack of supervision (Forth and Burke, 1998). Second, many of these studies rely on retrospective recall, a problematic strategy given the known deceitfulness of this population. Third, it is highly unlikely that these variables are causally related to psychopathy. There are no reasons why antisocial parents, parental alcoholism, inconsistent discipline, or a lack of supervision should give rise to the emotional difficulties seen in individuals with psychopathy (see chapters 4 and 8). This is not to say that these variables may not exacerbate the antisocial behavioral features of the disorder. Indeed, all of these variables are likely to increase the probability, and amount of, antisocial behavior in individuals with psychopathy, as they appear to do in non-psychopathic individuals (Lahey et al., 1995; Loeber et al., 1998). It is more likely that these family variables lead to the provision of models for antisocial behavior, or may provide actual motives for offending. A child who grows up viewing antisocial behavior may come to see it as a viable strategy for expressing anger or obtaining goals. The child sees the parent solve a dispute by violence and learns this strategy. Because of a lack of either self-esteem or economic resources, the child has an incentive to offend.

With respect to parenting in particular, there is, for most children, a weak but consistent association between the type of socialization practice used by the parent and the probability that the child will offend. Studies have shown, for example, that moral socialization is better achieved through the use of induction (reasoning that draws children's attention to the effects of their misdemeanors on others and increases empathy) than through harsh authoritarian or power assertive parenting practices which rely on the use of punishment (Baumrind, 1971, 1983; Hoffman and Saltzstein, 1967). Indeed, there have been suggestions that while empathy facilitates moral socialization, fear actually hinders it (Brody and Shaffer, 1982; Hoffman, 1994). Thus, if the parent fosters the child's empathic responding, the child is very unlikely to be antisocial. In contrast, if the parent typically socializes the child by physical punishment, the child is much more likely to offend. But this association does not apply to those children who show the emotional difficulties of a lack of guilt/remorse linked to psychopathy. Stunningly, with these children the type of parental socialization practice has no statistical bearing on the probability that the child will show antisocial behavior (Wootton et al., 1997). This suggests that the pathology associated with psychopathy substantially interferes with the ability to be socialized.

SUMMARY

In short, family variables appear to influence the behavioral component of psychopathy. Antisocial parents and, perhaps, parental alcoholism will provide the child with antisocial models (and may also reflect genetic load). Inconsistent discipline and a lack of supervision are likely to increase the child's opportunities for antisocial behavior. None of these variables are likely to be causal.

We have not considered the relationship between family variables and the probability of reactive aggression above. However, family variables will have a direct effect on the probability of reactive aggression if they either increase or decrease the level of environmental stress that the child experiences.

A socially based syndrome of antisocial behavior

In the sections above, we concluded that there was a genetic contribution to the emotional dysfunction seen in psychopathy as well as to the syndromes associated with an increased risk of reactive aggression. We also concluded that there were social variables (birth trauma and environmental stressors) that increased the risk of reactive aggression (though neither appear likely related to psychopathy on the basis of the currently available data). Finally, we considered various social variables that modulate the risk of instrumental/reactive aggression. However, the arguments made were based around the known neural architectures that mediate emotional responding; i.e., they were all biologically grounded. We will now consider an antisocial behavioral phenomenon that does not appear to be biologically but rather socially grounded: adolescent-limited conduct disorder. Importantly, one of the goals of this book is to demonstrate that individuals classified as presenting with conduct disorder or antisocial personality disorder are not a homogeneous group but rather a highly heterogeneous one. We consider that both these disorders are made up of a constellation of completely different disorders. We believe that one of these constellations is adolescent-limited conduct disorder.

As discussed in chapter 2, there is an explosion in antisocial behavior during adolescence. This rise in offending peaks at the age of 17 and then drops precipitously in young adulthood. The majority of criminal offenders are teenagers. By the early 20s, the number of active offenders decreases by over 50 percent, and by age 28, almost 85 percent of former delinquents have stopped offending (Blumstein and Cohen, 1987; Farrington, 1986). Terrie Moffitt has referred to such individuals, who begin to offend in their early teens but are no longer offending by their middle 20s, as *adolescent-limited* offenders (Moffitt, 1993a).

Importantly, for the arguments developed in this book, adolescent-limited offenders are not only engaging in reactive aggression; in fact, they are more likely to be engaged in instrumental antisocial behavior, albeit of a form which is often devoid of clear victims (shoplifting and fare dodging rather than robbery). In short, they are engaging in a particular form of goal-directed behavior, antisocial acts, for a limited period of time. Biological accounts of adolescent-limited offenders could be offered; i.e., that hormone/neurotransmitter level changes occurring around puberty increase the risk for aggression. If the increase in antisocial behavior represented an increase in reactive aggression, such accounts might even be plausible; the responsiveness of the basic threat response architecture which mediates reactive aggression is sensitive to a variety of hormones/ neurotransmitters (Gregg and Siegel, 2001; Panksepp, 1998). However, because adolescent-limited offenders engage in instrumental as well as reactive antisocial behavior, biological accounts of adolescent-limited antisocial behavior are unsatisfactory. That is, they would need to explain how a biological variable could affect this specific form of goal-directed behavior. The fact that the heritability of delinquency/aggression is particularly weak to non-significant in the adolescent period supports this contention (Goldsmith and Gottesman, 1996). This again suggests that a social, rather than a biological, explanation is appropriate for the explosion in antisocial behavior in adolescence.

Terrie Moffitt's (1993a) social account of the emergence of adolescent-limited antisocial behavior is of considerable interest. She argues that adolescent-limited youths learn to mimic the lifestyles of their life-course-persistent peers (her term for individuals such as those with psychopathy who begin their offending younger than 10 years of age and continue to offend long after the age of 20). Moffitt argues that teenagers experience a 5-10-year role vacuum, the "maturity gap," where they are "biologically capable and compelled to be sexual beings, yet they are asked to delay most of the positive aspects of adult life" (Moffitt, 1993a, p. 686); they have to live with their parents, cannot own significant material possessions, are constrained in their romantic lives, and their decisions may not be regarded as consequential by adults. Moffitt argues that youths see that the life-course-persistent individuals do not suffer from the maturity gap; they can steal for possessions and are likely to have engaged in sexual activity. "Viewed from within contemporary adolescent culture, the antisocial precocity of life-course-persistent youths becomes a coveted social asset" (Moffitt, 1993a, p. 687). Interestingly, while life-course-persistent children are ignored and rejected by other children because of their unpredictable, aggressive behavior (Coie et al., 1988a; Dodge et al., 1982), they are no longer rejected as adolescents (Coie et al., 1988b). By the end of the maturity gap, the young adult has many other ways to demonstrate his or her value as a being beyond antisocial behavior – ways that are likely to be more productive in the long run. Thus, the adolescent-limited offender desists from offending.

SUMMARY

In short, there is a population of individuals who present with CD during adolescence, but not during childhood or adulthood, individuals with adolescent-limited CD, for which a social explanation is the most appropriate.

Conclusion

The goal of this chapter was to consider the fundamental causes of aggression in the context of psychopathy and also syndromes associated with a heightened risk of reactive aggression. On the basis of the data, we can conclude that there is a genetic contribution to the emotional dysfunction seen in psychopathy. Our claim will be that genetic abnormalities give rise to a specific deficit in neurotransmitter function and neuro-development such that the emotional responsiveness of individuals with psychopathy is muted (see chapters 4 and 8). We can conclude also that it is highly likely that there are genetic contributions to the syndromes associated with a heightened risk of reactive aggression. Specifically, we can conclude that there are likely genetic contributions not only to the responsiveness of the basic threat circuitry but also to the functional integrity of the executive systems that regulate this circuitry.

We considered whether there might be social causes to psychopathy or syndromes associated with a heightened risk of reactive aggression. We considered that birth trauma and environmental stressors such as those occurring during physical and sexual abuse are unlikely to lead to the development of psychopathy. The neural systems reported to be damaged by birth trauma / environmental stressors are unlikely to be directly involved in the emotion dysfunction associated with psychopathy. Moreover, more general effects of environmental stressors on emotional responsiveness involve an increase, not a decrease, of the responsiveness of the neural and neurotransmitter systems involved in processing threat cues.

In contrast to psychopathy, we concluded that birth trauma and environmental stressors are likely causally related to an increased risk of reactive aggression. Birth trauma can damage frontal regions involved in the regulation of the basic threat circuitry. Environmental stressors can increase the basic responsiveness of this circuitry, making a reactive aggressive response more likely.

Beyond environmental threat, there are environmental variables that, although not causal for psychopathy or syndromes associated with reactive aggression, affect how the pathology is manifested. These include several family variables. We would argue that attachment difficulties are related to psychopathy but any causal link flows from the pathology associated with psychopathy to the disturbance in attachment. Any attachment account of psychopathy faces substantial difficulties with the current data.

In the final section of this chapter, we described a specific form of CD: *adolescent-limited* CD. Although this book fundamentally concerns psychopathy, in approaching this problem it is necessary to consider the DSM-IV diagnoses of CD and ASPD. The advantage of psychopathy is that this classification appears to identify a relatively homogeneous population. The difficulty with CD and ASPD is that these diagnoses identify highly heterogeneous populations (as is recognized by DSM-IV, at least for CD). We will delineate sub-populations within the diagnoses of CD and ASPD, in addition to psychopathy, as we progress through this book. In this chapter we describe the first of these sub-populations: adolescent-limited CD. This is a form of CD that appears entirely related to social factors.

CHAPTER FOUR

THE PSYCHOPATHIC INDIVIDUAL: THE FUNCTIONAL IMPAIRMENT

In chapter 1, we described the behavioral manifestation of psychopathy as detailed in the Psychopathy Checklist – Revised (PCL-R) (Hare, 1991). The purpose of this chapter is to consider the functional impairments presented by these individuals; i.e., their emotional and cognitive impairments.

Is psychopathy an anxiety disorder?

There has been an apparent conundrum in the understanding of the development of antisocial behavior. Many researchers have suggested that reduced anxiety levels lead to the development of antisocial behavior/psychopathy (Cleckley, 1976; Eysenck, 1964; Gray, 1987; Lykken, 1995; Patrick, 1994; Trasler, 1973). For example, Cleckley wrote: "Within himself he appears almost as incapable of anxiety as of profound remorse" (1976, p. 340). However, in apparent contradiction of this position, data has consistently indicated that high levels of antisocial behavior are associated with heightened levels of anxiety. Thus, there is a well-documented positive correlation between anxiety and antisocial behavior in children (Pine et al., 2000; Russo and Beidel, 1993; Zoccolillo, 1992) and adults (Robins et al., 1991). In other words, higher levels of anxiety are associated with higher levels of antisocial behavior.

We argue that this apparent conundrum is related to the problem, raised several times now, of assuming a unitary account for the explanation of all antisocial behavior. There have been reports that both the callous and unemotional

and the impulsive and conduct-disordered dimensions of psychopathy are independent of level of anxiety (Schmitt and Newman, 1999). This would suggest
that there is no relationship between anxiety and psychopathy. However, this
study did not examine the relationship between anxiety and the callous and
unemotional traits of psychopathy independently of the relationship between
anxiety and antisocial behavior. Studies that have removed the impact of the
relationship between anxiety and antisocial behavior have found that anxiety
level is *inversely* associated with the callous and unemotional dimension of
psychopathy. In the same studies, removal of the impact of the relationship
between anxiety and the callous and unemotional traits reveals that anxiety
level is *positively* associated with the impulsive and conduct-disordered dimension (Frick et al., 1999; Patrick, 1994; Verona et al., 2001). This strongly suggests
the existence of at least two populations at risk for the development of high
levels of antisocial behavior: individuals with psychopathy who present with
little anxiety and a second population whose antisocial behavior, we will argue,
is causally related to their heightened levels of anxiety (see chapters 7 and 8).

SUMMARY

In short, individuals with psychopathy present with reduced anxiety levels.
However, it is important to note, that another developmental pathway to
high levels of antisocial behavior is the consequence of elevated levels of
anxiety (see chapter 7). In the next section, we will consider indications of
emotional impairment in individuals with psychopathy that are consistent
with them presenting with atypically low levels of anxiety.

The response of individuals with psychopathy to threatening stimuli

David Lykken was one of the earliest theorists to associate psychopathy with
reduced anxiety (Lykken, 1957). His suggestion was that the psychopathic individual "has an attenuated experience, not of all emotional states, but specifically
anxiety or fear" (Lykken, 1995, p. 118). He argued that the reduced fearfulness
interferes with socialization (see below) and gives rise to the development of
psychopathy.

Lykken demonstrated low fearfulness in individuals with psychopathy in 1957
using two different tasks. With the first task, he examined the ability of individuals with psychopathy to show aversive conditioning. Aversive conditioning
involves learning that an unpleasant event (e.g., a loud noise or an electric

shock) is associated with an event in the world. In Lykken's study, the unpleasant event, the aversive unconditioned stimulus (US), was a harmless but painful electric shock. When participants receive electric shocks, they sweat. This is the automatic, unconditioned response (UR) to the electric shock. A participant's extent of sweating can be measured as the degree of electrodermal activity; i.e., the ease with which the skin can carry an electrical current. In Lykken's study, the event in the world, the conditioned stimulus (CS), was the sound of a buzzer. The buzzer would last for 5 seconds and then, immediately afterwards, the participant would receive the electric shock. Lykken was investigating whether, because of the pairing of the CS (buzzer) with the US (shock), the participant would learn to show a conditioned response (CR) to the CS. In line with the suggestion that individuals with psychopathy show impaired aversive conditioning, Lykken found that these individuals showed a significantly reduced electrodermal CR to the buzzer than the comparison individuals (for similar results, see also Flor et al., 2002; Hare and Quinn, 1971).

In related work, individuals with psychopathy have been found to either fail to generate, or generate to a lesser extent, emotional autonomic responses to other fear inducing stimuli. For example, imagine that you are about to receive an electric shock, the seconds are ticking down to when the pain will come: 5, 4, 3, . . . I am sure that you can imagine that you will become increasingly concerned as the pain comes closer. And if we measured your electrodermal response, in other words how much you are sweating, we would see that you sweat more as the seconds tick down. Non-psychopathic offenders also show this pattern of emotional responding. Remarkably, however, psychopathic offenders show very little emotional responding in this situation; they show smaller electrodermal responses than non-psychopathic offenders and these occur much closer to the shock than those of the non-psychopathic offenders (Hare, 1965, 1982; Hare et al., 1978; Ogloff and Wong, 1990). Individuals with psychopathy also show reduced emotional reactions (less electrodermal activity), relative to non-psychopathic individuals, when they are asked to imagine unpleasant or fearful experiences (Patrick et al., 1994). Thus, Patrick and colleagues (1994) asked participants to imagine situations such as "Taking a shower, alone in the house, I hear the sound of someone forcing the door, and I panic" or "I am relaxing on my living room couch looking out the window on a sunny autumn day." While the comparison individuals showed strong physiological reactions to the frightening events, the individuals with psychopathy showed a dramatically reduced response to these events.

Individuals with psychopathy also show reduced emotional responding to threatening stimuli in startle reflex paradigms. The startle reflex is the automatic jump reaction that you show when you are suddenly exposed to a basic threatening stimulus such as a loud noise or a looming object; i.e., your reaction when the monster suddenly rushes out of the closet in a horror movie. The startle reflex can be augmented by exposure to learnt threats immediately before the startle stimulus. Thus, in the horror movie, the creepy music leading up to the monster rushing out of the closet acts as a learnt threat, resulting in the activation of the basic systems in your brain that respond to threatening stimuli and giving rise to the augmentation of your startle reflex. Next time you watch a horror movie try watching it without the sound on and you will see that your reaction to the scary scenes will be greatly reduced.

Experimentally, the magnitude of the startle reflex can be modified by presenting a prime before the startle probe (a loud noise; 50 ms of 105 dB white noise). This prime can either be positive (e.g., erotic images), negative (e.g., assault scenes) or neutral (e.g., kitchen utensils). The startle reflex itself is measured by placing electrodes on the face around the eyes to measure the level of eye blink. Presenting a positive prime reduces the startle reflex with respect to the presentation of a neutral prime. Presenting a negative prime increases the startle reflex with respect to the presentation of a neutral prime (Lang et al., 1990; Levenston et al., 2000; Patrick, 1994). The magnitude of the startle reflex responses of non-psychopathic offenders can be altered by the presence of positive or negative primes. However, while psychopathic offenders do show some reduction in startle following positive (relative to neutral) primes, they present with significantly less augmentation of the startle reflex following negative visual primes (Levenston et al., 2000; Patrick, 1994).

Interestingly, when individuals with psychopathy are presented with threatening visual images such as a picture of a snarling dog, a pointed gun, or a mutilated body, they show equivalent electrodermal responses to those of comparison individuals (Blair et al., 1997; Levenston et al., 2000; Patrick et al., 1993). This may be considered a surprising result for those advocating reduced fear/anxiety in this population (Lykken, 1995; Patrick, 1994).

SUMMARY

In short, individuals with psychopathy show reduced responding to threatening stimuli. They show reduced aversive conditioning, reduced emotional responses in anticipation of punishment, reduced emotional responses when imagining threatening events, and reduced augmentation of the startle reflex by aversive primes. In the next section, we will consider their difficulties with emotional learning more generally.

Emotional learning in individuals with psychopathy

In the preceding section, we discussed the reduced responding to threatening stimuli shown by individuals with psychopathy. However, the emotional impairments shown by these individuals are more pervasive than difficulty with responding appropriately to negative stimuli. Individuals with psychopathy also present with difficulty in specific forms of instrumental learning, particularly when this is indexed through passive avoidance paradigms, and response reversal.

Instrumental learning involves learning to commit specific behavioral responses in order to gain reward or to avoid punishment. For example, passive avoidance learning involves learning to respond to stimuli that give rise to reward but learning to avoid responding to other stimuli that give rise to punishment. Alternatively, object discrimination learning involves learning to respond to one of two objects (one rewarded and one not rewarded) repeatedly presented in a pair-wise fashion over a series of trials. To achieve successful performance, some instrumental learning tasks (e.g., passive avoidance learning) require the formation of stimulus-reinforcement associations (i.e., the formation of an association between a stimulus and either reward or punishment). Other instrumental learning tasks (e.g., object discrimination) require the formation of stimulus – response associations (i.e., the formation of an association between a stimulus and a motor response). Individuals with psychopathy present with particular difficulty for instrumental learning tasks that require the formation of stimulus – punishment associations. However, they do not show impairment with instrumental learning tasks that require the formation of stimulus – response associations (this issue will be returned to, in far greater depth, in chapter 8).

To consider passive avoidance, David Lykken was the first to demonstrate that individuals with psychopathy were impaired in passive avoidance learning (Lykken, 1957). Since his original demonstration, there has been a series of replications of this result. Early work suggested that the nature of the negative reinforcer might affect the degree of impairment shown by individuals with psychopathy; the impairment might not be shown if the negative reinforcer were financial loss rather than electric shock (Schmauk, 1970). However, more recent studies have shown that, relative to comparison individuals, individuals with psychopathy commit more passive avoidance errors regardless of whether reinforcement is in the form of money, cigarettes, or confectionery (Newman and Kosson, 1986; Newman and Schmitt, 1998; Newman et al., 1985; Thornquist and Zuckerman, 1995).

Extinction and response reversal are the names given to specific forms of variants of tasks where participants must learn to withhold or change their behavioral response when they discover that their original response to a stimulus is now no longer rewarded but punished. One extinction task that has been used with individuals with psychopathy is a card playing task originally developed by Joe Newman and colleagues (Newman et al., 1987). In this task, the participant has to decide whether to play a card. Initially, the participant's choice to play is always reinforcing; if the participant plays the card he or she will win points or money. However, as the participant progresses through the pack of cards, the probability of reward decreases. Thus, initially ten out of ten cards are rewarded, then nine out of ten, then eight out of ten continuing on until zero out of ten cards are rewarded. The participant should stop playing the cards when playing means that more cards are associated with punishment rather than reward. That is, they should stop playing the cards when only four out of ten cards are associated with reward. Children with psychopathic tendencies and adult individuals with psychopathy have considerable difficulty with this task; they continue to play the cards even when they are being repeatedly punished and may end up losing all the points that they had gained (Fisher and Blair, 1998; Newman et al., 1987; O'Brien and Frick, 1996).

In extinction tasks like the card playing task described above, the participant learns to respond to a stimulus that gives rise to reward and then learns to avoid responding to this stimulus when responding to the stimulus gives rise to punishment. In response reversal tasks, the participant learns to respond to one of a series of objects to gain reward and then learns to reverse his or her responding, and respond to one of the other objects, when responding to the previously rewarded object gives rise to punishment. Individuals with psychopathy show pronounced impairment on response reversal tasks (although this appears to be less the case in children with psychopathic tendencies than in adults with the disorder) (Blair et al., 2001a; LaPierre et al., 1995; Mitchell et al., 2002; Roussy and Toupin, 2000).

Finally, there has been one investigation of the impact of emotion on episodic memory in individuals with psychopathy. In this study, memory for central versus peripheral details of visual images of negative events was investigated (Christianson et al., 1996). The central details of negative emotional events are the information that is connected with the source of emotional arousal. The peripheral details are the information preceding and succeeding emotional events or the irrelevant or spatially peripheral information within the emotional scenario. Previous research had shown that central details of negative emotional events are better retained than are peripheral details (see, for reviews, (Christianson, 1992; Goodman et al., 1991). Comparison individuals also showed this advantage for central relative to peripheral events. However, the individuals with psychopathy did not (Christianson et al., 1996).

SUMMARY

In short, individuals with psychopathy show difficulties in emotional learning. Specifically, they present with profound impairment in passive avoidance learning and response reversal. In addition, there are indications that individuals with psychopathy do not show modulation of episodic memory by affective stimuli. While the level of impairment shown by children with psychopathic tendencies and adults with psychopathy appears to be equivalent for passive avoidance learning, there is some suggestion that the impairment in response reversal may be more pronounced in adults with psychopathy (see chapter 8 for greater description of this issue).

Empathic responding in individuals with psychopathy

Appropriate empathic responding to victims has long been linked to the suppression of antisocial behavior (Eisenberg et al., 1996; Feshbach, 1987; Perry and Perry, 1974). Individuals presenting with high levels of antisocial behavior have been consistently reported to present with reduced empathic responses to the distress (notably the fear and sadness) of their victims (Chaplin et al., 1995; Perry and Perry, 1974). Indeed, one of the defining criteria of psychopathy as indexed by both the Antisocial Process Screening Device for children (Frick and Hare, 2001a) and the PCL-R for adults (Hare, 1991) is reduced empathic responding to victims.

There are several different types of paradigms that can be used to identify an individual's empathic responsiveness. One type of paradigm that has been frequently used involves self-report. The individual is given an empathy questionnaire, e.g., the Interpersonal Reactivity Index (Davis, 1983). The investigator determines whether there are group differences in self-reported empathy. This first approach has been of questionable use and data obtained with this technique will not be reviewed here. Its main problem is that it confounds the basic emotional responsiveness of empathy with the individual's linguistic and verbal capacities together with the enthusiasm, or lack of it, for self-disclosure. More verbally able individuals will have richer semantic knowledge bases to draw on when responding. Those who wish to look more empathic can learn to parrot empathic verbal responses.

A second paradigm type involves the direct measurement of the individual's autonomic responses to the distress of others (Aniskiewicz, 1979; Blair, 1999b; Blair et al., 1997; House and Milligan, 1976; Sutker, 1970); see figure 4.1. This technique thus directly assesses an individual's basic emotional response to the

Figure 4.1   The strongest of the distress cue stimuli used by Blair et al. (1997). The individuals with psychopathy were markedly reduced in their responsiveness to this stimulus.

distress of others. Of the existing five studies, three involved one type of paradigm while the other two used a second type of paradigm. In the first type of paradigm, the skin conductance responses of participants were recorded while they observed confederates whom they believed were being administered electric shocks. Using this methodology, two out of three studies reported reduced autonomic responsiveness in individuals with psychopathy relative to comparison individuals (Aniskiewicz, 1979; House and Milligan, 1976). In the second type of paradigm, the skin conductance responses of participants were recorded while they simply watched images presented on a screen. Using this methodology, both children with psychopathic tendencies and adults with psychopathy have been found to present with reduced autonomic responsiveness to the distress of others relative to comparison individuals (Blair, 1999b; Blair et al., 1997).

A third type of paradigm involves the naming of emotional expressions and vocal affect. It appears that the naming of emotional expressions recruits the neural architectures involved in the processing of these expressions (Blair and

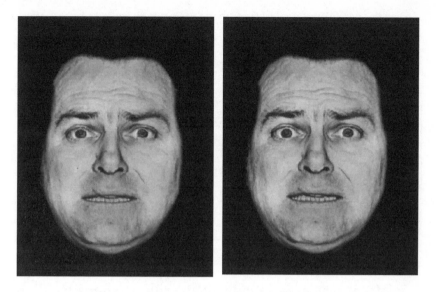

Figure 4.2 In the Blair et al. (2002) study, participants were presented with a facial stimulus displaying a neutral expression. This expression then began to display an expression (the participant was serially shown morphs that progressively displayed an emotional expression). (a) A 65 percent fearful morph (the level of expression necessary for successful recognition by comparison individuals); (b) a 75 percent fearful morph (the level of expression necessary for successful recognition by individuals with psychopathy).

Cipolotti, 2000; Calder et al., 1996). Indeed, neuropsychological and neuro-imaging data has identified at least three partially dissociable systems involved in the processing of emotional expressions: one principally responsive to fearful (and to a lesser extent sad) expressions, one principally responsive to disgusted expressions, and one responsive to a variety of expressions but particularly angry expressions (see also chapters 7 and 8). A series of studies have investigated the ability of children with psychopathic tendencies and adults with psychopathy to name the emotional expressions of others. These studies have revealed an impairment in the naming of fearful expressions (Blair et al., 2001b; Blair and Coles, 2000; Stevens et al., 2001) – though there has also been one report of impaired disgust recognition (Kosson et al., 2002b); see figure 4.2. In addition, there have been consistent reports of impairment in the naming of sad expressions in children with psychopathic tendencies. Three studies have also examined the naming of vocal affect, where it has been revealed that children with psychopathic tendencies and adults with psychopathy show impairment in recognizing fearful vocal affect and, though less consistently, sad vocal affect (Blair et al., 2001; Stevens et al., 2001).

SUMMARY

In short, individuals with psychopathy present with notable empathic impairment. Both children with psychopathic tendencies and adults with psychopathy present with reduced autonomic responses to the sadness of other individuals. In addition, they present with impaired recognition of fearful and sad facial expressions and vocal affect. Notably, adults with psychopathy and children with psychopathic tendencies do not present with impaired responding to angry, happy or surprised facial or vocal expressions.

Moral reasoning in individuals with psychopathy

Aversive conditioning, passive avoidance, and empathic responsiveness are processes that have been assumed to play a role in the moral socialization of the healthy developing child (Eysenck, 1964; Hoffman, 1988; Trasler, 1973). If these processes are dysfunctional in individuals with psychopathy, we might anticipate dysfunction in moral reasoning in individuals with psychopathy.

Typically, two paradigms have been used to assess moral reasoning in individuals with psychopathy: those of Kohlberg (Colby and Kohlberg, 1987; Kohlberg, 1969) and Turiel (1983). In Kohlberg's paradigm, the participant is first presented with a series of vignettes describing moral dilemmas and then asked how the protagonist should act in the dilemma situation and why they would act in this way. An example dilemma is described below:

In Europe, a woman was near death from a special kind of cancer. There was one drug that the doctors thought might save her. It was a form of radium that a druggist in the same town had recently discovered. The drug was expensive to make, but the druggist was charging 10 times what the drug cost him to make. He paid $200 for the radium and charged $2,000 for a small dose of the drug. The sick woman's husband, Heinz, went to everyone he knew to borrow the money, but he could only get together about $1,000, which is half of what it cost. He told the druggist his wife was dying, and asked him to sell it cheaper or let him pay later. But the druggist said "No, I discovered the drug and I'm going to make money from it." So Heinz got desperate and broke into the man's store to steal the drug for his wife.

Within this paradigm, the participant's judgment of whether Heinz should or should not steal is unimportant. What is important, with regards to determining the individual's level of moral reasoning, is the complexity of the participant's reasons as to why Heinz should or should not steal the drug. Crudely stated, the more complex the participant's reasoning, the higher their level of moral reasoning.

It has been consistently demonstrated that the moral reasoning of delinquents is at a lower level relative to comparison individuals (Blasi, 1980). However, it is much less clear that the moral reasoning of individuals with psychopathy is impaired as indexed by this task. Thus, although there have been some reports of individuals with psychopathy showing lower levels of moral reasoning than comparison non-psychopathic offenders (Campagna and Harter, 1975; Fodor, 1973; Jurkovic and Prentice, 1977), other studies have indicated that while the moral reasoning of delinquent psychopathic and non-psychopathic individuals is lower than that of individuals with no forensic history, there is no difference in level of moral reasoning between psychopathic and non-psychopathic offenders (Lee and Prentice, 1988; Trevethan and Walker, 1989). Also, there are considerable difficulties with the interpretation of performance on Kohlberg's paradigm. As noted above, the participant's level of moral reasoning is determined not by their decision as to how the protagonist should behave, but rather by the complexity of the justifications of their decision. Kohlberg's framework can therefore be considered to assess the individual's moral concepts, which is a reflection of their moral semantic memory. Indeed, according to Kohlberg, these conceptual structures drive moral reasoning and behavior (Colby and Kohlberg, 1987; Kohlberg and Kramer, 1969; Kohlberg et al., 1983). However, it is unclear that this is really the case. In fact, we will argue explicitly that this is not the case. Instead, if Kohlberg's moral judgment interview simply indexes the complexity level of an individual's semantic memory, we might expect performance on the measure to be highly sensitive to IQ and socioeconomic status (SES). Some measures of IQ specifically index the individual's semantic memory to provide the assessment of intelligence. Given that IQ and SES do indeed predict level of moral reasoning, it could be argued that Kohlberg's measure indexes IQ and the individual's cultural experiences rather than their moral reasoning *per se* (Shweder et al., 1987).

Turiel's paradigm is referred to as the moral/conventional distinction task (Turiel, 1983; see also Nucci and Nucci, 1982; Smetana, 1993). In this task, the participant is presented with stories involving moral and conventional transgressions. Moral transgression are actions defined by their consequences for the rights and welfare of other individuals (e.g., hitting another individual, damaging another individual's property) and conventional transgressions are defined by their consequences for the social order (e.g., talking in class, dressing in opposite-sex clothes). The participant is then asked to make a series of judgments about these transgressions (e.g., "How bad is the transgression?" "Why is the transgression bad to do?" and, crucially, "If there was no rule about people [doing the transgression], would it be OK to [do the transgression]?"). Healthy individuals distinguish between moral and conventional transgressions (Smetana, 1993; Turiel, 1983). The distinction between moral and conventional transgressions is made from the age of 39 months (Smetana and Braeges, 1990) and is found across cultures (Nucci et al., 1983; Song et al., 1987). There are several ways in which people differentiate between moral and conventional transgressions. Thus, first of all, people generally judge moral transgressions to be more *serious* than conventional transgressions (Nucci, 1981; Smetana and Braeges, 1990; Turiel, 1983). Second, people give different reasons for justifying why moral and conventional transgressions are wrong. Thus, for moral transgressions, people refer to the distress of the victim (i.e., it is wrong to hit someone because it will hurt them), but for conventional transgressions, people refer to the social disorder that may ensue (i.e., it is wrong to talk in class because you are there to learn) (Smetana, 1993; Turiel, 1983). Third, and more importantly, modifying the rule conditions (for example, by an authority figure removing the prohibition against the act) only affects the permissibility of conventional transgressions. Thus, even if there is no rule prohibiting the action, participants generally judge moral transgressions as non-permissible (i.e., they still think it is wrong to hit another individual even if there is no rule against it). In contrast, if there is no rule prohibiting a conventional transgression, participants generally judge the act as permissible (i.e., they think it is OK to talk in class if there is no rule against it). While participants do not always make the moral/conventional distinction in their seriousness judgments, they do always make the moral/conventional distinction in their modifiability judgments. Thus, children at certain ages have been found to judge some conventional and moral transgressions as equally serious (Stoddart and Turiel, 1985; Turiel, 1983). However, they still identify the moral transgressions as less rule contingent and less under authority jurisdiction than the conventional transgressions.

Children with psychopathic tendencies and adults with psychopathy have considerable difficulty with the moral/conventional distinction task (Blair, 1995, 1997; Blair et al., 1995a, 2001c). In addition, similar difficulties have been observed with more general populations of children presenting with antisocial behavior (Arsenio and Fleiss, 1996; Dunn and Hughes, 2001; Hughes and Dunn, 2000; Nucci and Herman, 1982). Children with psychopathic tendencies, adults with psychopathy, and other antisocial populations do generally regard moral transgressions as more serious than conventional transgressions. However, such populations are far less likely than comparison individuals to make reference to the victim of the transgression when justifying why moral transgressions are bad (Arsenio and Fleiss, 1996; Blair, 1995; Blair et al., 2001c; Dunn and Hughes, 2001; Hughes and Dunn, 2000). In addition, when the rules prohibiting the transgressions are removed, such populations are far less likely to make the distinction between moral and conventional transgressions that is seen in healthy individuals (Blair, 1995; Blair et al., 2001c; Nucci and Herman, 1982).

SUMMARY

In short, there are strong indications of impairment in moral reasoning in individuals with psychopathy. There are some indications of this using Kohlberg's moral judgment interview. However, the impairment is much more clearly evidenced by performance on the moral/conventional distinction test. Individuals with psychopathy, even when they are adult, fail to perform this task successfully even though a healthy developing individual shows successful performance from the age of 3 years.

Affect and language

In the above section, we described work investigating the moral semantic memory of individuals with psychopathy. We will argue below that any observed differences between psychopathic and non-psychopathic individuals in moral semantic memory is due to reduced affective input to semantic memory (see chapter 8). In this section, we will consider data concerning affective input to linguistic processing.

An individual's concepts are a product of his or her experience and cultural transmission. Concepts acquired in this way include those concerning emotional experience; i.e., what emotion an individual might experience in a given situation. We can therefore assume that if an individual lacked experience of a particular emotional experience, their concepts of this emotion might be atypical. One way to investigate the concepts of emotion that people have is by asking them to make inferences about the emotions that might be evoked by a given scenario. In an emotion attribution task, the participant is asked to state what emotion they think the individual in a given emotional situation might feel. Using this task, individuals with psychopathy have been found to show anomalous concepts for guilt but not for happiness, sadness, or embarrassment (Blair et al., 1995b).

A more direct investigation of the impact of affective input on linguistic processing is provided by studies using lexical decision tasks. In these tasks, the participant must decide as quickly and accurately as possible if a letter string forms a word (Graves et al., 1981; Strauss, 1983; Williamson et al., 1991). The letter strings are either neutral or emotional words or pronounceable pseudo-words. Replicating earlier work in healthy individuals (Graves et al., 1981; Strauss, 1983), non-psychopathic criminals responded faster to emotional words than neutral words. In addition, again replicating earlier work in healthy individuals (Begleiter et al., 1967), the non-psychopathic criminals showed larger evoked response potentials (ERPs) over central and parietal sites to emotional words. In contrast, the individuals with psychopathy failed to show any reaction time or ERP differences between neutral and emotional words (Kiehl et al., 1999a; Lorenz and Newman, 2002; Williamson et al., 1991). In comparable work, Day and Wong (1996) used a divided visual field paradigm where pairs of neutral and negative emotional words were presented simultaneously, one to the left and one to the right visual field (right and left hemisphere). Comparison individuals showed characteristically superior performance (lower error rates and shorter reaction times) when the emotional member of the pair was directed to their right hemisphere than when it was directed to their left hemisphere. However, the individuals with psychopathy did not show this superior performance for the right hemisphere (Day and Wong, 1996).

Two studies reported by Hare and colleagues are also of interest here (Hare et al., 1988b). The first study involved the participants being presented with word triads and having to select two words from each triad that best went together (Brownell et al., 1984). For example, one triad was "warm, loving, wise" while another was "foolish, shallow, deep." The task was scored for six types of word groupings. These were: (1) antonym (e.g., deep–shallow), (2) domain (e.g., loving–foolish – both relevant to domain of humans), (3) meta-phor (e.g., wise–deep); (4) polarity (e.g., foolish–shallow – both have a negative connotation), (5) domain and polarity (e.g., loving–wise – both are positively toned and pertain to humans), and (6) no relation (e.g., warm–foolish). In con-trast to the comparison individuals, the individuals with psychopathy made little use of emotional polarity. The pairings of the individuals with psychopathy appeared to be based on learnt associations between the words rather than on their emotional significance.

The second study reported by Hare et al. (1988b) involved participants being presented with emotional target phrases (e.g., "A man was thrown overboard a sinking ship") (Cicone et al., 1980). Each target phrase was accompanied by four test phrases. These were of the following types: (1) different descriptive features but of the same emotional tone (e.g., "A man running from a monster"), (2) similar descriptive features but opposite emotional tone (e.g., "A man surfing on a large wave"), (3) similar descriptive features but neutral emotional tone (e.g., "A woman standing on a yacht"), and (4) different descriptive characteristics and neutral tone (e.g., "A boy carrying a lamp into his room"). The participant was asked to select the test phrases that most closely matched the emotional tone of the target phrase. The comparison individuals had little difficulty in matching the emotional polarity of the target phrase with a test phrase. However, individuals with psychopathy, in contrast, were likely to make what the authors termed an "opposite polarity error." In other words, the individuals with psychopathy were significantly more likely than the comparison individuals to match the target phrase with a test phrase that was opposite in emotional polarity to the target phrase.

But are the results reviewed above of apparently reduced input of affect on linguistic processing just a reflection of a more generalized impairment in linguistic processing? Two recent findings, both using the lexical decision task, might suggest that individuals with psychopathy present with a more pervasive deficit in linguistic processing. Thus, Kiehl et al. (1999a) examined the influence of word concreteness on lexical decision. They found that the individuals with psychopathy made significantly more errors than comparison individuals in identifying abstract words as words. However, there were no group differences for concrete words. (On a related note, individuals with psychopathy have been reported to present with impairment when classifying words as abstract or concrete, if these words are presented to the right visual field (Hare and Jutai, 1988). Strikingly, however, individuals with psychopathy showed no impairment; indeed, they showed superior performance relative to comparison individuals, if the stimuli were presented to the left visual field. It is thus difficult to conclude that this result reflects an impairment in semantic processing.) In addition, Lorenz and Newman (2002), in their lexical decision task, found that whereas the comparison individuals were faster to state that high, rather than low, frequency words were words, individuals with psychopathy did not. However, one must be cautious when drawing conclusions from the previous two studies. Participant IQ was not recorded in the Kiehl et al. (1999a) study, thus group differences might be due to potential group differences in intelligence. In the Lorenz and Newman (2002) study, the high and low frequency words were made up of both emotional and neutral words. Thus, it is unclear whether the individuals with psychopathy received less benefit from a given word's higher frequency because of an insensitivity to this higher frequency or because, in healthy individuals, the influence of affect and frequency interacted. Thus, healthy individuals may have been particularly fast to state that a high-frequency emotional, relative to a high-frequency neutral, word was a word. In other words, the reduced effect of frequency shown by the individuals with psychopathy may actually still reflect the reduced effect of affect.

A third study indicating more generalized impairment in linguistic/semantic processing in individuals with psychopathy used a rather different paradigm (Newman et al., 1997). In this task, participants were instructed to determine whether two pictures or two words were conceptually related. At the same time as the two target stimuli were presented, a distracter stimulus was also presented (a word if the judgment was of two pictures or a picture if the judgment was of two words). Whereas healthy individuals (Gernsbacher and Faust, 1991) and low anxious comparison individuals in this study were faster to state that two target stimuli were unrelated if the distracter stimulus was not conceptually related to either of the target stimuli, low anxious individuals with psychopathy were not; they showed no interference of the distracter stimulus on the processing of the target stimuli.

Three further studies, however, suggest no generalized semantic processing impairment in individuals with psychopathy. Thus, one study examined the extent to which individuals with psychopathy and comparison individuals used the meaning of a word to prime, and thus facilitate, the processing of a second word. Each trial consisted of a prime word followed by a target stimulus that was either a word or a non-word (with a 50/50 ratio of words to non-words). For the word trials, the prime was either semantically related (e.g., doctor–nurse) or semantically unrelated (e.g., knife–cotton). In this study, both individuals with psychopathy and comparison individuals identified words more quickly when they were preceded by a related word; i.e., both groups displayed comparable priming (Brinkley et al., in press). Similarly, in a semantic priming task where the participant had to judge whether the target word was either an animal or a fruit following the presentation of either a congruent (e.g., ape–cat) or incongruent (e.g., apple–cat) word prime, both individuals with psychopathy and comparison individuals showed semantic priming and there were no group differences (Blair et al., in preparation). Finally, Brinkley et al. (in press) examined level of interference in a Stroop task as a function of semantic relatedness of the target response to the distracter. Thus, it is generally found that Stroop interference is greater if "yellow" is written in green ink than if "lemon" is written in green ink. In this study, both groups demonstrated Stroop interference and this was modulated by level of semantic relatedness between the color naming response and the distracter word.

SUMMARY

In short, individuals with psychopathy present with notably reduced affective input to linguistic processing. They present with reduced conceptual knowledge concerning moral emotions, reduced influence of affect information during lexical decision, and notable absences of appropriate affect input on specific tasks investigating semantic knowledge. In addition, there is some suggestion of more generalized impairment in linguistic/semantic processing.

Attention

There have been various suggestions of attentional abnormalities in individuals with psychopathy (Howland et al., 1993; Jutai and Hare, 1983; Jutai et al., 1987; Kiehl et al., 1999b; Kosson, 1996, 1998; Kosson and Newman, 1986; Raine and Venables, 1988). In line with these suggestions, there have been several demonstrations of atypical performance on attentional paradigms in individuals with psychopathy. Unfortunately, however, this body of work has been hampered by a loose definition of attention. Paradigms investigating the processing of distractor stimuli during goal-directed task performance (Jutai and Hare, 1983) have sometimes been considered together with data from dual-task paradigms (Kosson and Newman, 1986) as measuring "attention" even though the neurocognitive functions mediating task performance in these two types of task can be dissociated. We will briefly review the literature in this section.

Jutai and Hare (1983) recorded autonomic and electrocortical activity while prison inmates with high and low ratings of psychopathy were presented with a series of binaural tone pips, either by themselves (passive attention) or while video games were being played (selective attention). The N100 component of the auditory evoked potential was used as an index of attention paid to the tone pips, while performance on the video games was considered to be a reflection of attentiveness to the primary task. The individuals with psychopathy displayed normal N100 responses to the tone pips presented alone. However, the individuals with psychopathy gave small N100 responses to the tone pips during each trial, including the first one, when they were engaged in playing the video game. In contrast, the comparison individuals gave large N100 responses to tone pips during the first trial and small responses during later trials. This data would suggest an attentional abnormality in individuals with psychopathy. Specifically, it would suggest an over-focusing of attention in the individuals with psychopathy such that representations of the competing distractor stimuli were more greatly suppressed (an explanation consistent with the proposals of Jutai and Hare, 1983).

Howland and colleagues (1993) examined the attentional performance of psychopaths and non-psychopaths on an exogenously-cued Posner task. They found that performance was generally comparable across groups, but that psychopaths made more errors than non-psychopaths on invalidly cued trials with left-side imperative stimuli. Psychopaths also made more errors than controls on neutral trials for which the imperative stimulus appeared in the right visual field.

Three studies have investigated ERPs during phonemic or visual stimulus using "oddball" paradigms or the closely related continuous performance test (Jutai et al., 1987; Kiehl et al., 1999a; Raine and Venables, 1988). In oddball paradigms, the participant is searching for one target stimulus (the oddball) in a temporally separated stream of identical non-target stimuli. In the continuous performance test, the participant is searching for one target stimulus in a temporally separated stream of non-identical non-target stimuli. None of these studies found behavioral differences with respect to task performance. With respect to the ERP data, the picture is very mixed. Jutai et al. (1987), who used a phonemic oddball paradigm, found no group differences in the P300 component of the ERP. Jutai et al. (1987) recorded ERPs during the phonemic oddball paradigm both while participants performed the oddball task alone (single-task condition), and while participants simultaneously performed a distractor video-game task (dual-task condition). In the dual-task conditions, individuals with psychopathy did show P300 responses to the target that were notable for an overlapping positive slow wave (primarily at vertex and left-hemisphere sites). The functional significance of this result remains unknown and such a result has not been reported since.) Kiehl et al. (1999a), who used a visual oddball paradigm, reported significantly reduced P300 amplitude for target stimuli in the individuals with psychopathy. Raine and Venables (1988), who used a visual continuous performance task, reported, in contrast, significantly *enhanced* P300 amplitude for target stimuli in the individuals with psychopathy. In short, given the absence of behavioral effects and the inconsistent P300 effects, there are, currently, no clear indications of impairment in individuals with psychopathy in the detection of target stimuli amidst temporally separated distractors.

Two additional studies to that of Jutai et al. (1987) have investigated the ability of individuals with psychopathy to perform dual-task paradigms (Kosson, 1996; Kosson and Newman, 1986). In the Kosson and Newman (1986) study, participants performed a visual search task (counted the number of targets that appeared across each set of eight test frames) and a go/no-go task, in which they were to respond as quickly as possible to low-pitched, but not high-pitched, tones. Kosson (1996) presented participants with two simultaneous classification tasks. Participants were asked to classify symbol-strings as all numbers, all letters, or a mixture (50 percent), but only if the string appeared in a horizontal rather than vertical frame. They were also asked to classify a four-tone sequence as increasing in pitch, maintaining constant pitch, or a mixture, but only if the tones were relatively low-pitched. In the Kosson and Newman (1986) study, individuals with psychopathy made more visual-search errors than comparison individuals if they were asked to divide attention equally between the two tasks (i.e., the dual-task condition) but not if they were asked to focus on the visual search task. This would suggest difficulties in dual-task performance in individuals with psychopathy. However, in contrast, Kosson (1996) found no group differences in dual-task performance. However, the individuals with psychopathy responded to a higher percentage of secondary-task distractors. This cannot be taken to represent an attentional impairment *per se*. The representation of the stimuli was sufficient to guide behavior such that there were no group differences in the group task performance. However, the results do echo the impairments seen in individuals with psychopathy when performing response control tasks such as go/no-go or the stop-signal task (LaPierre et al., 1995; Roussy and Toupin, 2000); see chapter 8. They again suggest that individuals present with impairment regulating previously primed behavioral responses.

Kosson (1998) examined psychopaths' performance on a divided visual field task with two lateralized stimuli per trial. Participants were to classify symbol-strings as all numbers, all letters, or a mixture, but only if the string appeared in green rather than yellow font. Attention to the two stimuli was manipulated by target frequency; in one condition (relatively spatially focused attention) targets were more frequent in one visual field, while in the other condition (equally divided attention) targets were equi-probable in either visual field. This study did indicate attentional abnormalities in the individuals with psychopathy. Thus, under the relatively spatially focused attention condition, psychopaths misclassified more secondary targets and marginally more primary targets than non-psychopaths. An explanation of these results is a non-trivial task. They suggest that the comparison participants were better able than the individuals with psychopathy to take advantage of the relatively spatially focused condition but that this particularly helped their representation of targets in the non-focused field. However, the task was complex and the functional significance of the results will need to be unpacked in future work.

One interesting result from Kosson (1998) was that the individuals generally over-responded to distractors under the relatively spatially focused condition. This result again suggest the impairment in individuals with psychopathy in response control tasks seen in other studies (Kosson, 1996; LaPierre et al., 1995; Roussy and Toupin, 2000).

SUMMARY

There have been considerable suggestions of attentional abnormalities in individuals with psychopathy. However, the evidence is currently not overwhelming. Studies by Jutai and Hare (1983), Howland et al. (1993), and Kosson (1998) might suggest attentional abnormalities. However, they implicate such disparate forms of attentional processing that they suggest that individuals with psychopathy are marked by widespread attentional difficulties. In contrast, findings with oddball/continuous performance tasks (Jutai et al., 1987; Kiehl et al., 1999a; Raine and Venables, 1988) and dual performance tasks (Kosson, 1996; Kosson and Newman, 1986) are highly inconsistent. In addition, many of the studies in this field have not been

evaluated in the context of current formulations of attentional abnormalities from a cognitive neuroscience perspective. In short, it is unclear
whether individuals with psychopathy do present with attentional abnormalities or, if they do, what form they take.

Conclusions

In this chapter, we considered the functional impairment shown by individuals
with psychopathy. We began with a cautionary note: the apparent contradiction
between data indicating reduced anxiety in individuals with psychopathy and
data indicating that anxiety levels correlated with levels of antisocial behavior.
However, we pointed out that this contradiction was one of a number of apparent contradictions that can occur if care is not used to distinguish between
instrumental aggression and reactive aggression. Elevated levels of instrumental
aggression and psychopathy are associated with reduced anxiety. Elevated levels
of reactive aggression can be associated with increased anxiety.

Within the chapter, we reported that individuals with psychopathy are marked
with a constellation of impairments that primarily affect emotional processing.
Individuals with psychopathy present with reduced responses to threatening
stimuli, reduced emotional learning and relearning, reduced empathic responding, difficulties with aspects of moral reasoning, and difficulties with affect-laden
language. Such data were predicted by, and have led to the development of, the
fear and empathy (violence inhibition mechanism) dysfunction accounts that
will be described in chapter 5 and the integrated emotion systems model to be
considered in chapter 8.

Finally, we also noted that there are a few impairments seen in individuals
with psychopathy that are not linked to impairments in emotional processing;
e.g., impairments in some tasks related to semantic processing and attention.
These data are not predicted by the emotion-based models but will be returned
to as conundrums to be solved in chapter 9.

CHAPTER FIVE

COGNITIVE ACCOUNTS OF PSYCHOPATHY

In chapter 4, we described many of the functional impairments seen in individuals with psychopathy. The goal of this chapter is to consider a series of models that have attempted to account for these functional impairments. All of the models included in this chapter are cognitive models. By cognitive, we mean information processing models; i.e., models of what the brain is doing rather than where the brain is doing it. Cognitive here is not used to exclude emotion-based accounts. Within our perspective, cognitive is information processing, whether it is affect-based or non-affect-based.

The models that we will consider in this chapter are the response set modulation hypothesis (Newman, 1998), the fear dysfunction models (Eysenck and Gudjonsson, 1989; Lykken, 1995; Patrick, 1994), and the violence inhibition mechanism (VIM) model (Blair, 1995). Other theories such as the left hemisphere activation hypothesis (Kosson, 1996), various positions proposing frontal lobe dysfunction (Moffitt, 1993b; Raine, 2002a), and the somatic marker hypothesis (Damasio, 1994) will not be discussed here because these theories' primary focus is at the neural level. Instead, they will be considered in chapter 6.

The response set modulation hypothesis

An influential model of psychopathy is the response modulation hypothesis of Newman and colleagues (Newman 1998; Patterson and Newman, 1993). Response modulation involves "a rapid and relatively automatic (i.e., non-effortful or involuntary) shift of attention from the effortful organization and implementation of goal-directed behavior to its evaluation" (Newman et al., 1997). This "brief and highly automatic shift of attention . . . enables individuals to monitor and, if relevant, use information that is peripheral to their dominant response set (i.e., deliberate focus of attention)" (Lorenz and Newman, 2002, p. 92). The initial physiological basis of the model (Gorenstein and Newman, 1980) was based on the work of Gray and others on the implications of septo-hippocampal lesions for emotional learning (Gray, 1971). "In animal studies, deficient response modulation typically involves response perseveration or a tendency to continue some goal-directed behavior (e.g., running down the arm of a maze) despite punishment or frustrative nonreward (i.e., extinction)" (Newman, 1998, p. 85).

It is this proposed reduced automatic processing in individuals with psychopathy that is at the core of Newman's model. Thus:

> Whereas most people automatically anticipate the consequences of their actions, automatically feel shame for unkind deeds, automatically understand why they should persist in the face of frustration, automatically distrust propositions that seem too good to be true, and are automatically aware of their commitments to others, psychopaths may only become aware of such factors with effort.
>
> *(Newman, 1998, p. 84)*

Newman argues that it is not that individuals with psychopathy are incapable of regulating their behavior, only that self-regulation is more effortful for psychopaths because of the lack of these "relatively automatic processes" to guide actions.

The response modulation hypothesis is an attention-based model. According to the model, "the impulsivity, poor passive avoidance, and emotion-processing deficits of individuals with psychopathy may all be understood as a failure to process the meaning of information that is peripheral or incidental to their deliberate focus of attention" (Lorenz and Newman, 2002, p. 92).

The response set modulation hypothesis has generated a considerable body of experimental work. Thus, it has been used to explain the observed impairment in passive avoidance learning presented by individuals with psychopathy described in chapter 4 (Newman and Kosson, 1986). Indeed, the most frequently used measure of passive avoidance learning in individuals with psychopathy is the computerized number task introduced by Newman and Kosson (1986). In this task, participants are presented with a series of two-digit numbers some of which, when responded to, result in reward while others result in punishment (Kosson et al., 1990; Newman and Kosson, 1986; Newman et al., 1990). Participants must learn which stimuli, when responded to, result in reward and which result in punishment. In the original investigation using this task, Newman and Kosson (1986) found that individuals with psychopathy committed more passive avoidance errors than comparison individuals. This finding has been consistently replicated (Kosson et al., 1990; Newman and Kosson, 1986; Newman et al., 1990; Thornquist and Zuckerman, 1995).

A second major paradigm introduced by Newman and related to response set modulation is the one-pack card playing task (Newman et al., 1987). The task was described in detail in chapter 4, but briefly. In this task, the participant has to decide whether to select a card from a deck. Initially, the participant's choice to play is always reinforcing; if the participant plays the card he/she will win points or money. However, as the participant progresses through the pack of cards, the probability of reward decreases. The participant should terminate his/her responding before he/she receives greater levels of punishment than reward. Children with psychopathic tendencies and adults with psychopathy have considerable difficulty with this task; they continue to play the cards even when they are being repeatedly punished, and may end up losing all the points that they had gained (Fisher and Blair, 1998; Newman et al., 1987; O'Brien and Frick, 1996).

According to the response set modulation hypothesis, the poor performance of individuals with psychopathy on both the passive avoidance and one-pack card playing tasks are related to their inability to shift their attention from their goal of responding to gain reward to the peripheral punishment information. However, the response set modulation hypothesis has also been used to explain data that is not derived from emotional learning tasks. In the lexical decision task, which we also discussed in chapter 4, participants are presented with letter strings and must respond when the letter strings presented to them form a word. Healthy individuals respond faster, and show larger evoked response potentials (ERPs) over central and parietal sites, to emotional than neutral words (Begleiter et al., 1967; Graves et al., 1981). In contrast, individuals with psychopathy fail to show any reaction time or ERP differences between emotional and neutral words (Kiehl et al., 1999a; Lorenz and Newman, 2002; Williamson et al., 1991). Interestingly, as regards the response set modulation hypothesis, while healthy individuals are faster to respond to high frequency versus low frequency words, individuals with psychopathy are not (Lorenz and Newman, 2002). According to the response set modulation hypothesis, the absence of emotion and frequency effects on lexical decision performance in individuals with psychopathy is due to their inability to use the peripheral affective or frequency information because of their focus of attention on the dom-inant response set (deciding whether the stimulus was a word or not).

The response set modulation hypothesis has thus been associated with the development of an assortment of interesting paradigms. However, it is not without difficulties. In particular, while the response modulation hypothesis is an attentional account, it is unclear to what extent this account is compatible with contemporary models of attention.

Probably the current dominant model of attention is the biased competition model (Desimone and Duncan, 1995). This model stresses that attention is a

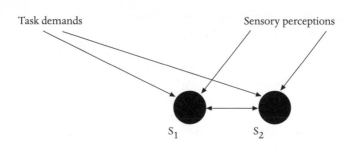

Figure 5.1   A simplified representation of the Desimone and Duncan (1995) model. Potential stimuli (S_1 and S_2) that might be attended to compete for activation. Representations of these stimuli are mutually inhibitory.

result of the competition for neural representation which occurs when multiple stimuli are present (Desimone and Duncan, 1995; Duncan, 1998). Which stimuli win this competition and are "attended to", can be a product of both (1) bottom-up sensory processes; thus there are enduring bottom-up biases to objects that are moving, bright, and large, for example (Jonides and Yantis, 1988; Triesman and Gormican, 1988); and (2) top-down influences on the basis of task demands (Desimone and Duncan, 1995). For example, if a person is told to search for objects of a particular color, units responding to that color will be primed in one or more systems within which color is coded. Objects of the desired color will then gain a competitive advantage in the primed system (Duncan et al., 1997). Alternatively, directed attention to a particular location in space facilitates processing of stimuli presented at that location. In this way, even objects that are not physically salient may win the competition and influence ongoing behavior. In short, an object may become the focus of attention because either it is intrinsically salient or top-down feedback processes bias its processing.

Figure 5.1 represents a simplified representation of the Desimone and Duncan (1995) model. In this representation, only two stimuli can be attended to: S_1 and S_2. In the absence of task demand information, which stimulus is attended to (or whether both might be) will be a function of bottom-up processes. If S_1 is moving, bright, and large for example, and S_2 is not, units representing S_1 will be highly active and suppress, though the inhibitory connections, those units representing S_2 (S_1 will be attended to). However, if the task demands stipulate a search for the still, dim, and small S_2 stimulus, the units representing this stimulus will be primed and their activity boosted such that the units representing S_1 will be suppressed (S_2 will be attended to).

There are two ways in which to consider the response modulation hypothesis with respect to this framework. According to the response modulation hypothesis, the difficulty faced by individuals with psychopathy is that the "relatively automatic processes" are less likely to guide actions. The first way of interpreting this idea within the biased competition model would be to suggest that the impact of bottom-up sensory-driven mechanisms is reduced in individuals with psychopathy. While such an interpretation makes some interesting novel predictions, for example that individuals with psychopathy would be less sensitive to pop-out effects of stimulus salience in a visual array, it is less clear that it is in line with the spirit of the response modulation hypothesis. The hypothesis stresses that the problems for individuals with psychopathy should emerge when they are engaged in goal-directed behavior. However, reduced functioning of bottom-up sensory-driven mechanisms would be apparent in behavior whether the individual was engaged in goal-directed action or not.

The second way of interpreting the response modulation hypothesis makes reference to attentional top-down feedback. According to the biased competition model, the degree to which a stimulus is processed (i.e., attended to) is determined by the degree to which it survives the competition process in sensory systems. The degree to which a stimulus that is not the focus of attention survives the competition process is thought to be a function of task load (Lavie, 1995). Under difficult task conditions (high load conditions), where processing of additional stimuli may fatally disrupt the goal-directed processing of the target stimuli, top-down processes will result in a tight focus on the target stimulus. As a consequence, the representation of the unattended stimuli will be sufficiently suppressed by the target stimulus as not to be processed. In contrast, under less difficult task conditions (low load conditions), where the processing of additional stimuli will not disrupt the goal-directed processing of the target stimulus, the unattended stimuli can survive the competition and be processed. For example, determining whether a centrally presented word stimulus is bisyllabic or not (high task load) prevents the identification of whether a peripherally presented non-target stimulus is moving. In contrast, determining whether the centrally presented word stimulus is written in upper or lower case (low task load) does not (Rees et al., 1997).

As regards the response modulation hypothesis, the suggestion would therefore be that individuals with psychopathy always operate under high load conditions during goal-directed activity or that top-down directed attention processes are so effective that they fail to incorporate other stimulus dimensions. That is, attention to the target stimuli dimensions so suppresses the representation of the unattended stimuli that they are not processed. At first glance, such an interpretation is attractive. It would appear to explain reduced processing of punishment information during goal-directed attention to stimuli associated with reward (Newman and Kosson, 1986; Newman et al., 1987) as well as reduced interference in Stroop-type tasks (Newman et al., 1997).

However, such an interpretation would not explain the lexical decision data (healthy individuals respond faster to emotional than neutral words while individuals with psychopathy do not). If the stimulus to be identified as a word or not is being attended to (as must be the case to achieve the task), then the stimulus should automatically activate associated affective input; this would not be a function of attention, it would be an inevitable function of the word's associations. Indeed, it should occur to an even greater extent; just as the suppression of competitor stimuli should be enhanced, the processing of associated information should be enhanced. The only way that the word should not activate this input would be independent of an attentional account; i.e., if the learnt emotional associations in individuals with psychopathy are profoundly impaired.

Moreover, an attentional account of the impairment seen in individuals with psychopathy in passive avoidance learning and response reversal as indexed by the one-pack card playing task is only superficially attractive. In the passive avoidance and response reversal paradigms (Newman and Kosson, 1986; Newman et al., 1987), the punishment information is presented in the absence of distracting information. According to models of attention (Desimone and Duncan, 1995; Lavie, 1995), it would be difficult to see why this information should not be attended to/processed given the absence of competing stimuli. The fact that the punishment information does not modulate the behavior of individuals with psychopathy would tend to suggest that these individuals have difficulties learning from this information, rather than that they cannot attend to it. Such a suggestion is made by the fear and integrated emotion systems accounts (Blair, 2003a; Fowles, 1988; Lykken, 1995; Patrick et al., 1994).

SUMMARY

In short, the response set modulation hypothesis has resulted in the development of an assortment of interesting paradigms. However, at present it is unclear the extent to which this attention-driven hypothesis is compatible with contemporary positions on attention.

The dysfunctional fear hypotheses

One of the main positions regarding the emotional impairment shared by individuals with psychopathy is that there is impairment in the neurophysiological systems modulating fear behavior (Cleckley, 1976; Eysenck, 1964; Fowles, 1988; Gray, 1987; Lykken, 1995; Mealey, 1995; Patrick, 1994; Pichot, 1978; Trasler, 1973, 1978). For example, Cleckley (1976) wrote: "Within himself he appears almost as incapable of anxiety as of profound remorse" (p. 340). The dysfunctional fear positions all assume that moral socialization is achieved through the use of punishment (Eysenck and Gudjonsson, 1989; Trasler, 1978). In essence, they assume that the healthy individual is frightened by punishment and associates this fear with the action that resulted in the punishment, thus making the individual less likely to engage in the action in the future. The suggestion is that individuals with psychopathy, because they are less aversively aroused by punishment, make weaker associations and thus are more likely to engage in the punished action in the future than healthy individuals.

The variants of the fear dysfunction hypothesis have generated a considerable body of empirical literature. Indeed, the earliest formal experimental investigations of psychopathy were based around the fear dysfunction hypothesis (Lykken, 1957). Thus, the fear dysfunction positions predict the observed findings of impairment in individuals with psychopathy in aversive conditioning (Flor et al., 2002; Lykken, 1957), in generating autonomic responses to anticipated threat (Hare, 1982; Ogloff and Wong, 1990), in the augmentation of the startle reflex to visual threat primes (Herpertz et al., 2001; Levenston et al., 2000), in passive avoidance learning (Lykken, 1957; Newman and Kosson, 1986), and in response reversal (Mitchell et al., 2002; Newman et al., 1987).

However, despite this empirical success, the variants of the fear dysfunction hypothesis face several problems. First, for the most part, the variants are underspecified at both the cognitive and neural levels. The various authors do not provide many details concerning the computational properties of the fear system. For example, it is difficult to be certain about the range of inputs to any putative fear systems or how the fear system operates in response to these inputs. The only more detailed account of a fear system that has been used in relation to explaining psychopathy is the behavioral inhibition system model (Gray, 1987; Gray and McNaughton, 1996; McNaughton and Gray, 2000). This model is depicted in figure 5.2. The suggestion here is that there is a unitary fear system, the behavioral inhibition system, which is thought to generate autonomic responses to punished stimuli (through classical conditioning) as well as inhibiting responding following punishment (through instrumental conditioning).

The behavioral inhibition system model does provide us with a putative range of inputs to a fear system and outputs from this system. However, it assumes that there is a unitary fear system, a claim implicit in all the variants of the fear dysfunction hypothesis. However, and this brings us to the second problem for the fear dysfunction hypothesis, the empirical literature strongly suggests that there is no single fear system but rather that there are a series of at least partially separable neural systems that are engaged in specific forms of processing that can be subsumed under the umbrella term fear. For example, aversive conditioning and instrumental learning are two forms of processing in which the fear

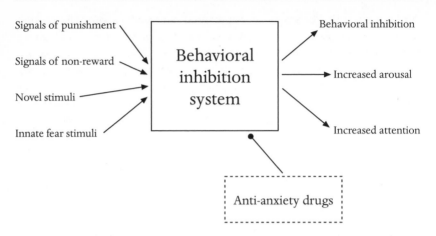

Figure 5.2   The behavioral inhibition system postulated by Gray (1982). This system is held to be activated by each of the classes of stimuli on the left-hand side and to produce each of the outputs on the right-hand side. Anti-anxiety drugs are held to act specifically on the behavioral inhibition system. Adapted from Gray (1982) with permission.

system is thought to be involved (Lykken, 1995; Patrick, 1994). Yet the neural circuitry to achieve aversive conditioning and instrumental learning are doubly dissociable (Killcross et al., 1997). Thus, a lesion to the central nucleus of the amygdala will prevent aversive conditioning but still allow instrumental learning to occur. In contrast, a lesion to the basolateral nucleus of the amygdala will prevent instrumental learning but still allow aversive conditioning to occur. Moreover, early amygdala lesions result in a massive reduction of neo-phobia; the infant monkey is no longer fearful of novel objects. However, the same infant monkeys with amygdala lesions show heightened social phobia; i.e., their fear response to another infant monkey is actually heightened (Amaral, 2001; Prather et al., 2001). These findings strongly suggest partially separable "fear" systems: for aversive conditioning/instrumental learning and for social threats.

The third problem faced by the fear dysfunction hypothesis is that it is unclear why the fear theories should predict the very high level of antisocial behavior shown by individuals with psychopathy. As noted several times previously, psychopathy is a disorder where the afflicted individual engages in instrumental antisocial behavior including aggression with striking frequency; the psychopathic individual uses antisocial behavior to achieve his/her goals (Cornell et al., 1996; Williamson et al., 1987). This has usually been taken to indicate that the psychopathic individual has failed to be socialized away from using antisocial behavior (Eysenck and Gudjonsson, 1989; Trasler, 1978).

However, the assumption that conditioned fear responses play a crucial role in moral socialization has been questioned (Blackburn, 1988; Blair and Morton, 1995). Thus, the developmental literature indicates that moral socialization is not achieved through the formation of conditioned fear responses but rather through the induction and fostering of empathy (Hoffman, 1984); see also chapter 8. Studies have shown, for example, that moral socialization is better achieved through the use of induction (reasoning that draws children's attention to the effects of their misdemeanors on others and increases empathy) than through harsh authoritarian or power assertive parenting practices which rely on the use of punishment (Baumrind, 1971, 1983; Hoffman and Saltzstein, 1967). Indeed, there have been suggestions that while empathy facilitates moral socialization, fear actually hinders it (Hoffman, 1994). Thus, in a review of a large number of studies of disciplinary methods, it was concluded that punishment-based power assertion had an adverse effect on moral socialization regardless of age (Brody and Shaffer, 1982). Indeed, it has been suggested that the primary utility of power assertion is to prevent the parent from being ignored while the child is transgressing (Hoffman, 1988).

In addition, according to conditioning theory and data, the conditioned stimulus (CS) that ends up being associated with the unconditioned stimulus (US) is the CS that most consistently predicts the US (Dickinson, 1980). To achieve socialization through aversive conditioning, it would therefore be crucial to ensure that the relevant CS (a representation of the transgression activity that the caregiver is attempting to ensure the child will find aversive) consistently predicts the US (the caregiver hitting the child). However, this is very difficult to achieve. In houses using punishment-based techniques, the punishment is rarely contiguous with the performance of the transgression. This means that the desired CS rarely predicts the US of the caregiver's punishment. Instead, the CS predicting the US is more likely to the individual who delivers the US. Thus, in these households, aversive conditioning may occur but the US – CS association will be physical pain and a particular parent, rather than physical pain and antisocial behavior. Indeed, in households using punishment-based techniques, the punished child frequently does not show fear of committing transgressions (the poorly predictive CS) but does show fear of the person who is likely to punish them (the highly predictive CS) (Hoffman, 1994).

A fourth problem faced by the fear positions is also related to the idea embedded in them, that socialization should be achieved through punishment. If healthy individuals learn to avoid antisocial behavior because of fear of punishment, it must be assumed that the healthy child judge all rules / transgressions in a similar way. In other words, if we learn to avoid talking in class and hitting other individuals because we are punished when we commit these actions, there is no reason for us to distinguish between these two transgressions. However, as noted in chapter 4, healthy developing children make a distinction between moral (victim-based) and conventional (social-order-based) transgressions from the age of 36 months (Smetana, 1981, 1985, 1993). In other words, children do not judge all transgressions the same. Instead, they differentiate between those transgressions that result in harm to another and those that simply cause social disorder.

SUMMARY

In short while the fear positions have generated a considerable body of data, they currently face many difficulties as models of the development of psychopathy. This is not to say that they are wrong but rather that they are under-specified. Indeed, in many respects the model that we will be describing in chapter 8 can be considered a development of these fear positions. Certainly, the neurocognitive architecture that will be described is considered to mediate fear processing.

Violence inhibition mechanism model

The importance of empathy for moral socialization was one of the reasons for the development of the original violence inhibition mechanism (VIM) model of psychopathy (Blair, 1995; Blair et al., 1997). This model has changed considerably since its earliest formulation but basically rests on the phenomenon that many social animals, including humans, find the experience of the distress of conspecifics aversive. Thus, both rats and monkeys will learn to make instrumental responses (pressing levers/pulling chains) which terminate unpleasant occurrences to conspecifics (Church, 1959; Masserman et al., 1964; Rice, 1965; Rice and Gainer, 1962). For example, if a rat learns that pressing a bar will lower another, suspended, rat to the ground (a distressing experience for the suspended rat), the rat will press the lever (Rice and Gainer, 1962). Alternatively, in a study with rhesus monkeys, the animals were trained to pull two chains to receive different levels of reward. After the initial training, the experimenters altered the task such that pulling the chain with the larger reward caused another monkey in sight of the test animal to receive an electric shock. After the participants witnessed the shock of the conspecific, 10 out of the 15 test animals preferred the non-shock chain even though it resulted in half as many rewards. Of the remaining 5 test animals, one stopped pulling the chains altogether for 5 days and another for 12 days after witnessing the shock of the object. Variables that particularly induced a cessation of high-reward/conspecific-pain lever

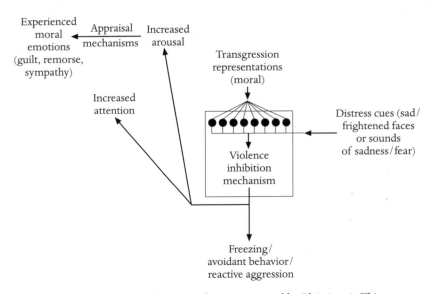

Experienced moral emotions (guilt, remorse, sympathy) ← Appraisal mechanisms Increased arousal

Transgression representations (moral)

Increased attention

Distress cues (sad/ frightened faces or sounds of sadness/fear)

Violence inhibition mechanism

Freezing/ avoidant behavior/ reactive aggression

Figure 5.3 The violence inhibition mechanism proposed by Blair (1995). This system is held to be activated by distress cues and also stimuli associated with these distress cues (moral transgressions). It is thought to give rise to threat-related behavior (e.g., freezing), increased attention, and arousal.

pressing included visual rather than auditory cues, experience by the test animal of shock, and enhanced familiarity with the shocked individual (Masserman et al., 1964).

The suggestion is that most humans are also predisposed to find the distress of conspecifics aversive (Blair, 1995; Blair et al., 1997). In short, they are punished by signals of another human's sadness or fear. This will reduce their probability of engaging in actions that gave rise to another individual's distress (as the rhesus monkeys showed in Masserman et al.'s (1964) study) or increase their probability of engaging in actions that remove another individual's distress (as the rats showed in Rice and Gainer's (1962) study). The distress of another individual is considered aversive by most humans (Bandura and Rosenthal, 1966). Moreover, the presentation of cues indicating another individual's sadness or fear reduces the probability of future physical aggression (Perry and Perry, 1974), disputes over property ownership (Camras, 1977), and aggressive sexual activity (Chaplin et al., 1995).

At its simplest, the VIM is thought to be a system that when activated by distress cues, the sad and fearful expressions of other individuals, results in increased autonomic activity, attention, and activation of the brainstem threat response system (usually resulting in freezing) (Blair, 1995); see figure 5.3.

According to the model, moral socialization occurs through the pairing of the activation of the mechanism by distress cues with representations of the acts that caused the distress cues (i.e., moral transgressions, such asone person hitting another) (Blair, 1995). Through association these representations of moral transgressions become triggers for the mechanism. The appropriately developing child thus initially finds the pain of other individuals aversive and then, through socialization, thoughts of acts that cause pain to others become aversive also. It is proposed that individuals with psychopathy have disruption to this system such that representations of acts that cause harm to others do not become triggers for the VIM (Blair, 1995).

In its original form, the VIM model was meant to detail a cognitive model of the prerequisites for moral development. It suggested the existence of an early developing system which leads to distress cues generating an aversive emotional reaction in observers. It suggested that this system was necessary for moral socialization and that it was dysfunctional in individuals with psychopathy. The model was able to provide an explanation of much of the existing data. For example, the model provided an account for why individuals distinguished between moral and conventional transgressions (Smetana, 1993; Turiel et al., 1987). It was predicted that individuals with psychopathy would be less able to distinguish between moral and conventional transgressions, a prediction that has been confirmed (Arsenio and Fleiss, 1996; Blair, 1995, 1997; Blair et al., 1995a, 2001c; Nucci and Herman, 1982). It was predicted that this impairment would be related to reduced responsiveness to sad and fearful facial expressions. Research has shown that psychopathic individuals show reduced autonomic responses to the distress of other individuals (Aniskiewicz, 1979; Blair, 1999b; Blair et al., 1997; House and Milligan, 1976). Moreover, it has been shown that while "victim" scenes prime up the threat system in healthy individuals such that after this prime, the participant presents with an augmented startle response, this is not the case in individuals with psychopathy (Levenston et al., 2000). In addition, individuals with psychopathy, in childhood and adulthood, present with impairment even in the naming of sad and particularly fearful facial and vocal affect (Blair et al., 2001b, in press; Stevens et al., 2001).

However, while the original VIM model could provide an account of the emergence of instrumental antisocial behavior in individuals with psychopathy and while it did generate a variety of predictions that have been empirically confirmed, it faced a serious difficulty: it could not account for the data associated with the response set modulation and fear hypotheses. Moreover, it could not account for data on the interaction of temperament and socialization practice on the development of moral development/conscience. Kochanska has stressed the role of fearfulness as the important temperamental factor (Kochanska, 1993, 1997). Indeed, she and others have found fearful children to show higher levels of moral development/conscience using a variety of measures (Asendorpf and Nunner-Winkler, 1992; Kochanska, 1997; Kochanska et al., 1994; Rothbart et al., 1994). In addition, Kochanska has stressed that different socialization practices may promote moral development in children with different temperaments (Kochanska, 1993, 1997). In line with this, she found that for fearful children, maternal gentle discipline promoted moral/conscience development. In contrast, for "fearless" children, alternative socialization practices, presumably capitalizing on mother – child positive orientation (secure attachment, maternal responsiveness), promoted the development of conscience (Kochanska, 1997).

SUMMARY

In short, while the original VIM model does provide a plausible account of the emergence of the instrumental antisocial behavior displayed by individuals with psychopathy, it cannot account for the range of impairments shown by such individuals. In particular, the VIM account cannot explain much of the data associated with the response set modulation and fear hypotheses. This has resulted in an expansion of the model at both the cognitive and neural levels: the integrated emotion systems model. This expanded model will be described in chapter 7.

General conclusions

The goal of this chapter was to discuss the three main cognitive accounts of psychopathy: the response set modulation account, the fear dysfunction hypotheses, and the VIM model. Each of these models has been associated with the development of new, or adaptation of old, paradigms to use with individuals with psychopathy. Each of these models has been associated with novel predictions, many of which have been empirically confirmed. However, none of them can be considered a full account of psychopathy. The response set modulation account struggles with some of the empirical literature within the field of psychopathy but faces even more difficulty with the empirical literature beyond psychopathy. A theory of psychopathy needs to be a theory of healthy cognition together with an account of how the system(s) can become dysfunctional so that the disorder can emerge. The response set modulation account of attention does not appear compatible with current theory and empirical data within the field of attention.

The fear dysfunction positions face a different set of problems. These are mostly related to the fact that, with the exception of the behavioral inhibition system account, they tend to be highly under-specified. This is particularly a problem given more recent data suggesting that there is not a unitary fear system but rather a collection of systems that are interconnected to a greater or lesser degree. As yet, no fear dysfunction position has attempted to grapple with the dissociations within the neural architecture mediating the response to threat, or considered what it might mean for an account of psychopathy.

The VIM account has the advantage that it can provide a ready explanation for the emergence of instrumental aggression in individuals with psychopathy. However, it cannot be considered a full explanation of the disorder. There are too many empirical results connected to the functional impairment in individuals with psychopathy for which it can provide no insight.

In short, none of these three cognitive accounts can provide a complete explanation of psychopathy. In chapter 6, we will consider neural accounts of the development of psychopathy.

CHAPTER SIX

NEURAL ACCOUNTS OF PSYCHOPATHY

In chapter 5, we described the three main cognitive accounts of psychopathy but concluded that none could provide a full explanation of the disorder. The goal of this chapter is to consider a series of models that have attempted to account for the functional impairments shown by individuals with psychopathy by reference to neural architecture. These models are the left hemisphere activation hypothesis (Kosson, 1996), various positions proposing frontal lobe dysfunction (Moffitt, 1993b; Raine, 2002a), and the somatic marker hypothesis (Damasio, 1994). Each will be considered in turn.

The left hemisphere activation hypothesis

There have been speculations that individuals with psychopathy may present with "weak or unusual lateralization of language function, and that psychopaths may have fewer left hemisphere resources for processing language than do normal individuals" (Hare and Jutai, 1988, p. 329). Such speculations were prompted by a series of studies in the 1980s. Thus, for example, Hare and Jutai (1988) presented word stimuli to the participant's left or right visual field. Participants had to state whether the word stimuli matched either a previously presented word, a semantic category, or an abstract category. Strikingly, individuals with psychopathy showed pronounced difficulty for the abstract category discrimination if the stimuli were presented to the right visual field. However, their performance was superior to that of comparison individuals if the stimuli were presented to the left visual field. There were no significant effects of visual field if the participant was making stimulus word matching or semantic category judgments.

Similarly, in a dichotic listening task, individuals with psychopathy and comparison individuals were presented with words played to the right or left ear and asked to report what they had heard (Hare and McPherson, 1984). The individuals with psychopathy were impaired in their reporting of words that were played to the right ear but not to the left ear relative to comparison individuals. This result was later replicated in a population of adolescent individuals with psychopathic tendencies (Raine et al., 1990).

This position of "weak or unusual lateralization of language function" in individuals with psychopathy (Hare and Jutai, 1988) has been developed into the left hemisphere activation (LHA) hypothesis (Kosson, 1998). According to this position, individuals with psychopathy present with deficits in cognitive processing that are state-specific, occurring only under conditions that selectively and differentially activate left hemisphere resources. The LHA hypothesis suggests that information processing in general (i.e., not specifically that subserved by the left hemisphere) will be disrupted in individuals with psychopathy when the left hemisphere is substantially and differentially activated by processing demands (Kosson, 1998). According to Kosson, differential activation of the left hemisphere can be achieved by demands that may be incidental to the given task; e.g., responding differentially with the right hand, or attending disproportionately to the right visual field.

While the data from the three studies described above (Hare and Jutai, 1988; Hare and McPherson, 1984; Raine et al., 1990) have been taken in support of the LHA position by Kosson, it is unclear to what degree they are in line with the predictions of the model. Thus, while Hare and Jutai (1988) found that individuals with psychopathy showed pronounced difficulty for the abstract category discrimination if the stimuli were presented to the right visual field, the performance of these individuals was *superior* if the stimuli were presented to the left visual field. The latter result remains to be explained by the LHA. Moreover, there were no significant effects of visual field if the participant was making stimulus word matching or semantic category judgments; i.e., in contrast, to the LHA, processing *in general* was not disrupted. With respect to the Hare and McPherson (1984) and Raine et al. (1990) findings, the individuals with psychopathy were only impaired in their reporting of words that were played to the right ear; i.e., again processing was not generally disrupted.

Kosson has published several direct tests of his position (Kosson, 1996, 1998). Using complex tasks that will not be fully described here, Kosson (1996, 1998) presented participants with eight-character strings that were either made up of consonants, numbers, or a mixture of the two. In line with Kosson's position, use of the right hand for visual discriminations (i.e., the condition differentially activating the left hemisphere) was associated with impaired performance in the individuals with psychopathy relative to comparison individuals. Interestingly, however, and unexplainable by the LHA position though in line with the results of Hare and Jutai (1988), the individuals with psychopathy presented with superior performance relative to the comparison individuals when they were using their left hand.

Currently, the main difficulty for the LHA position is its lack of specificity. It remains unclear why greater activation of left hemisphere systems should generally disrupt cortical functioning. It remains unclear which left hemisphere systems, when over-activated, generally disrupt cortical functioning. It remains unclear how to quantify greater left hemisphere activation: should responding with the right hand be taken as an equivalent "left hemisphere stressor" to greater target presentations in the right visual field? Given this lack of specificity, the utility of the model is currently limited.

SUMMARY

There do appear to be indications of "weak or unusual lateralization of language function" in individuals with psychopathy. However, the functional significance of these findings is difficult to discern (this issue will be revisited in chapter 9). There are no obvious reasons why these impairments should give rise to the development of psychopathy. Currently, the LHA variant of this position is in need of refinement. The evidence that excessive activation of the left hemisphere has a general effect on cognitive processing is not overwhelming.

The frontal lobe dysfunction hypothesis

Frontal lobe and consequent executive dysfunction have long been related to antisocial behavior (Barratt, 1994; Elliot, 1978; Gorenstein, 1982; Moffitt, 1993a; Raine, 1997, 2002a). This has led to suggestions that either psychopathy in particular or antisocial behavior more generally is due to frontal lobe dysfunction (Gorenstein, 1982; Moffitt, 1993a; Raine, 2002a, b). These suggestions have been prompted by three sets of data: (1) data from patients with acquired lesions of frontal cortex; (2) data from neuropsychological studies of individuals presenting with antisocial behavior; and (3) data from neuro-imaging studies of individuals presenting with antisocial behavior. The implications of these three sets of data for psychopathy in particular and antisocial behavior more generally will be discussed in turn.

Data from patients with acquired lesions of frontal cortex

There is a consistent literature indicating that patients with acquired lesions of frontal cortex may present with emotional and personality changes such as euphoria, irresponsibility, lack of affect, lack of concern for the present or future, and increased aggression (Hecaen and Albert, 1978; Stuss and Benson, 1986). However, it is important to note that such patients present with increased levels of reactive aggression and not instrumental aggression (Anderson et al., 1999; Blair and Cipolotti, 2000; Burgess and Wood, 1990; Grafman et al., 1996; Pennington and Bennetto, 1993). This is the case even if the lesions are acquired very early in life (Anderson et al., 1999; Pennington and Bennetto, 1993). Moreover, as is shown in figure 6.1, frontal cortex corresponds to almost half of the cortex (Fuster, 1980) and has been implicated in a variety of putative processes (Baddeley and Della Sala, 1998; Burgess and Shallice, 1996; Luria, 1966; Pennington and Ozonoff, 1996; Roberts et al., 1998). At its simplest, a division is usually made between dorsolateral, orbital, and medial frontal cortex (see figure 6.1). Analysis of the lesion locations of patients presenting with increased levels of aggression has shown that it is orbital (ventral) and medial frontal cortex, but not dorsolateral prefrontal cortex, that are involved in the regulation of (reactive) aggression (Damasio, 1994; Grafman et al., 1996; Volavka, 1995).

There are, therefore, two important implications of this neurological literature. First, patients with acquired lesions of orbitofrontal cortex show key differences in presentation relative to individuals with psychopathy even if the lesion is acquired early in life. This does not necessarily disprove a frontal lobe account of psychopathy but does mean that such an account is in need of considerably greater specification than those currently available. Second, these data do strongly indicate that orbital (ventral) and medial frontal cortex pathology can give rise to an increased risk of antisocial behavior. This issue will be returned to in chapter 7.

Data from neuropsychological studies of individuals presenting with antisocial behavior

There are considerable data indicating that individuals with antisocial behavior show impaired performance on measures of executive functioning (see, for reviews of this literature, Kandel and Freed, 1989; Moffitt, 1993b; Morgan and Lilienfield, 2000; Pennington and Ozonoff, 1996). However, it is noteworthy that within this literature, distinction is rarely made between different regions of

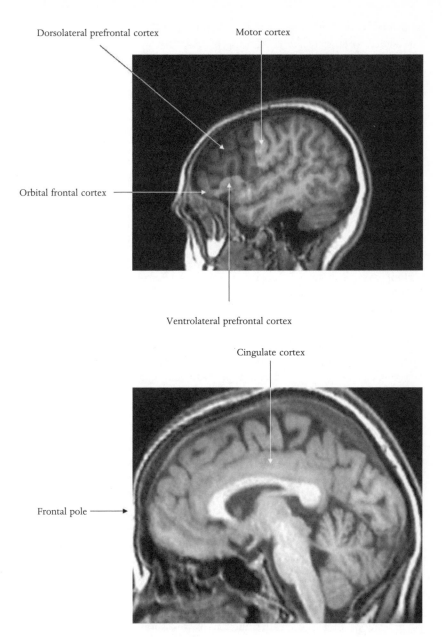

Figure 6.1 (a) Two main subdivisions of the frontal lobes: dorsolateral prefrontal cortex and orbital frontal cortex. (b) The third subdivision of the frontal lobes, medial frontal cortex, consisting of anterior regions of the cingulate as well as the cortex immediately surrounding the cingulate.

prefrontal cortex or different forms of executive function. Instead, the literature has tended to concentrate on the use of tasks that index executive functions commonly linked to dorsolateral prefrontal cortex (DLPFC); e.g., the Wisconsin Card Sorting Task (WCST) and the Controlled Oral Word Association Test (COWAT). This is problematic as the neurological literature described above has shown that it is orbito- (ventral) and medial frontal cortex and specifically *not* DLPFC that are involved in the regulation of (reactive) aggression (Damasio, 1994; Grafman et al., 1996; Volavka, 1995); see chapter 7.

So how can one explain the ample evidence that individuals with antisocial behavior do show impaired performance on measures of DLPFC executive functioning? We suggest two possibilities. First, it is worth remembering here that there is significant comorbidity of conduct disorder (CD)/psychopathic tendencies and attention deficit hyperactivity disorder (ADHD); see chapter 2. ADHD has been associated with dysfunction of right-sided DLPFC prefrontal-striatal systems (Castellanos et al., 1996; Giedd et al., 2001). Individuals with ADHD present with pronounced impairment on measures of executive functioning (Barkley, 1999; Pennington and Ozonoff, 1996). It is thus possible that the association of antisocial behavior with impaired performance on executive function tasks is due to individuals with ADHD presenting with antisocial behavior. ADHD may be a risk factor for dysfunction that leads to antisocial behavior even if the pathology associated with ADHD itself does not lead to antisocial behavior (see chapter 9). Indeed, in line with this suggestion, Pennington and Ozonoff (1996) noted in their review that individuals with CD who were not comorbid for ADHD presented with no indications of executive dysfunction.

Of course, an alternative explanation of the association between impairment of executive functions thought to rely on the DLPFC and antisocial behavior is that these executive function measures index the severity of the executive impairment. Individuals with a greater degree of DLPFC impairment may be more likely to also have a greater impairment of executive functions thought to rely on orbital and medial frontal cortex. According to this explanation, the association between impairment of executive functions thought to rely on the DLPFC and antisocial behavior is correlational rather than causal.

In short, there are clear data indicating an association between executive function and antisocial behavior. However, the causal significance of this association is questionable. But is psychopathy related to executive dysfunction? In contrast to generally antisocial populations, individuals with psychopathy show no indications of executive dysfunction on measures linked to dorsolateral prefrontal cortex (Kandel and Freed, 1989; LaPierre et al., 1995; Mitchell et al., 2002). Thus, individuals with psychopathy have been found to show no impairment on the WCST (LaPierre et al., 1995), the COWAT (Roussy and Toupin, 2000; Smith et al., 1992), or the ED-shift component of the intradimensional/

extradimensional (ID/ED) task (Mitchell et al., 2002). However, individuals with psychopathy do appear to show executive dysfunction on measures linked to orbital frontal cortex dysfunction; e.g., the Porteus maze test, motor go/no-go tasks, and measures of response reversal/extinction such as the ID/ED task and the one-pack card playing task (LaPierre et al., 1995; Mitchell et al., 2002; Newman et al., 1997; Roussy and Toupin, 2000). Thus, individuals with psychopathy do present with frontal lobe dysfunction, albeit dysfunction that is selective to those executive functions mediated by orbital frontal cortex rather than DLPFC.

Data from neuro-imaging studies of individuals presenting with antisocial behavior

A series of brain imaging studies of aggressive individuals have suggested that these individuals are marked by reduced frontal functioning (Critchley et al., 2000; Goyer et al., 1994; Raine et al., 1994b, 1997, 1998a, b, 2000; Schneider et al., 2000; Volkow and Tancredi, 1987; Volkow et al., 1995; Wong et al., 1997). For example, Volkow and Tancredi (1987) examined cerebral blood flow (CBF) under rest conditions using positron emission tomography (PET) in four reactively violent psychiatric patients. Two of these patients presented with reduced CBF in frontal cortex (all four presented with reduced CBF in the left temporal lobe). In a follow-up study, Volkow and colleagues (1995) examined CBF under rest conditions using PET in eight reactively violent psychiatric patients and eight comparison individuals. As a group, the violent individuals showed significantly less CBF in medial temporal and frontal cortex than the comparison individuals.

Similarly, Raine and colleagues (1994b, 1997) examined CBF using PET during performance of a continuous performance task in murderers pleading not guilty by reason of insanity and matched comparison individuals ($N = 22$ and $N = 41$ in both groups in the 1994 and 1997 studies, respectively). Raine and colleagues (1994b) found reduced CBF in prefrontal cortex in the murderers pleading not guilty by reason of insanity. Raine and colleagues (1997) found reduced CBF in the murderers pleading not guilty by reason of insanity in the prefrontal cortex, superior parietal gyrus, left angular gyrus, and the corpus callosum, while abnormal asymmetries of activity (left hemisphere lower than right) were also found in the amygdala, thalamus, and medial temporal lobe. Finally, Raine and colleagues (2000) also investigated prefrontal white and gray matter volumes in individuals taken from the community who scored highly on the PCL-R against those of two comparison individuals. This study reported reduced prefrontal gray, but not white, matter volume in the individuals scoring highly on the PCL-R.

There are difficulties with these studies however. The Volkow and Tancredi (1987) and the Raine and colleagues (1994b, 1997, 1998a, 2000) studies included violent individuals with known organic brain damage (this was the case for over 50 percent of the murderers in some of these studies) and, in the studies conducted by Raine and colleagues, patients with schizophrenia. Organic damage to frontal regions will be associated with reduced frontal activity whether the patient is aggressive or not. Schizophrenia, whether the patients are aggressive or not, is associated with prefrontal cortical atrophy (Roth et al., 2004; Shallice et al., 1991). Thus, the atypical blood flow reported may reflect organic damage or schizophrenia that may, or may not, be related to their aggressive behavior. Interestingly, Wong and colleagues (1997) investigated CBF under rest conditions using PET, and structural abnormalities using MRI, in 20 repetitive violent schizophrenic offenders and a matched group of 19 non-repetitive violent schizophrenics. This study reported no group differences in functioning or structure. Moreover, a recent study of impulsive – aggressive male personality disordered (PD) patients, who were screened for axis I pathology and brain abnormalities, reported that temporal lobe volumes were 20 percent smaller in PD patients than comparison individuals but there were no group differences in frontal lobe volume (Dolan et al., 2002).

In addition, the vast majority of the above studies did not examine subregions of the frontal lobes differentially despite data that it is only orbital (ventral) and medial frontal cortex that have been implicated in the regulation of (reactive) aggression (Damasio, 1994; Grafman et al., 1996; Volavka, 1995). However, two studies did subdivide frontal cortex. Dolan et al. (2002) found reduced medial frontal volumes in her impulsive–aggressive male PD patients. A second study examined the CBF under rest conditions using PET of 17 patients with personality disorder (antisocial, borderline, dependent, and narcissistic) and 43 comparison individuals. They compared CBF to their patients' history of (mostly reactive) aggression and found that lower normalized CBF in orbitofrontal cortex (BA 47) correlated with a history of aggression (Goyer et al., 1994).

There have been a growing number of neuro-imaging studies of individuals with psychopathy (Kiehl et al., 2001; Laakso et al., 2002; Muller et al., 2003; Raine et al., 2000; Schneider et al., 2000; Soderstrom et al., 2002; Tiihonen et al., 2000; Veit et al., 2002). With respect to structural imaging studies, as noted above, Raine et al. (2000), in his study of individuals taken from the community who scored highly on the PCL-R, reported reduced prefrontal gray, but not white, matter volume in individuals scoring highly on the PCL-R. Soderstrom et al. (2002) correlated regional cerebral blood flow (rCBF) in prior specified regions of interest (ROIs) against PCL-R scores and its constituent factors. They reported significant negative correlations between the callous and unemotional interpersonal Factor 1 and frontal and temporal perfusion. In other words, the higher the levels of callous and unemotional characteristics, the less blood flow that was observed in frontal and temporal regions.

There are, however, concerns with both of these studies. As noted above, there was a confound in the Raine et al. (2000) study; 33 percent of these individuals with psychopathic tendencies also presented with schizophrenia spectrum disorders. With respect to the Soderstrom et al. (2002) work, all of the participants were subjects of pre-trial forensic psychiatric investigations. In short, the sample had been selected on the basis of prior concerns about the potential presence of organic abnormalities. In other words, this sample may not be representative of individuals with psychopathic tendencies. In addition, no statistical corrections for performing multiple comparisons were conducted in this work. This would be problematic generally but is particularly the case here where some of the effects, particularly the frontal effects, were very small.

There is also the difficulty that both of these studies investigated frontal cortex as a global entity and did not distinguish between its constituent regions. Laakso and colleagues (2002) did subdivide frontal cortex into dorsolateral, orbitofrontal, and medial frontal volumes in 24 non-psychotic, violent male subjects presenting with psychopathic tendencies in combination with type 2 alcoholism, and 33 age-matched control males. The individuals with psychopathic tendencies did present with significantly smaller volumes of all three cortical regions on the left, but this significance disappeared after controlling for differences in education and duration of alcoholism.

With respect to functional imaging paradigms, four studies can be considered (Kiehl et al., 2001; Muller et al., 2003; Schneider et al., 2000; Veit et al., 2002). Muller et al. (2003) examined the neural responses of individuals with psychopathy and comparison individuals to positive and negative emotional pictures. Schneider and colleagues (2000) explored rCBF during aversive conditioning in high PCL-R scoring individuals relative to the comparison individuals. Surprisingly, both of these studies reported greater frontal activity in individuals with psychopathy in relation to these pictures relative to comparison individuals. However, it should be noted that Schneider and colleagues (2000) also reported superior aversive conditioning in their individuals with psychopathy. This finding is inconsistent with previous research (see chapter 4). Individuals with psychopathy are notable for their poor emotional learning (Lykken, 1957; Newman and Kosson, 1986; Newman et al., 1987). Moreover, they found very similar findings in a population of individuals presenting with social phobia (Schneider et al., 1999). Patients with this disorder exhibit some characteristics that are the antithesis of psychopathy. Thus, these results should be considered tentative, particularly since Veit et al. (2002), in a similar study of aversive conditioning in individuals with psychopathy, individuals with social phobia, and comparison individuals, found reduced orbital frontal cortex and anterior cingulate activity to CS+s in the individuals with psychopathy but increased activity in these regions in the social phobics; see figure 6.2. Importantly, the Veit et al. (2002) study recorded their participants' autonomic responses to the CS+s and CS–s to confirm that aversive conditioning was occurring (albeit weakly in the individuals with psychopathy). Kiehl et al. (2001) presented an affective memory task to individuals with psychopathy and comparison individuals. They also reported decreased anterior cingulate activity in the individuals with psychopathy.

In short, the picture with respect to frontal activity in individuals with psychopathy is mixed. Two studies have reported generally increased activity while two have reported generally decreased activity in the individuals with psychopathy relative to comparison individuals. However, given the concerns with the Schnieder et al. (1999) study and given also the neuropsychological results described above, we are confident that there are indications of orbital and medial frontal cortex dysfunction in individuals with psychopathy.

Conclusions

There are reasons to believe that frontal dysfunction can increase the probability of aggression. Patients with orbital and medial frontal cortex lesions are more likely to display aggression, generally aggressive individuals present with impaired performance on executive function tasks, and generally aggressive individuals present with reduced frontal activity during rest conditions.

However, the frontal lobe positions themselves remain rather underspecified. Typically, they do not distinguish between different regions of prefrontal cortex, different forms of executive function, or, at the behavioral level, between reactive and instrumental aggression. Moreover, the frontal lobe positions usually fail to provide any detailed cognitive account as to why damage to functions mediated by frontal cortex should lead to an increased risk of aggression. The data does allow some constraint of these positions. First, it is clear that a frontal lobe explanation is more appropriate for reactive rather than instrumental aggression (see chapter 7); patients with frontal lesions present with reactive and not instrumental aggression. Second, while dorsolateral executive dysfunction may be associated with reactive antisocial behavior, the association is likely to be correlational rather than causal. The association between dorsolateral executive dysfunction and reactive antisocial behavior probably reflects that the individuals with this dysfunction also have dysfunction in ventral-medial and orbital frontal cortex. Ventral-medial and orbital frontal cortex dysfunction are causally related to a heightened risk of reactive aggression (Anderson et al., 1999; Blair and Cipolotti, 2000; Grafman et al., 1996; Pennington and Bennetto, 1993). Third, with respect to psychopathy, there are also reasons to

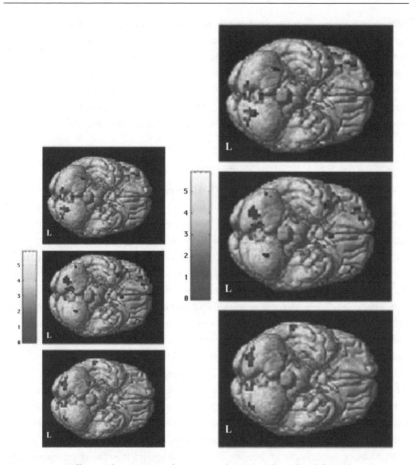

Figure 6.2 Differential activations for CS 1 and CS 2 in the orbital frontal cortex for (a) the healthy comparison individuals, (b) patients with social phobia, and (c) individuals with psychopathy ($p < 0.01$ uncorrected for visualization). From Veit et al. (2002).

consider that the disorder may be association with orbital and medial frontal cortex dysfunction. Individuals perform poorly on measures of response reversal, a function in which orbital frontal cortex is known to play a role. Moreover, there are indications of reduced orbital and medial frontal cortex activity in individuals with psychopathy during the performance of emotional tasks. To what extent this dysfunction is causal will be considered more fully in chapter 8.

Finally, considerable work needs to be done to provide an account of why frontal lesions increase the probability of reactive aggression/psychopathy. Most accounts do not adequately specify a mechanism by which frontal cortex dysfunction might give rise to these difficulties. Frequently, reference is made to reduced "inhibition"/dysfunction in inhibitory mechanisms following frontal dysfunction. However, such claims are difficult to interface with the known absence of inhibitory connections from frontal cortex to posterior systems. One position that has attempted to specify a functional theory and to account for the emergence of antisocial behavior following dysfunction in the putative mechanism is the somatic marker hypothesis. This will be described below.

The somatic marker hypothesis

According to Damasio and colleagues, ventromedial frontal cortex (orbitofrontal and medial frontal cortex) acts as a repository, and is involved in the formation of recorded dispositional linkages between factual knowledge and bio-regulatory states (Bechara et al., 2000a; Damasio, 1994). When emotionally significant decisions are being made (i.e., decisions involving rewards and/or losses), bio-regulatory (bodily) states provide affective coloring that automatically bias the individual toward or away from the available response options. In essence, the bodily feedback, or "somatic marker," provides an automated way of labeling a particular option as either good or bad, thereby influencing the likelihood that that particular response will be made. This rapid labeling can occur via a "body loop" in which a "somatic marker" is conveyed to somato-sensory cortices, but it can also occur via an "as-if body loop," in which the body is bypassed and reactivation signals are conveyed to the somato-sensory structures. Under either loop, the somato-sensory structures then adopt an appropriate pattern that constrains option – outcome reasoning. In short, the somato-sensory pattern marks the scenario as either good or bad, allowing the rapid rejection/endorsement of specific option – outcome pairs.

Two major findings are associated with the somatic marker hypothesis. First, patients with lesions to ventromedial frontal cortex fail to show autonomic responses to visually presented social stimuli (scenes of social disaster, mutilation, and nudity) under passive viewing conditions (Damasio et al., 1990, 1991). Passive viewing conditions require the participant to only look at the pictures of scenes. It should be noted that these patients did, however, show appropriate autonomic responses to the same stimuli under active viewing conditions. These involved attention-inducing instructions such as to describe the pictures. Second, patients with lesions to ventromedial frontal cortex perform poorly on the four-pack card playing task (Bechara et al., 1994, 1999, 2000b). In this task, participants are presented with four packs of cards. Two packs result in high rewards but even higher punishments and, if played continuously, result in a net loss. Two packs result in low rewards but even lower punishments and, if played continuously, result in a net gain. The participants have to learn to avoid the high reward, net loss packs in favor of the low reward, net gain packs. Healthy participants learn to take from the low reward packs and show skin conductance responses (i.e., warning somatic markers) before the selection of a card from the disadvantageous packs. In contrast, patients with ventromedial damage continued to choose from the disadvantageous packs and failed to show skin conductance responses before their choices from these packs.

The somatic marker hypothesis has generated considerable interest. However, it faces the same problem that most unitary accounts of antisocial behavior face. That is, it is unclear whether it should be considered an account of instrumental or reactive aggression. To be fair, Damasio and Bechara were developing an account of the functions of ventromedial frontal cortex, not developing a model of aggression. However, Damasio, in particular, has suggested that psychopathy might be the developmental form of acquired sociopathy (Damasio, 1994; Damasio et al., 1990). Yet the data from patients with ventromedial frontal lesions suggests that these regions are involved in the regulation of reactive but not instrumental aggression (Anderson et al., 1999; Blair and Cipolotti, 2000; Grafman et al., 1996; Pennington and Bennetto, 1993). Any account of ventromedial function and antisocial behavior must take into account the inflated rates of reactive as opposed to instrumental aggression found in patients with such lesions. It is unclear how the somatic marker hypothesis would predispose a patient with damage to this system toward one or other particular form of aggression.

As an account of psychopathy, the somatic marker hypothesis should predict that individuals with psychopathy will present with reduced autonomic responses to visually presented social stimuli as well as impaired performance on the four-pack card playing task. While children and adults with psychopathy do present with impaired performance on the four-pack card playing task (Blair et al., 2001a; Mitchell et al., 2002), they do not present with generally reduced autonomic responses to visually presented social stimuli (Blair, 1999b; Blair et al., 1997; Levenston et al., 2000; Patrick et al., 1993). In short, individuals with psychopathy appear to generate somatic markers even if they do show impairment on the four-pack card playing task.

With regard to reactive aggression within this model, we could speculate that an option – outcome pair is activated such as "hit that person but be punished later." In a healthy individual, there will be activation of the linkage between knowledge of hitting and punishment and the emotional aversion to punishment. The consequent aversive somatic marker should then guide the individual away from hitting the other. However, if there is damage to the somatic marker system, there will be no somatic marker to guide behavior. We would expect a similar option – outcome pair for instrumental aggression; however, individuals with lesions to this region are not known for high levels of instrumental aggression.

SUMMARY

The somatic marker hypothesis is an interesting model of ventromedial prefrontal cortex functioning. However, its application to the understanding of aggression and antisocial behavior has been less successful. Its predictions for the performance of individuals with psychopathy have only been partially confirmed. Moreover, the pattern of data would tend to indicate that individuals with psychopathy may be able to generate somatic markers even if the data from the four-pack gambling task would suggest that they do not use them very appropriately. At a more theoretical level, the somatic marker system has been extensively criticized (Rolls, 1997; Tomb et al., 2002). Specifically, for our purposes, it is unclear to what extent it is informative as an account of reactive/instrumental aggression.

General conclusions

The goal of this chapter was to consider three models that have attempted to account for the functional impairments shown by individuals with psychopathy by reference to neural architecture. These models were the left hemisphere activation hypothesis (Kosson, 1996), various positions proposing frontal lobe dysfunction (Moffitt, 1993b; Raine, 2002a), and the somatic marker hypothesis (Damasio, 1994).

We would argue that several clear conclusions can be drawn. First, there does appear to be "weak or unusual lateralization of language function" in individuals with psychopathy. However, it is unlikely that this is causally related to the development of psychopathy.

With respect to the frontal lobe positions, it is clear that frontal lobe dysfunction can lead to increases in aggression. However, on the basis of the empirical literature, these positions can be further specified. First, it is clear that a frontal lobe explanation is more appropriate for reactive rather than instrumental aggression. Second, while dorsolateral executive dysfunction may be associated with reactive antisocial behavior, the association is likely to be correlational rather than causal. In contrast, ventral-medial and orbital frontal cortex dysfunction are causally related to a heightened risk of reactive aggression. Third, with respect to psychopathy, there are reasons to consider that the disorder may be associated with orbital and medial frontal cortex dysfunction. To what extent this dysfunction is causal will be considered more fully in chapter 8. Fourth, considerable work needs to be done to provide an account of why frontal lesions increase the probability of reactive aggression/psychopathy. The somatic marker hypothesis can be considered such an account. However, this account, in turn, has not been very informative regarding accounting for reactive aggression.

In the next two chapters, we will develop models of reactive and instrumental aggression.

CHAPTER SEVEN

A NEUROCOGNITIVE ACCOUNT OF REACTIVE AGGRESSION

In chapters 5 and 6, we described a series of cognitive/neural models of psychopathy/aggression. However, one problem with many of these accounts was the effective assumption that aggression was a unitary phenomenon and that all individuals displaying elevated levels of aggression share the same pathology. There have been few attempts to provide accounts specifically tailored to the emergence of either reactive or instrumental aggression. Nor have there been many attempts to develop a model of those individuals who present with predominantly reactive aggression that is different from an account of those individuals who present with both reactive and instrumental aggression. The purpose of this chapter is to describe an account of reactive aggression and the pathologies that put the individual at risk for displaying elevated levels of reactive aggression. Following this, an account of instrumental aggression/psychopathy will be offered in chapter 8.

Reactive aggression can be considered to be the ultimate mammalian response to a threat. Mammals have a very gradated response to threat. Mammals, including humans, freeze to distant threats, attempt to escape from closer threats, and then launch explosive attacks (reactive aggression) against threats that cannot be escaped (Blanchard et al., 1977).

It is important to note here that reactive aggression is not inappropriate *per se*. In fact, reactive aggression can be an adaptive response to a highly threatening stimulus. However, reactive aggression can be maladaptive, and will gain clinical attention, if it is expressed to stimuli that are not conventionally considered sufficiently threatening. In other words, reactive aggression to an individual who has cornered you in a dark alley is appropriate; reactive aggression to an individual who has accidentally knocked into you on the street is not. The

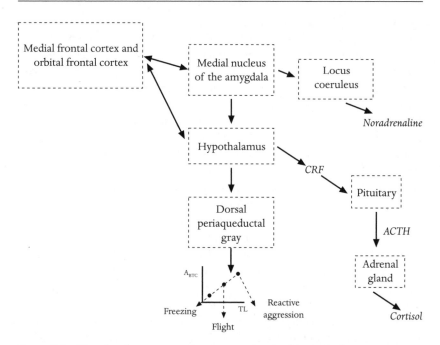

Figure 7.1 Neural and neurotransmitter systems involved in the basic response to threat. The graph relates threat level (TL) to activation of the basic threat circuitry (A_{BTC}) in a simple linear fashion. The points on the graph reflect levels of activation of the basic threat circuitry necessary for specific threat-related behaviors.

explosive aggression may be mediated by the same neural architecture. However, the aggression in the second instance suggests that the architecture has become dysregulated. In this chapter, we will consider how this dysregulation might occur.

The basic architecture

Reactive aggression is the ultimate natural response to a frustrating or threatening event shown by mammalian species. It is mediated by a neural circuit that is shared with other mammalian species (Gregg and Siegel, 2001; Panksepp, 1998); see figure 7.1. This circuit mediates the basic, gradated response to threat. This neural architecture runs from medial amygdaloidal areas downward, largely via the stria terminalis to the medial hypothalamus, and from there to the dorsal half of the periaqueductal gray (PAG). The system is organized in a hierarchical manner such that aggression evoked by signals sent from the amygdala will result in aggression only if the medial hypothalamus and PAG are functioning properly, but aggression evoked by signals from the PAG does not depend on the functional integrity of the amygdala (Bandler, 1988; Gregg and Siegel, 2001; Panksepp, 1998). In other words, we could elicit reactive aggression by stimulating the neuron in the PAG depicted in figure 7.1 even if the amygdala had been lesioned. However, we could not elicit reactive aggression by stimulating the neuron in the amygdala if the PAG had been lesioned. This system mediates the animal's gradated response to threat. A description of the animal's response to threat has been elegantly charted through the work of Robert and Caroline Blanchard (Blanchard et al., 1977). They have shown that at low levels of stimulation from a distant threat, the animal will freeze. At higher levels of stimulation from a closer threat, the animal will attempt to escape the environment. At higher levels still, when the threat is very close and escape is impossible, the animal will display reactive aggression (Blanchard et al., 1977).

In figure 7.1, we have also depicted two important neurochemical systems that respond to stress/threat and are likely to contribute to reactive aggression (Charney, 2003; Francis and Meaney, 1999).

First, the hypothalamic – pituitary – adrenal (HPA) axis: stress stimulates release of corticotropin-releasing factor (CRF) from the paraventricular nucleus (PVN) of the hypothalamus. CRF is released by the PVN neurons into the portal blood supply of the anterior pituitary, where it provokes the synthesis and release of adrenocorticotropic hormone (ACTH) from the pituitary. This results in increases of cortisol from the adrenal gland. High levels of cortisol, through negative feedback, decrease both CRF and NE synthesis at the level of the PVN, and thereby constrain the PVN.

Second, the noradrenergic system: there is a second population of CRF neurons in the central nucleus of the amygdala. These neurons project to the locus coeruleus, resulting in increased noradrenaline release from the terminal fields of this ascending noradrenergic system.

Regulation of the basic architecture

As depicted in figure 7.1, regions of frontal cortex, in particular orbital, ventrolateral, and medial frontal cortex (see also figure 6.1), are involved in the regulation of the basic circuitry that is responsible for responding to threat. Damage to these regulatory systems is likely to dysregulate this circuitry. Indeed, as reviewed in chapter 6, both the animal and human neuropsychological literature suggest that the frontal cortex is involved in the modulation of the subcortical circuit mediating reactive aggression (Anderson et al., 1999; Grafman et al., 1996; Gregg and Siegel, 2001; Panksepp, 1998; Pennington and Bennetto, 1993). Damage to medial and orbital/ventrolateral frontal cortex is associated with increased risk for the display of reactive aggression in humans whether the lesion occurs in childhood (Anderson et al., 1999; Pennington and Bennetto, 1993) or adulthood (Grafman et al., 1996). Neuro-imaging data have revealed reduced frontal functioning in patients presenting with reactive aggression (Raine et al., 1998a; Soderstrom et al., 2000; Volkow and Tancredi, 1987; Volkow et al., 1995). Within this literature there are suggestions that ventrolateral frontal cortex is particularly impaired in patients presenting with elevated levels of reactive aggression (Goyer et al., 1994).

Medial, orbital, and ventrolateral frontal cortex are involved in at least two processes that modulate the subcortical systems mediating reactive aggression (Blair, 2004). The first is the computation of expectations of reward and identifying whether these expectations have been violated (Rolls, 2000). Frustration has long been linked to the display of reactive aggression (Berkowitz, 1993). Frustration occurs following the initiation of a behavior to achieve an expected reward and the subsequent absence of this reward. Medial, orbital, and ventrolateral frontal cortices are necessarily involved in resolving situations where reinforcement expectations have been violated; i.e., damage to these systems will give rise to an individual who will be frustrated more often.

The second process can be considered to be a component of social cognition. It has been suggested that neurons in orbitofrontal cortex are recruited by a system (termed the social response reversal system; Blair and Cipolotti, 2000) that is crucial for social cognition and the modulation of reactive aggression but which is separable from the system computing violations of reward expectancies (Blair, 2001; Blair and Cipolotti, 2000). The social response reversal system is thought to be activated by (1) aversive social cues (negative valence expressions: disgust, fear, sadness, and particularly anger) and (2) situations associated with social disapproval. The suggestion is that this system modulates current behavioral responding, in particular the modulation of reactive aggression, but that this modulation is a function of the position in the dominance hierarchy of the other individual. Thus, for example, the angry expression of an individual higher in the dominance hierarchy will suppress reactive aggression and lead to alterations in current instrumental behavior. In contrast, the angry expression of an individual lower in the dominance hierarchy will lead to activation of the subcortical circuitry for reactive aggression. In line with this, there is data from work with primates demonstrating that reactive aggression is modulated by the individual's position in the dominance hierarchy. Thus, stimulated animals will

A S
L C
LIBRARY
LRS

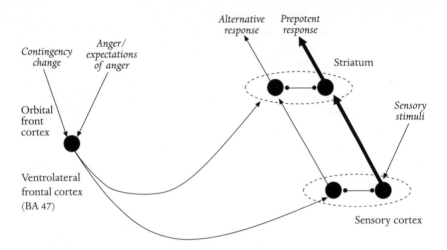

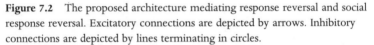

Figure 7.2 The proposed architecture mediating response reversal and social response reversal. Excitatory connections are depicted by arrows. Inhibitory connections are depicted by lines terminating in circles.

We show a sensory stimulus activating a prepotent response; the sensory stimulus activates a representation in sensory cortex and triggers the prepotent motor response. We depict our suggestion that ventrolateral prefrontal cortex achieves response reversal and social response reversal by increasing attention to competing stimuli in the environment (the activation of the sensory representation competing with the representation of the sensory stimulus) and increasing the activation of competing potential motor responses (the activation of the motor response competing with the prepotent motor response).

vent their rage on more submissive animals and avoid confrontations with more dominant ones (Alexander and Perachio, 1973).

We depict the commonalities between the system for response reversal and the system for social response reversal in figure 7.2. The suggestion is that the basic problem that individuals have to solve to avoid frustration is to prevent inappropriate responses. In figure 7.2, we depict a sensory stimulus activating a prepotent response (the bold pathway in the figure). The sensory stimulus is represented in sensory cortex and it elicits the prepotent motor response. For example, the individual might have learnt that whenever a red and a blue triangle are present in the environment, pressing the red triangle gives a reward of $100. Assuming enough experience with the red and blue triangles, a prepotent response will be formed; the individual will be reaching for the red triangle as soon as it is seen. The situation is good as long as pressing the red triangle does give the $100.

However, suppose there is a change in contingencies. Pressing on the red triangle now loses the individual $100 (though pressing on the blue triangle will gain $100). In short, the individual needs to rapidly learn to avoid pressing the red triangle in favor of the blue triangle. Continuing to press the red triangle and losing $100 when you were expecting to win $100 will be very frustrating. The individual needs to learn to reverse his or her responding from the red to the blue triangle. Medial, orbital, and ventrolateral prefrontal cortices are crucial for this reversal of responding. We suggest that medial and orbital frontal cortices are involved in the detection of the contingency change; i.e., that responding to the red triangle is no longer rewarding. We suggest, and depict in figure 7.2, the role of ventrolateral prefrontal cortex in the reversal of responding. We suggest that it increases attention to competing stimuli in the environment (i.e., the representation of the blue triangle) and that it has a role in increasing the activation of competing potential motor responses (thus suppressing the activation of the prepotent response).

We suggest that ventrolateral prefrontal cortex has the same role with respect to social response reversal. The difference is that, in this case, the system is not triggered by the detection of a contingency change but rather by the expectation or the sight of a dominant conspecific's anger. To give an example, an individual might have developed a prepotent response such that they always put their feet up on their desk. Every time they put their feet up on their own desk, they become highly relaxed. However, one day they are invited to their boss's office. The sight of their boss's desk might elicit the prepotent response. However, in a healthy individual, the expectation of the boss's anger should prevent this response being elicited.

In short, the response control units involved in both response reversal and social response reversal are thought to be implemented by lateral orbital frontal cortex (Brodmann's Area 47). Neuro-imaging data indicates a clear role of BA 47 in response reversal (Cools et al., 2002). Moreover, this region is activated by negative emotional expressions; in particular, anger but also fear and disgust (Blair et al., 1999; Kesler-West et al., 2001; Sprengelmeyer et al., 1998), though this response in BA 47 can be modulated by the behavioral demands of the task (Kringelbach and Rolls, 2003). In addition, this region is activated if an individual is induced to feel angry (Dougherty et al., 1999) or when processing situations that are likely to cause anger (others' socially inappropriate behavior) (Berthoz et al., 2002). This concentration of neuro-imaging data on the role of BA 47 in these functions, which we assume are crucial for the regulation of reactive aggression, is particularly interesting in the context of the results of Goyer and colleagues discussed earlier; they found that the functioning of BA 47 was particularly compromised in their patients presenting with elevated levels of reactive aggression (Goyer et al., 1994).

Dysfunctional regulation

In short, there is a basic threat system that mediates reactive aggression and there are regions of frontal cortex that regulate this system. In this section, we will consider ways in which these systems can become dysregulated. Specifically, we will identify four potential ways in which this can occur. The first two relate to reasons for elevation of the baseline responsiveness of the basic neural circuit. The third and fourth relate to the regulatory systems for this circuitry.

Heightened threat circuitry sensitivity as a result of prior exposure to significant environmental threats

As noted above, reactive aggression is displayed when the basic threat circuitry (medial nucleus of the amygdala, medial hypothalamus, and dorsal PAG) has been activated to a sufficient degree by an environmental threat. But the probability of reactive aggression to an environmental threat is not only determined by the intensity of the current threat but also by exposure to past threats.

Animal work has shown that repetitive electrical stimulation of the superior colliculus, a region of the threat basic response circuitry (Gregg and Siegel, 2001; Panksepp, 1998), can have long-term (at least 3 months) effects on anxiety-related behavior (King, 1999). In other words, environmental threats may change the baseline activation of the basic threat circuitry such that reactive aggression is more likely. To illustrate, suppose reactive aggression is displayed whenever an individual's basic threat circuitry reaches 0.8 units of activation. This 0.8 units of activation will be far more easy to achieve if the resting state of the basic threat circuitry, because of past exposure to environmental threats, is already high (0.5 units of activation) rather than if it is low because the individual has not previously been threatened (0 units of activation). In short, a less intense environmental threat will be required to elicit reactive aggression.

The neurochemical response to threat (see figure 7.1) can be profoundly affected by prior threat experience, particularly if this occurs early in life. Thus, stressors in early life have profound and long-term effects on HPA function (Bremner and Vermetten, 2001; Charney, 2003). Both prenatal and early deprivation stress result in increased glucocorticoid responses to subsequent stressors, which in turn augments future stress responses (Levine et al., 1993; Stanton et al., 1988). Early postnatal adverse experiences alter hypothalamic CRF mRNA, hippocampal glucocorticoid receptor mRNA, median eminence CRF content, and stress-induced CRF, corticosterone, and ACTH release (Heim et al., 1997; Liu et al., 1997; Plotsky and Meaney, 1993).

Chronic stress is also associated with potentiated release of noradrenaline following exposure to subsequent stressors (Nisenbaum et al., 1991) and a general lifelong increase in the sensitivity of the noradrenergic system (Francis et al., 1999). Repetitive stress is associated with an increased turnover and release of noradrenaline in the cortex, hippocampus, amygdala, hypothalamus, and locus coeruleus (Nisenbaum et al., 1991; Tanaka et al., 2000). Maternal separation results in an increased release of noradrenaline in the paraventricular nucleus of the hypothalamus. Maternal separation also results in a decrease in the alpha-2 autoreceptors of the locus coeruleus (Liu et al., 2000). Since the alpha-2 receptor is inhibitory, this would be expected to result in an increase in locus coeruleus activity, with increased noradrenergic reactivity.

There is considerable evidence in humans of an association between physical and sexual abuse and increased risk of aggression (Farrington and Loeber, 2000). Moreover, there is a heightened risk for the display of reactive aggression in patients with post-traumatic stress disorder (PTSD) (Silva et al., 2001). This is particularly interesting as patients with PTSD show an elevated startle to basic aversive stimuli in comparison to healthy individuals (Morgan et al., 1996, 1997). This elevated startle is indicative of greater baseline activity in the basic threat system.

One feature that animals display when they feel themselves to be in a threatening environment or if they have experienced repetitive stimulation of the basic threat response circuitry (King, 1999) is hyper-vigilance; the animal is highly sensitive to threat. This has interesting parallels with one of the processing styles seen in children who present with heightened levels of reactive aggression. Reactively aggressive children direct their attention selectively towards hostile social cues and have difficulty diverting attention away from these cues (Gouze, 1987). This hyper-vigilance may lead to aggressive children interpreting stimuli in hostile ways and reacting accordingly (Crick and Dodge, 1994). Kenneth Dodge and colleagues have demonstrated that in situations where a provacateur's actual intent is ambiguous, aggressive children are about 50 percent more likely to infer hostile intent than are non-aggressive children (Dodge, 1980). This result has been replicated on many occasions (see, for reviews, Crick and Dodge, 1996; Dodge, 1991; Quiggle et al., 1992). These hostile attribution biases are associated with the display of reactive rather than instrumental aggression (Dodge and Coie, 1987). Moreover, in an elegant study, Dodge and colleagues assessed almost 600 children for the lifetime experience of physical abuse through clinical interviews with mothers prior to the child's matriculation in kindergarten. They observed that early abuse increased the risk of teacher-rated externalizing outcomes in Grades 3 and 4 by fourfold, and this effect could not be accounted for by confounded ecological or child factors. Abuse was associated with the formation of hostile attribution biases, which, in turn, predicted later externalizing outcomes (Dodge et al., 1995).

Heightened threat circuitry sensitivity as a result of innate biological predispositions

In the illustration above, we supposed that reactive aggression is displayed whenever an individual's basic threat circuitry reaches 0.8 units of activation and drew the obvious conclusion that this level of activation is easier to achieve if the resting state of the circuitry is higher than if it is lower. The baseline level of activation is a product of previous experience of environmental threats (see above). However, it is also highly likely to be a product of innate biological predispositions. It is probable that endogenous factors may predispose an individual's basic threat responsiveness to be either high or low.

An increased risk of reactive aggression is seen in children, and adults, with depression and anxiety. Indeed, a positive correlation between anxiety and antisocial behavior has been well documented in children (Pine et al., 2000; Russo and Beidel, 1993; Zoccolillo, 1992) and adults (Robins et al., 1991). Recent positions on depression and anxiety stress the role of over-activity in the basic threat circuitry, particularly within the amygdala (Drevets, 2003; Kagan and Snidman, 1999). It is plausible that this over-activity has a genetic basis (Hettema et al., 2001; Johnson et al., 2002). In short, it is possible that the endogenous factors that predispose an individual to depression and anxiety may also increase the probability that they will express reactive aggression.

Reduced regulation of threat circuitry due to disturbance of orbital and medial frontal cortical regions

As depicted in figure 7.1, regions of frontal cortex, in particular orbital and medial frontal cortex, are involved in the regulation of the basic circuitry mediating the response to threat. Damage to these regulatory systems is likely to dysregulate this circuitry. Indeed, as noted above and in chapter 6, both the animal and human neuropsychological literature suggest that frontal cortex is involved in the modulation of the subcortical circuit mediating reactive aggression (Anderson et al., 1999; Grafman et al., 1996; Gregg and Siegel, 2001; Panksepp, 1998; Pennington and Bennetto, 1993). Certainly, damage to medial frontal and orbital frontal cortex is associated with increased risk for the display of reactive aggression in humans, whether the lesion occurs in childhood

(Anderson et al., 1999; Pennington and Bennetto, 1993) or adulthood (Grafman et al., 1996).

In addition, there are considerable neuro-imaging data showing reduced frontal functioning in patients presenting with reactive aggression (Raine et al., 1998a; Soderstrom et al., 2000; Volkow and Tancredi, 1987; Volkow et al., 1995). It is important to note here that these neuro-imaging studies have been conducted exclusively in adults. While the results almost certainly apply to understanding reactive aggression in children, they are in need of empirical confirmation. Moreover, the above neuro-imaging studies have placed little emphasis on considering the separable regions of frontal cortex. This is despite the fact that the neuropsychological data strongly suggest that only medial and orbital frontal cortex are involved in modulating reactive aggression; dorsolateral prefrontal cortex appears to have little role (Grafman et al., 1996). However, one of the few studies to dissociate functional regions of frontal cortex with regard to aggression was conducted by Goyer and colleagues, who examined the CBF under rest conditions using PET of 17 patients with personality disorder (antisocial, borderline, dependent, and narcissistic) and 43 comparison individuals (Goyer et al., 1994). The patients' aggression was predominantly reactive. They found that it was lower normalized CBF in lateral orbital frontal cortex (BA 47) that correlated with a history of reactive aggression.

We argued above that medial, orbital, and ventrolateral frontal cortices are involved in at least two processes that modulate the subcortical systems mediating reactive aggression (Blair, 2004): response reversal and social response reversal. Dysfunction in either system would dysregulate the systems mediating reactive aggression.

Disruption of the regulation of the basic threat circuitry need not occur only following acquired neurological damage to frontal cortex. There are at least two psychiatric conditions that appear to be related to disruption of these regulatory systems: intermittent explosive disorder/impulsive aggressive disorder (Coccaro, 1998) and childhood bipolar disorder (McClure et al., 2003). Patients with both disorders express irritability and are at higher risk for reactive aggression. Patients with both disorders show difficulty on response reversal paradigms requiring expectation violation computations and error detection (Best et al., 2002; Gorrindo et al., in press). In addition, patients with both disorders show impairment in the ability to recognize facial expressions, suggesting difficulties with social cue processing (Best et al., 2002; McClure et al., 2003).

Reduced regulation of threat circuitry due to serotonergic abnormalities

Serotonin has long been implicated in the modulation of aggression, in particular reactive aggression (Lee and Coccaro, 2001). Generally, experimental manipulations which increase serotonin receptor activation have been found to decrease aggression, and those which decrease receptor activation have been found to increase aggression (see Bell et al., 2001; Shaikh et al., 1997). Thus, selective destruction of serotonin (5-HT) neurons in the raphe complex in cats and rats lead to increases in aggression (File and Deakin, 1980). In humans, there have been consistent reports of a relationship between low cerebrospinal fluid (CSF) concentrations of 5-HIAA and reactive aggression, and CSF concentration of 5-HIAA has been successfully used to predict risk of aggression (Virkkunen et al., 1989).

Specific gene knock-out studies on mice have reported increased aggressiveness for several knock-outs affecting serotonergic functioning, including the 5-HT_{1B} receptor (Ramboz et al., 1996) and monoamine oxidase (MAO) A but not B (Shih et al., 1999). In addition, a human family with a stop codon of the MAO_A gene has been reported where the males were affected by mild mental retardation and sexually aggressive behaviors (Brunner et al., 1993). Recent work has suggested the possibility that the emergence of aggression might require the interaction between environmental stressors with particular genetic contributions to the functioning of the serotonergic system (Moffitt et al., 2002). Thus, Caspi et al. (1995) observed that a functional polymorphism in the gene encoding the neurotransmitter-metabolizing enzyme monoamine oxidase A (MAOA) moderated the effect of maltreatment. Maltreated children with a genotype conferring high levels of MAOA expression were less likely to develop antisocial problems than maltreated children with a genotype conferring low levels of MAOA expression.

Pharmacological challenge studies also suggest that serotonin plays a role in the modulation of reactive aggression. Thus, the prolactin elevation in response to a single dose of a 5-HT agonist can be used to index central 5-HT activity. Peak prolactin responses to the 5-HT releasing agent, fenfluramine, correlate significantly inversely with an interview-assessed life history of aggression in males (though not females) (Manuck et al., 1998). Tryptophan depletion increases laboratory aggression in both men and women (Bjork et al., 2000; Bond et al., 2001). Moreover, there is now data suggesting that the aggressive effect of tryptophan depletion is mediated via the 5-HT_{1A} receptor (Cleare and Bond, 2000). Cleare and Bond (2000) found that participants in whom aggression can be provoked or inhibited by tryptophan depletion or enhancement, respectively, show a blunted hypothermic response to ipsapirone. Since ipsapirone acts specifically to stimulate 5-HT$_{1A}$ receptors, the blunted hypothermic response is likely to represent impaired 5-HT$_{1A}$ receptor function in the aggressive individuals. Moreover, animal work has demonstrated a selective suppressive action of 5-HT$_{1A}$ receptors on the PAG neurons mediating defensive rage (see Gregg and Siegel, 2001).

Summary and conclusions

There is a population of individuals who present with predominantly reactive aggression. The reactive aggression of these individuals can be severe and repeated. Work with animals has identified a neural circuit that runs from the medial nucleus of the amygdala to the medial hypothalamus, and from there to the dorsal half of the periaqueductal gray. This circuitry allows the expression of reactive aggression in mammalian species, including humans. This circuitry can become dysregulated. We identify four potential ways in which this can occur. The first two relate to the basic neural circuit that responds to threat and allows the expression of reactive aggression. Individuals for whom the sensitivity of this basic circuitry is elevated, either as a result of physical/sexual abuse or endogenous factors, are at greater neurobiological risk of displaying reactive aggression. The third and fourth relate to regulatory systems for this circuitry. Thus, the functioning of medial and orbital frontal systems involved in the regulation of the basic threat circuitry can be compromised. This appears to occur in individuals who present with bipolar disorder and intermittent explosive disorder. Alternatively, or perhaps a contributory factor to the compromising of the frontal regulatory systems (Lee and Coccaro, 2001), the serotonergic system may be disturbed.

The ideas and data summarized in this chapter are depicted as a causal model in figure 7.3. Causal modeling is a technique developed by Morton and Frith (1993) to formally illustrate accounts of developmental causality. Causal models are divided into four levels: social, biological, cognitive, and behavioral (Morton and Frith, 1993). The relationship of connected elements within a causal model is one of causality. Thus, we represent two developmental routes for the elevation of the responsiveness of neurons in the amygdala, hypothalamus, and PAG (the basic threat circuitry, at the cognitive level). These are extreme/repeated experiences of environmental threat (e.g., through physical or sexual abuse) or genetic factors. Both routes will increase the probability of reactive aggression and may result in the child receiving a diagnosis of conduct disorder (CD) or the adult a diagnosis of antisocial personality disorder (ASPD). A child or adult with

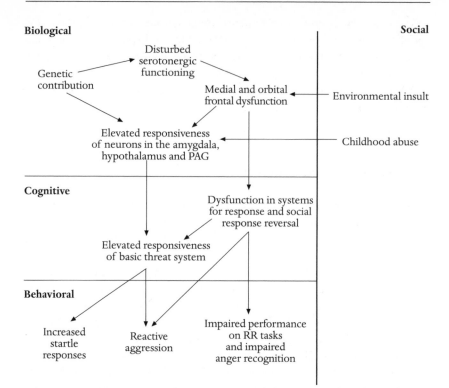

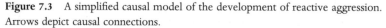

Figure 7.3   A simplified causal model of the development of reactive aggression. Arrows depict causal connections.

It is considered that there may be a genetic contribution to both disturbed serotonergic functioning and elevated responsiveness of neurons in the neural systems making up the basic threat system (though this is unlikely to represent the same genes). Alternatively, medial and orbital frontal cortex dysfunction may occur through environmental insult (including birth trauma) while responsiveness of neurons in the neural systems making up the basic threat system may occur as a consequence of extreme threat experiences, e.g., as occurring through childhood abuse. Medial and orbital frontal cortex dysfunction will lead to reduced regulation of the basic threat systems (and probably, over time, an elevation in their responsiveness). Both dysfunction in the executive regulatory systems mediating response and social response reversal and increased responsiveness of the basic threat systems should lead to increased levels of reactive aggression. However, dysfunction in the executive regulatory systems will also be associated with, for example, impaired performance on response reversal while increased responsiveness of the basic threat systems will be associated with, for example, increased startle responses.

reactive aggression due to these factors would be expected to show an elevated startle response.

We also represent several developmental routes for dysfunction in medial and orbital frontal regions involved in the regulation of the basic threat circuitry (comparator unit for response reversal and social response reversal at the cognitive level). This dysfunction could be a result of environmental insult (see chapter 3 for reference to birth trauma as a risk factor for antisocial behavior) or possibly disturbances in the serotonergic system. Dysfunction in medial and orbital frontal regions will increase the risk for reactive aggression and may result in the child receiving a diagnosis of CD or the adult a diagnosis of ASPD. A child or adult with reactive aggression due to these factors would be expected to show impaired response reversal/social response reversal.

In short, this chapter has detailed a model of reactive aggression. Moreover, it has described several developmental routes that might prompt a diagnosis of CD or ASPD. These join the route described in chapter 3. In chapter 8, we will consider other routes for another form of CD/ASPD, psychopathic tendencies.

CHAPTER EIGHT

A NEUROCOGNITIVE ACCOUNT OF PSYCHOPATHY

In chapter 7, we described a neurocognitive account of reactive aggression. The purpose of this chapter is to provide a neurocognitive account of a disorder linked to elevated levels of instrumental and reactive aggression; i.e., psychopathy (Cornell et al., 1996; Williamson et al., 1987).

Figure 8.1 represents the account as a causal model (the modeling process was introduced in chapter 7). As depicted in the model, and as described in chapter 3, there is growing evidence of a genetic contribution to psychopathy. In particular, two recent studies have indicated a genetic contribution to the emotional impairment seen in individuals with psychopathy (Blonigen et al., 2003; Viding et al., submitted). We suggest that the genetic anomalies disrupt the functioning of the amygdala (Blair, 2001, 2002; Blair et al., 1999; Patrick, 1994). We believe that the amygdala is functioning atypically from an early age in individuals with psychopathy. Furthermore, we believe that it is this problem in amygdala functioning that leads to the psychopathic individual's impairment in emotional learning. We believe that this impairment in emotional learning is at the root of psychopathy. As depicted in figure 8.1, individuals with this impairment will present with the problematic behaviors identified through Factor 1 of the PCL-R (i.e., a lack of guilt and a lack of empathy). In addition, individuals with this impairment will present with impaired performance on specific tasks such as passive avoidance learning and the recognition of fearful facial expressions (see below). Importantly, though, we do not believe that the presence of the emotional dysfunction necessarily leads to the full syndrome of psychopathy. It need not necessarily result in an elevated level of Factor 2 behaviors. The argument is that the emotional dysfunction increases the probability that the individual will learn antisocial motor programs for the

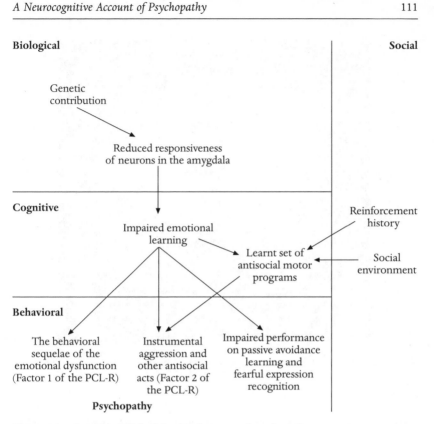

Figure 8.1 A causal model of the development of psychopathy.

achievement of goals. Whether they do or not will depend on the individual's social environment and learning history; i.e., a wealthy child might have more prosocial ways to gain reward available to them (see chapter 3). We will further unpack the proposed model below.

The amygdala and psychopathy

The amygdala is an almond-shaped structure located bilaterally in the forebrain (see figure 8.2). The term "amygdala" was initially used to describe a mass of gray matter in the anterior portion of the human temporal lobe by Burdach (1819–1826). In later work, Johnston investigated the amygdala region in several mammalian and non-mammalian vertebrates. He named its constituent nuclei on the basis of their relative positions within his "amygdaloid complex." These

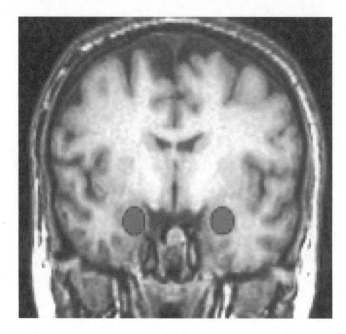

Figure 8.2   A coronal slice showing the location of the amygdala within the brain.

were the central, medial, cortical, basal, accessory basal, and lateral nuclei (Johnston, 1923). Burdach's "amygdala" corresponds to the basolateral nuclei later identified by Johnston. Johnston claimed that the amygdala "consists of two parts: the central and medial nuclei constituting an old part . . . and the basal, lateral and cortical nuclei" (Johnston, 1923). This dichotomy between the basolateral (BLA) and central nuclei (CeN) is prevalent in the amygdala literature today. The amygdala is one of the most crucial regions in the neural circuitry that processes emotion, and is at the center of what Joe LeDoux termed "the emotional brain" (1998).

Figure 8.3 depicts the integrated emotion systems (IES) model, a model of the functional interactions between various neural systems involved in emotional processing. Within the figure are depicted the three major connectional "systems" that involve the amygdala with other regions of the brain (Price, 2003). These are:

1   A largely forebrain system providing sensory input to the amygdala (both BLA and CeN). The structures providing this sensory input include olfactory cortex, ascending taste/visceral pathways, posterior thalamus, and

sensory association cortical areas. Many of the connections between these structures and the amygdala are reciprocal. They thus probably allow the amygdala to modulate sensory processing.

2   A system of projections to the brainstem (extending from the hypothalamus, to the medulla and even the spinal cord). These pathways are implicated in the modulation of visceral function in relation to emotional stimuli and mostly extend from the CeN.

3   A system of connections to regions of the forebrain. These regions include ventromedial frontal, rostral insular, and rostral temporal cortex, the medial thalamus, and the ventromedial basal ganglia. These connections are reciprocal. It is believed that they allow the amygdala to influence goal-directed behavior. They mostly extend from the BLA.

Learning functions of the amygdala

The amygdala allows the formation of three types of conditioned stimulus association (Everitt et al., 2003). These associations can be both appetitive and aversive. The types of association are:

1   Conditioned stimulus (CS)–unconditioned response (UR) associations. Examples of behavior generated as a result of a CS–UR association are salivation to a tone that has been previous associated with food or a galvanic skin response to a colored shape that has previously been associated with the presentation of a loud noise. The CeN, but not the BLA, is necessary for the formation of CS–UR associations (Everitt et al., 2003; Killcross et al., 1997).

2   Conditioned stimulus (CS)–affect representation associations (e.g., fear or the expectation of reward). The suggestion is one of "an emotional 'tone' that is tagged to a stimulus" (Everitt et al., 2003, p. 234). Such a concept is widely used in theories of emotional learning (Dickinson and Dearing, 1979). The BLA, but not the CeN, is necessary for the formation of these associations.

3   Conditioned stimulus (CS)–valenced sensory properties of the unconditioned stimulus (US) associations. The CS can be associated with specific sensory properties of the US (e.g., visual appearance, sound, and smell) and also "consumatory" qualities such as its taste. The BLA, but not the CeN, is necessary for the formation of these associations. The suggestion from reinforcer devaluation studies is that these associations are not stored in the amygdala (Pickens et al., 2003). We believe, as is depicted in figure 8.3, that they are stored within the insula.

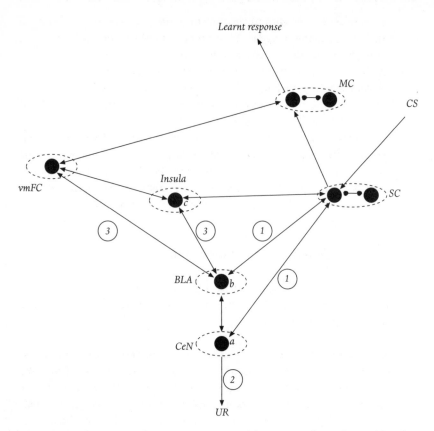

Figure 8.3 The integrated emotion systems model. Arrows indicate the transfer of information. Bidirectional arrows indicate this transfer is reciprocal.

(1) Corresponds to the transfer of information to both the basolateral (BLA) and central (CeN) nuclei of the amygdala from a subset of the systems providing sensory input to the amygdala. Sensory association cortex (SC) is depicted but other structures would include olfactory cortex, ascending taste / visceral pathways, and posterior thalamus. (2) Corresponds to projections to the brainstem. (3) Corresponds to the transfer of information to forebrain systems, including the depicted ventromedial frontal cortex (vmFC) and insula. MC, Motor cortex but also includes other regions necessary for the implementation of a motor response (e.g., basal ganglia); CS, conditioned stimulus; UR, unconditioned response. Hebbian learning at *a* allows a represented CS to become associated with a UR (i.e., the formation of a CS–UR association). Hebbian learning at *b* allows a represented CS to become associated with an affect representation (i.e., the formation of a CS–affect representation association). CS–valenced sensory properties of the US associations are stored at *c*.

For the purposes of the arguments to be developed in this chapter, we will contrast the three types of association listed above with stimulus–response associations. CS–CR associations involve the formation of an association between a stimulus and a particular response. CS–CR association formation is of particular interest because although it can be considered a form of emotional learning (the individual must learn to do a particular response to the stimulus as a function of reward/punishment information), it is a form of emotional learning for which the amygdala is not necessary. Lesions of the amygdala do not disrupt the formation of stimulus–response associations (Baxter and Murray, 2002).

SUMMARY

In short, the amygdala is necessary for the formation of CS–UR associations and CS–reinforcement associations, but not CS–CR associations. CS–UR and CS–reinforcement associations can be both appetitive and aversive. In this chapter, we will argue that individuals with psychopathy are impaired in the formation of both of these types of association but that the dysfunction is more significant for aversive rather than appetitive associations.

The amygdala and the expression of basic emotional reactions

The architecture depicted in figure 8.3 was a simplification of the systems which allow aversive/appetitive conditioning. Aversive/appetitive conditioning is the learning process through which a CS can come to elicit an unconditioned response. This can either occur either (1) as a direct association of the CS through the CeN to a specific UR (e.g., salivation to the bell that has been paired with food) or (2) following the formation of a CS–affect representation association through BLA and then onto CeN. The rat experiencing a shock following a tone will learn a CS–affect representation; i.e., a tone–"fear" association. The rat will freeze when hearing the tone. We know that the rat has not learnt a CS–UR association because the UR to shock is to demonstrate escape behaviors. If the rat had learnt a CS–UR association, it should flee when hearing the tone. Instead, when the rat hears the tone, the CS(tone)–affect(fear) association is activated and the rat freezes to the potential threat. This control of behavior by the CS–affect association is mediated through the BLA and then onto CeN (Everitt et al., 2003).

Our argument is that amygdala dysfunction is a central focus of the pathology associated with psychopathy. The first indications of this pathology come through studies demonstrating impaired aversive conditioning in individuals with psychopathy (Flor et al., 2002; Hare, 1970; Lykken, 1957); see chapter 3. While we currently cannot be sure whether the failure of individuals with psychopathy to demonstrate a conditioned skin conductance response to, for example, a neutral face CS paired with a noxious odor (Flor et al., 2002) represents reduced ability to form CS–UR or CS–affect representation associations, either possibility is consistent with amygdala dysfunction. Indeed, in line with this suggestion (Blair, 2001; Blair et al., 1999), recent neuro-imaging work has demonstrated reduced amygdala activity during aversive conditioning in individuals with psychopathy (Veit et al., 2002).

A paradigm frequently used as a measure of anxiety in animals is the augmented startle reflex paradigm (Davis, 2000). This paradigm has been used in work with humans also, and three studies have applied it to the study of psychopathy (Levenston et al., 2000; Pastor et al., 2003; Patrick et al., 1993); see chapter 4. Considerable data suggests that the amygdala is necessary for the modulation of the startle response by CSs (Angrilli et al., 1996; Davis, 2000). We depict in figure 8.3 the suggestion that a visual prime, a CS, can increase the activity of brainstem neurons mediating the startle reflex through the CeN via the BLA as a result of a CS–affect representation (a CS–UR association would mean that the CS itself induced a startle response) (Everitt et al., 2003). Dysfunction in either CeN or BLA would give rise to the reduced augmentation of the startle reflex by visual threat primes seen in individuals with psychopathy (Levenston et al., 2000; Pastor et al., 2003; Patrick et al., 1993).

As depicted in figure 8.3, one route to the activation of autonomic responding is through the amygdala. However, it is not the only route (Tranel and Damasio, 1994). The existence of these multiple routes may explain some of the inconsistent findings with respect to autonomic responses to CSs in individuals with psychopathy (see chapter 4). Individuals with psychopathy show appropriate SCRs to visual threats, even to the same visual threats that do not prime their startle responses (Blair et al., 1997; Levenston et al., 2000; Pastor et al., 2003; Patrick et al., 1993). In contrast, individuals with psychopathy show reduced SCRs to facial expressions of sadness (Blair, 1999b; Blair et al., 1997), imagined threat scenes (Patrick et al., 1994), anticipated threat (Hare, 1965, 1982; Hare et al., 1978; Ogloff and Wong, 1990), and emotionally evocative sounds (e.g., a male attack sound or a baby's laugh) (Verona et al., 2004). The argument here must be that individuals with psychopathy show impairment in the generation of SCRs when this relies on the integrity of the amygdala. SCRs to visual threats appear to be more disrupted by lesions of orbital frontal cortex rather than the amygdala (Tranel and Damasio, 1994); i.e., the ability of individuals with psychopathy to generate autonomic responses to these stimuli is consistent with the amygdala position. As yet, it is unknown whether amygdala lesions disrupt SCRs to facial expressions of sadness, imagined threat scenes, or emotionally evocative sounds. However, the model makes the clear prediction that they would. Recent neuro-imaging work has indicated that the amygdala plays a crucial role in generating SCRs to anticipated threat (Phelps et al., 2001). The reduced ability of individuals with psychopathy to generate SCRs to anticipated threat is thus in line with the model.

SUMMARY

The amygdala influences the behavioral expression of basic emotional reactions. It influences the level of the startle reflex by priming the subcortical basic threat circuitry as a result of activation by conditioned stimuli. In addition, it allows conditioned stimuli to come to elicit unconditioned responses. Failures in these functions in individuals with psychopathy are strongly indicative of pathology within the amygdala.

The amygdala and stimulus selection ("attention")

In figure 8.4, the suggested role of the amygdala in biasing stimulus selection, in "attention," is depicted (see also figure 8.1). Attention is considered to be the result of the competition for neural representation which occurs when multiple stimuli are present (Desimone and Duncan, 1995; Duncan, 1998). Which stimuli win this competition, and are "attended to," is a product of both top-down influences such as directed attention and bottom-up sensory processes such as stimulus salience (Desimone and Duncan, 1995). In figure 8.4, we see top-down "executive" processes operating on the representation of the shape, "priming" it such that if the shape is present in the environment, it is more likely to win the competition for representation; i.e., it will be attended to.

In figure 8.4, we also see the influence on attention of a particular type of salience, emotional salience. There is now a growing body of work showing that the amygdala does indeed enhance attention to emotional information relative to neutral information (Anderson and Phelps, 2001; Vuilleumier et al., 2001). In relation to the model, the suggestion is that a CS will activate CS–affect representation associations. As the connections of these representations with the representation of the CS are reciprocal, the activation of the CS in turn

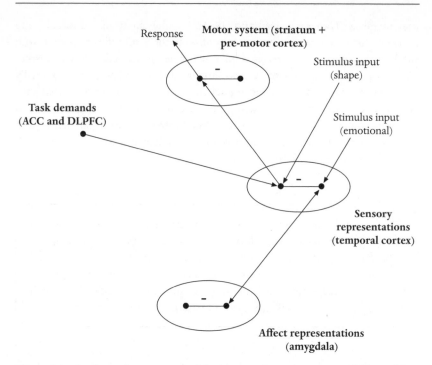

Figure 8.4   A subset of components of the integrated emotion systems (IES) model involved in the emotional modulation of attention. ACC = Anterior cingulate; DLPFC = dorsolateral prefrontal cortex.

will be augmented. Representations of the CS are therefore more salient (strongly activated) than the representations of any competing environmental stimuli, all other things being equal.

The model suggests that if individuals with psychopathy present with amygdala dysfunction they will receive markedly reduced augmentation of the representation of the CS from the reciprocal connections with the amygdala. This makes two clear predictions: (1) if the CS is the target stimulus, performance will be impaired in individuals with psychopathy relative to comparison individuals (a weaker representation should be less able to control behavior), and (2) if the CS is the distracter to ongoing behavior, performance will be superior in individuals with psychopathy relative to comparison individuals (a weaker representation will be less of a competitor for the stimulus that should be controlling behavior). Both of these predictions have been confirmed (Day and Wong, 1996; Lorenz and Newman, 2002; Mitchell et al., under revision; Williamson et al., 1991).

Emotional words (e.g., murder) are CSs. Emotional words should, and do, activate the amygdala (Hamann and Mao, 2002). This activation should be, and is, associated with augmentation of the representation of the word in temporal cortex (Nakic, unpublished work). Augmentation of the representation of the word stimulus should make lexical decision easier; i.e., it should be easier to state that an emotional word is a word than that a neutral word is a word. Healthy participants are faster to state that an emotional word is a word than a neutral word (Graves et al., 1981; Strauss, 1983). Moreover, they show larger evoked related potentials (ERPs) over central and parietal cortical sites to emotional words (Begleiter et al., 1967). In contrast, but again in line with the hypothesis developed here, psychopathic individuals show significantly reduced reaction time and ERP differences between neutral and emotional words (Day and Wong, 1996; Lorenz and Newman, 2002; Williamson et al., 1991); see also chapter 4.

In the emotional interrupt task (Mitchell et al., under revision) , participants are instructed to make one response if a square is presented and another response if a triangle is presented on a computer screen. The participant is presented with either a positive, negative, or neutral visual image for 200 ms before the target stimulus (presented for 150 ms) and for 400 ms after the target stimulus. Healthy participants are slower to respond to the square/triangle if it is temporally bracketed by emotional stimuli rather than neutral stimuli. In terms of the model, the representation of the emotional CS is boosted by reciprocal feedback from the valence representations and stimulus–affect representation associations. It therefore becomes a more effective competitor for the square/triangle target stimulus. In contrast, but in line with the position developed here, individuals with psychopathy perform similarly whether the square/triangle is temporally bracketed by an emotional stimulus or a neutral stimulus (Mitchell et al., under revision).

SUMMARY

Reciprocal connections from the affect representations, implemented by the amygdala, and CS representations, implemented by sensory cortex, should lead in healthy individuals to improved performance if the CS is the target stimulus for goal-directed behavior and impaired performance if the CS is a distracter for goal-directed behavior. Healthy individuals do show superior processing of emotional words in lexical decision tasks (according to the model, the activation of the emotional word CS is boosted by the reciprocal connections with the affect representations). In addition, healthy individuals do show impaired performance on the emotional interrupt task (according to the model, the activation of the emotional *distractors* is greater because of the reciprocal connections with the affect representations). Individuals with psychopathy should, and do, show reduced evidence of these effects.

The amygdala and instrumental learning

Instrumental learning involves the individual learning to perform an action to a stimulus if this action results in reward and to withhold from performing an action to a stimulus if this action results in punishment. The amygdala, and particularly the BLA, are implicated in some, but not all, forms of instrumental learning (Ambrogi Lorenzini et al., 1999; Baxter and Murray, 2002; Everitt et al., 2000; Killcross et al., 1997; LeDoux, 2000).

In the IES model depicted in figure 8.3, two modules of units are depicted that have received little, or no, attention up to now. The first of these corresponds to units coding motor responses (implemented by regions that include the striatum and pre-motor cortex). The second corresponds to units coding expectation of reward (implemented by medial orbital frontal cortex/rostral anterior cingulate). These units allow rapid decision making.

As regards the second module, implemented by medial orbital frontal cortex, here a claim is being made about a commonality of function of medial orbital frontal cortex with other regions of frontal cortex. There have been several recent suggestions that left dorsolateral prefrontal cortex is involved in the selection of a verbal response option when more than one is in competition (Frith, 2000; Robinson et al., 1998). These have been elegantly modeled computationally (Usher and Cohen, 1999). Very briefly, the Usher and Cohen (1999) model assumes the existence of modality-specific posterior units that are limited by temporal decay, while anterior units use active reverberations which can sustain themselves and which are limited by displacement from competing new information. The anterior units, by being self-excitatory but mutually inhibitory, allow rapid selection between competing, multiple active posterior response options (Usher and Cohen, 1999). The suggestion here is that the "decision" units in orbital frontal cortex may serve a similar function over units in pre-motor cortex that mediate motor responses. The "decision" units would receive information in order to solve response competition on the basis not only of the activation of units coding the motor response but also expectations of reinforcement as a result of previously formed CS–affect representations and CS–valenced sensory representations (i.e., from the amygdala and insula). The more active a unit from expectation information, the more likely it will "win" the representational competition and the response associated with this unit will be initiated.

As noted above, the amygdala is necessary for the formation of CS–UR, CS–affect representation, and CS–valenced sensory properties of the stimulus associations. It is not necessary for the formation of stimulus – response associations (Baxter and Murray, 2002). Some instrumental learning tasks are reliant on the formation of CS–affect representation/CS–valenced sensory properties of the stimulus associations. For example, in passive avoidance learning, the participant is presented with stimuli. Some stimuli, if responded to, engender reward. Others, if responded to, engender punishment. The participant's task is to learn to respond to the "good" stimuli and avoid responding to the "bad" stimuli. Computationally, the participant must code the valence associated with a particular stimulus; the participant must learn which stimuli to approach and which to avoid. In terms of the model depicted in figure 8.3, passive avoidance learning can be solved on the basis of stored CS–affect representations. If the individual has formed a CS–positive affect association, the individual will approach (respond to) this stimulus. If the individual has formed a CS–negative affect association, the individual will avoid (fail to respond to) this stimulus. Amygdala lesions disrupt passive avoidance learning (Ambrogi Lorenzini et al., 1991).

Other instrumental learning tasks must be solved through the formation of stimulus–response associations (Baxter and Murray, 2002). For example, object discrimination learning involves learning to respond to one of two objects (one rewarded and one not rewarded) repeatedly presented in a pair-wise fashion over a series of trials. In other words, the participant must learn that when Stimulus A and Stimulus B are present they should respond toward A. Conditional learning involves learning to perform a particular motor response in the presence of a particular stimulus (press left button if green light is on, but right button if red light is on). In conditional learning, the participant must learn that when Stimulus A is present they should do Response 1.

In object discrimination/conditional learning tasks, and unlike in passive avoidance learning tasks, the participant cannot learn that some of the stimuli are "good" or "bad" and should therefore be approached or avoided. In object learning tasks, the compound stimulus (A plus B) can either be "good" or "bad" – what determines whether it is is not the quality of the stimulus (this is always repeated) but the quality of the response made to the stimulus. This is even clearer with respect to conditional learning tasks. Again, the value of the stimulus is determined by the individual's action to the stimulus; the same stimulus can give rise to reward or punishment depending on the individual's actions.

Such tasks cannot be solved by stimulus–affect representation associations. Amygdala lesions do not disrupt performance on these tasks (Baxter and Murray, 2002; Burns et al., 1999; Malkova et al., 1997; Petrides, 1982, 1985).

Given these data, we can make two clear predictions with respect to instrumental learning and individuals with psychopathy. First, task performance on instrumental learning tasks reliant on the formation of CS–affect representation/CS–valenced sensory properties associations (e.g., passive avoidance learning) should be impaired in individuals with psychopathy. In line with this prediction, individuals with psychopathy are impaired in passive avoidance learning (Blair et al., 2004; Newman and Kosson, 1986; Newman and Schmitt, 1998). Second, task performance on instrumental learning tasks reliant on stimulus–response associations (e.g., object discrimination learning and conditional learning) should not be impaired in individuals with psychopathy. In line with this prediction, individuals with psychopathy show no difficulty on object discrimin-ation or conditional learning tasks (Blair et al., 2001a; Mitchell et al., 2002).

SUMMARY

Some instrumental learning tasks are reliant on the formation of CS–affect representation/CS–valenced sensory properties of the stimulus associations (e.g., passive avoidance learning). Successful performance on these tasks is reliant on the integrity of the amygdala. Other instrumental learning tasks must be solved through the formation of stimulus–response associations (e.g., object discrimination and conditional learning). The amygdala is not necessary for the formation of stimulus–response associations. Individuals with psychopathy show impairment on instrumental learning tasks reliant on the formation of CS–affect representation/CS–valenced sensory properties of the stimulus associations. In other words, individuals with psychopathy show impairment on those instrumental learning tasks that rely on the amygdala. They do not show impairment on instrumental learning tasks reliant on stimulus–response associations.

The relationship between the IES, fear dysfunction, and VIM models

In chapter 5, we discussed the clear limitations of the fear dysfunction (Lykken, 1995; Patrick, 1994) and violence inhibition mechanism (VIM) (Blair, 1995) dysfunction positions. One major limitation of these models was that the data generated from predictions of the fear dysfunction models could not be explained by the VIM model, while the data generated from predictions of the VIM model could not be explained by the fear dysfunction accounts. The IES model can be considered an extension of the fear dysfunction and VIM accounts. It suggests a fundamental impairment in the affect representations implemented by the amygdala (particularly those for negative affect; see below). These affect representations are considered to be crucial for the formation of the CS–affect representation associations necessary for performance of such tasks as aversive conditioning and passive avoidance learning, tasks that the fear dysfunction position correctly generated predictions for (see above). These affect representations are also considered to be involved during the processing of fearful and sad expressions and moral socialization, functions that the VIM account was concerned with. The affect representations are directly activated by fearful and sad expressions, albeit to a weaker degree in individuals with psychopathy (see below). In short, the IES model allows an integration of the fear dysfunction and VIM models.

In addition, the IES model refines the fear dysfunction accounts. The early fear dysfunction accounts assumed that fear-related behaviors were mediated by a unitary fear system (Fowles, 1988; Lykken, 1995; Patrick, 1994); see chapter 5. Such models now require refinement. The empirical literature suggests that there is no single fear system but rather a series of at least partially separable neural systems engaged in specific forms of processing that can be subsumed under the umbrella term fear (Amaral, 2001; Blair and Cipolotti, 2000; Killcross et al., 1997; Prather et al., 2001). Specifically, with reference to the IES model and the argument introduced in the section on "The amygdala and instrumental learning," punishment information can be used when learning about an object (i.e., when forming a CS–affect representation association). But it can also be used when learning about how to respond to an object (i.e., when forming a CS–response association). The amygdala is crucially involved in the formation of CS–affect representations. However, the amygdala is not necessary for the formation of CS–(learnt) response associations (Baxter and Murray, 2002). In short, the punishment positions need to distinguish learnt threats from specific types of social threat (Amaral, 2001; Blair and Cipolotti, 2000) and the different forms of association that can be formed with a conditioned stimulus as a function of punishment information (Baxter and Murray, 2002; Killcross et al., 1997). The extension of the fear dysfunction positions, the IES model, does make these distinctions.

The above argument is important because the fear dysfunction positions (Fowles, 1988; Lykken, 1995; Patrick, 1994) were repeatedly, and correctly, attacked by Newman and colleagues on the basis of results with variants of the passive avoidance paradigm (Newman, 1998). As stated above, in the standard passive avoidance paradigm, participants must learn to respond to some stimuli (to gain reward) while not responding to others (if they do, they are punished). In punishment-only "passive avoidance learning," participants must learn to respond to some stimuli (if they do not, they are punished) and not to respond to others (if they do, they are punished). While individuals with psychopathy present with impairment on standard passive avoidance learning tasks (Blair et al., 2004; Newman and Kosson, 1986; Newman and Schmitt, 1998), they show no impairment on punishment-only "passive avoidance learning" tasks (Newman, 1998).

These data are problematic for the fear dysfunction positions because these positions should predict difficulties whenever punishment information needs to be processed (Newman, 1998). If these positions were correct, individuals with psychopathy should learn poorly in both the standard passive avoidance paradigm and the punishment-only paradigm. However, the model developed above provides a principled reason for this dissociation: punishment-only task variants cannot be solved through the formation of CS–affect representation associations. In these variants of the passive avoidance task, there are no "good"/"bad" stimuli; both S+s and S–s can give rise to reward or punishment. Instead of forming a stimulus – reinforcement association, the participant must form a stimulus–response association: if S+ do R1 (respond), if S– do R2 (respond differently). In short, the punishment-only versions of the task are very similar to conditional learning tasks and, given their dependence on stimulus–response associations, should be, and are, solvable by individuals with psychopathy.

SUMMARY

The IES model allows an integration of the earlier empathy dysfunction/ VIM and fear dysfunction models. In addition, it represents constraints on these models, particularly the fear dysfunction models. There is no single, unitary fear system but rather several partially dissociable systems that are involved in the processing of aversive cues, only some of which are impaired in psychopathy.

Implications of amygdala dysfunction: moral socialization

In figure 5.3, we depicted the violence inhibition mechanism. In figure 8.5, we depict the extension of this model within the IES account. As can be seen, the putative functions of the VIM are those of the affect representations implemented by the amygdala. These representations allow the association of

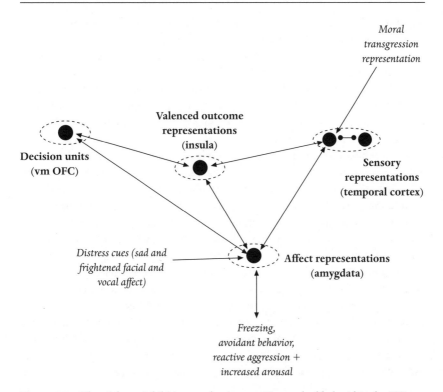

Figure 8.5   The violence inhibition mechanism position embedded within the IES. Vm OFC = ventromedial orbital frontal cortex.

potential CS (in this case, moral transgressions) with US (in this case, distress cues such as another individual's fear). This association is thought to occur through Hebbian learning (Hebb, 1949). Recent data at the cellular level confirms this characterization of learning within the amygdala as Hebbian (Blair et al., 2001d). Potential outputs of the affect representations include freezing/reactive aggression as well as increased arousal. These can be activated by the US (distress cues) and, after learning, the CS (the sight/thought of moral transgressions). Increased attention, also thought to be a consequence of VIM activation, is related in the IES model to the reciprocal connections between the affect representations and the sensory representations (see the section on "The amygdala and stimulus selection").

There are two developments of the VIM account within the IES model. The first is the claim that while the affect representations are crucial for learning about the "badness" of moral transgressions (i.e., associating representations of moral transgressions with the aversive US of another individual's distress), the learnt associations are stored outside of the affect representations as valenced outcome representations (potentially, we suggest, within the insula; see the section on "Learning functions of the amygdala"). In other words, patients with acquired amygdala lesions in adulthood would not be expected to lose knowledge about the "badness" of moral transgressions or to begin to behave immorally. Second, decision units have been added. The role of these units in selecting between response choices will be discussed below (see below, "Orbital/ ventrolateral frontal cortex and response reversal").

We will now consider moral socialization with reference to the IES account. Socialization is the name given to the process by which caregivers, and others, reinforce behaviors that they wish to encourage and punish behaviors that they wish to discourage. Socialization involves aversive conditioning and instrumental learning. The unconditioned stimulus (US; the punisher) that best achieves socialization as regards instrumental antisocial behavior is not physical pain (Hoffman, 1994). Physical pain is rarely contiguous with the antisocial behavior and only occurs when the individual willing to use force is available. In addition, according to conditioning theory and data, the conditioned stimulus (CS) that is associated with the US is the CS that most consistently predicts the US (Dickinson, 1980). Indeed, in households using physical punishment, the CS predicting the US is rarely the antisocial behavior but rather the individual who delivers the US. Thus, in these households, aversive conditioning may occur but the US–CS association will be physical pain and a particular parent, rather than physical pain and antisocial behavior (Hoffman, 1994).

A US that is often present whenever antisocial behavior is committed, particularly in childhood, is the distress of the victim. The suggestion is that the sadness and fearfulness of the victim act as a US eliciting aversive conditioning and instrumental learning. Thus, in order to learn that hitting another individual is bad, a representation of this action must be associated with an aversive unconditioned stimulus (i.e., the distress of the victim). Similarly, learning to avoid committing moral transgressions involves either personally committing, or viewing another commit, a moral transgression and then being "punished" by the aversive response of the victim's distress (Blair, 1995).

Sad and fearful expressions are thought to act as aversive unconditioned stimuli and an appropriate response to these stimuli is crucial for socialization (Blair, 1995). Functional imaging studies have shown, with a few exceptions (Kesler-West et al., 2001), that fearful and sad expressions all modulate amygdala activity (Baird et al., 1999; Blair et al., 1999; Breiter et al., 1996; Drevets et al., 2000; Morris et al., 1996; Phillips et al., 1997, 1998; Schneider et al., 1994). In line with the amygdala dysfunction hypothesis, psychopathic individuals show pronounced impairment in processing sad and fearful expressions. Thus, they show reduced autonomic responses to these expressions (Aniskiewicz, 1979; Blair et al., 1997) and, particularly in childhood, impaired ability to recognize these expressions (Blair et al., 2001b).

One early index of appropriate moral socialization is the demonstration of the moral/conventional distinction. From the age of 3.5 years, children distinguish in their judgments between moral (victim-based) and conventional (social-disorder-based) transgressions (Smetana, 1993; Turiel et al., 1987). Crucially, normally developing children best discriminate in their judgments between the two types of transgressions when they are asked to imagine situations where there are no rules prohibiting the transgressions. In healthy children and adults, the non-permissibility of moral transgressions is relatively uninfluenced by the presence of rules prohibiting their commission (e.g., you would probably judge that hitting another individual for no reason is bad even if it was not against the law). However, the permissibility of conventional transgressions is highly influenced by the existence of rules (e.g., you would probably judge that drinking in the pub after 11.00 p.m. in the UK is OK even though it is against the law). Adults with psychopathy and children with psychopathic tendencies are least likely to make a discrimination under these conditions (Blair, 1995, 1997; Blair et al., 1995a, 2001c). Moreover, similar difficulties have been observed with more general populations of children presenting with antisocial behavior (Arsenio and Fleiss, 1996; Dunn and Hughes, 2001; Hughes and Dunn, 2000; Nucci and Herman, 1982). In addition, psychopathic adults show reduced comprehension of situations likely to induce guilt although they show appropriate comprehension of happiness, sadness, and even complex emotions such as embarrassment (Blair et al., 1995b).

There is also good direct evidence that the impairment shown by psychopathic individuals interferes with socialization. Thus, while it has been repeatedly shown that the use of empathy-inducing positive parenting strategies by caregivers decreases the probability of antisocial behavior in healthy developing children, it does not decrease the probability of antisocial behavior in children who present with the emotional dysfunction of psychopathy (Wootton et al., 1997).

The amygdala dysfunction position also allows an understanding of a potential conundrum related to the socialization literature: that despite the fact that aversive conditioning and other punishment-based techniques are not associated with successful socialization (Brody and Shaffer, 1982; Hoffman, 1994), the temperamental factor "fearfulness" *is* associated with successful socialization (Kochanska, 1993, 1997). However, if we consider that the temperamental factor "fearfulness" reflects the integrity of the amygdala (Blair, 2001), as the data presented above suggest, the conundrum is removed. It is not fearfulness *per se* that is important in socialization but rather it is the integrity of the amygdala. The amygdala responds to the fear and sadness of victims and allows the formation of moral transgression–victims' distress associations (i.e., a particular form of stimulus–punishment association). Within this framework, empathy induction, a parenting technique that is associated with successful socialization (see chapter 4), is so successful because it focuses the transgressor's attention on the victim and therefore boosts the punishment value of the victim's distress. Individuals who are less fearful due to early amygdala dysfunction (i.e., individuals with psychopathy according to our account) will not find the distress of others aversive, and therefore will be difficult to socialize (cf. Wootton et al., 1997).

SUMMARY

Socialization involves aversive conditioning and instrumental learn-ing, potentially particular instrumental learning reliant on stimulus–reinforcement associations; i.e., socialization involves the amygdala. The unconditioned stimulus (US; the punisher) that best achieves socialization as regards instrumental antisocial behavior is the distress of the victim. It is thought that the amygdala dysfunction seen in psychopathy disrupts socialization.

Qualifying the amygdala dysfunction position

Reward and punishment processing

Our basic argument is that, at the neural level, psychopathy is associated with amygdala dysfunction. At the cognitive/computational level, the suggestion with respect to psychopathy is that the affect representations implemented by the amygdala are either less responsive or learning on the basis of the activation of these representations is disrupted. The affect representations are activated by the fear and distress of others. Reduced responsiveness to these expressions interferes with moral socialization, leading to an individual who is at risk for learning to use antisocial behavior as a method for achieving his/her goals.

A principal function of the amygdala is the formation of stimulus–reward and stimulus–punishment associations; animals with amygdala lesions present with impairment in both reward- and punishment-related behavior (Baxter and Murray, 2002). This is the specifics of the functional impairment depicted at the cognitive level in figure 8.3. Many of the impairments seen in individuals with psychopathy can be attributed to the impaired formation of stimulus–punishment associations/reduced representation of aversive stimuli. Thus, both aversive conditioning and passive avoidance learning involve the formation of stimulus–punishment associations. In addition, in the startle reflex paradigms, the visual stimulus that primes the brainstem to augment the startle to a loud noise is a conditioned stimulus (a stimulus that has been previously associated with punishment). Finally, sad and fearful expressions have been considered to be aversive unconditioned stimuli (Blair, 2003b).

However, while it is clear that individuals with psychopathy do present with impairment in the formation of stimulus–punishment associations/reduced representation of aversive stimuli, the extent to which individuals with psychopathy present with impairment in the formation of stimulus–reward associations/reduced representation of appetitive stimuli is less clear (Levenston et al., 2000; Blair et al., submitted a, submitted b). Individuals with psychopathy show appropriate suppression of the startle reflex following the presentation of positive visual primes but reduced augmentation of the startle reflex following the presentation of negative visual primes (Levenston et al., 2000; Pastor et al., 2003; Patrick et al., 1993). This suggests that individuals with psychopathy are unimpaired in processing positive material. However, as noted above, in lexical decision-making tasks where participants must identify words versus non-words, comparison individuals are faster to identify positive and negative emotional words than neutral ones, but individuals with psychopathy do not show this emotional advantage (Lorenz and Newman, 2002; Williamson et al., 1991). In addition, Verona and colleagues reported reduced skin conductance responses to both positive and negative auditory stimuli in individuals with psychopathy (Verona et al., 2004). Finally, in recent work within our own group, using both affective priming (Blair et al., submitted c) and decision-making paradigms (Blair et al., submitted a), we have found impaired processing of both positive and negative material, but that this impairment is particularly severe for negative material.

The results of the differential reward and punishment learning task are particularly interesting in this regard (Blair et al., submitted a). In this task, the participant has to choose between two objects presented on a computer screen. However, there are ten different objects to choose between. Each of these ten objects is randomly assigned a value at the beginning of the testing session (−1600, −800, −400, −200, −100, 100, 200, 400, 800, or 1600). The two objects presented to the participant on any one trial can either involve one rewarding and one punishing object, two objects with different levels of punishment, or two objects with different levels of rewards. The participant has to choose the object that will gain the most points or lose the least points. This task allows an assessment of an individual's sensitivity to variations in reward/punishment levels; choosing between the object that gives 1600 points and the object giving

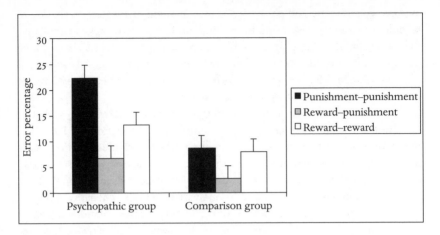

Figure 8.6   Data from the differential reward/punishment task.

100 points should be, and is, easier than choosing between the object that gives 1600 points and the object giving 800 points. Individuals with psychopathy show pronounced difficulty with this task (Blair et al., submitted a). Strikingly, and very unlike comparison individuals, their impairment is far more pronounced when choosing between objects that give rise to different levels of punishment as opposed to choosing between objects that give rise to different levels of reward; see figure 8.6.

   In short, all of the above data suggest that both the affect representations coding reward and punishment information are impaired in individuals with psychopathy. However, taken together, they suggest that the affect representations coding punishment information are more dysfunctional than those coding reward. We would suggest two potential accounts to these data. Both accounts assume that the positive affect representations are less dysfunctional than the negative ones in individuals with psychopathy; i.e., the formation of stimulus–reward associations is less impaired that the formation of stimulus–punishment associations. However, the first account suggests that the inconsistent results reflect chance factors. According to the account, inconsistent findings regarding the level of impairment in the formation/responding on the basis of stimulus–reward associations would reflect the inconsistent impact of task demands on the less impaired form of processing. Of course, this is an unsatisfactory account. It provides no principled way of determining the level of reward-related impairment on any individual task. In addition, the very consistent findings of appropriate levels of suppression of the startle reflex by appetitive primes, despite differences between the studies, argues against an account based on stochastic influences (Levenston et al., 2000; Pastor et al., 2003; Patrick et al., 1993).

The second account echoes the data that forced the development of the fear dysfunction models. As noted above, there is no single "fear" system, but, rather, partially separable systems, only some of which are impaired in individuals with psychopathy. Reward-related processing is somewhat less well understood. However, concepts of reward-related processing are likely to be refined into suggested separable systems. The contrast between the data obtained by Verona et al. (2004) and Mitchell et al. (under revision) and the modulation of the startle reflex data may be highly informative in this regard (cf. Blair et al., submitted a). One possibility is that the suppression of the basic threat circuitry mediating the startle response can be suppressed by positive information by a route bypassing the amygdala. Indeed, while there is considerable data that amygdala lesions disrupt the augmentation of the startle response by visual threat primes (Angrilli et al., 1996; Davis, 2000), to our knowledge there is no literature demonstrating that amygdala lesions disrupt the suppression of the startle response by visual appetitive stimuli. If the account we develop here is correct, the clear prediction is that amygdala lesions will not disrupt the suppression of the startle response by visual appetitive stimuli. Of course, it remains unclear why in the tasks described by Verona et al. (2004) and Mitchell et al. (under revision), the impairment seen in individuals with psychopathy was equally marked for positive and negative stimuli, while in the studies on the lexical decision task (Lorenz and Newman, 2002; Williamson et al., 1991), affective priming (Blair et al., submitted c), and the differential reward/punishment task (Blair et al., submitted a), the impairment was notably more marked for negative rather than positive information. However, it is likely that advances in the understanding of reward-related processing in the affective cognitive neuroscience literature will be highly informative in this regard.

SUMMARY

In short, we assume that the affect representations implemented by the amygdala are dysfunctional but that the impairment for negative affect representations is more marked than the impairment for positive affect representations. In other words, the formation of, and responding to, stimulus–punishment associations is more impaired in individuals with psychopathy than the formation of, and responding to, stimulus–reward associations.

Social cognition

The amygdala has been considered to play a role in certain aspects of social cognition; in particular, affect-related judgments of facial stimuli (Adolphs, 2003; Baron-Cohen et al., 2000). Thus, in one paradigm, participants were shown pictures of individuals in natural poses and asked to judge the trustworthiness of these individuals. While healthy individuals typically judge some individuals' faces less trustworthy than others, patients with amygdala lesions present with atypical judgment patterns (Adolphs et al., 1998). Further support for the suggestion of an amygdala involvement in the judgment of trustworthiness comes from recent neuro-imaging work indicating that healthy individuals show greater amygdala activation to faces judged to be untrustworthy relative to faces judged to be trustworthy (Winston et al., 2002). In a second paradigm, participants must judge the complex social emotion being displayed by an individual based on information from the eye region only (Baron-Cohen et al., 1997). Individuals with amygdala lesions show impairment on this task (Adolphs et al., 2002; Stone et al., 2003) and neuro-imaging complements these findings by demonstrating amygdala activation during the performance of this task (Baron-Cohen et al., 1999). However, despite this apparent role of the amygdala in these two aspects of social cognition, individuals with psychopathy do not present with impairment in either the making of trustworthiness judgments (Richell et al., in press) or the judging of complex social emotions from the eyes (Richell et al., 2003).

At present, no formal model of these aspects of social cognition has been proposed. There have been no attempts to tie these aspects of social cognition to the known role of the amygdala in the formation of stimulus–reward and stimulus–punishment associations. It is even conceivable that these aspects of social cognition do not involve the amygdala *per se* but rather cortex adjacent to the amygdala or even fiber tracts that pass through the amygdala. However, if we assume that they do involve the amygdala then we must qualify the amygdala position that we have developed. It is not that all aspects of amygdala functioning are necessarily impaired in individuals with psychopathy; only those concerned with the formation of stimulus–reinforcement associations are impaired and even in this case, the formation of stimulus–punishment associations is far more marked that the formation of stimulus–reward associations.

SUMMARY

Those aspects of social cognition in which the amygdala has been implicated, affect-related judgments of facial stimuli, are not dysfunctional in individuals with psychopathy. This reinforces the suggestion made on the basis of the differential stimulus–punishment/stimulus–reward impairment that not all aspects of amygdala functioning are equivalently impaired in individuals with psychopathy.

Potential implications of these qualifications

Individuals with psychopathy do not present with equivalent impairment to patients with amygdala lesions. Functions that appear to require the amygdala such as the formation of stimulus–reward associations and certain aspects of social cognition are only mildly impaired, or even intact, in individuals with psychopathy. This suggests that the genetic anomalies that we assume are the fundamental causes of psychopathy do not lead to the development of the disorder through a global disruption of the functioning of the amygdala. Instead, they may have a more selective effect, perhaps by disrupting the functioning of specific neurotransmitter(s) which are involved in specific aspects of amygdala functioning.

We suggest that the genetic anomalies we assume to underlie psychopathy give rise to disturbance in neurotransmitter functioning such that the ability of the amygdala to perform stimulus–punishment associations is particularly compromised. Polymorphisms of particular genes can alter the functioning of specific neurotransmitter systems (Lichter et al., 1993; Shih et al., 1999; Vandenbergh et al., 1992). However, it remains unclear which neurotransmitter systems might be dysfunctional in individuals with psychopathy. One possibility is that the noradrenergic response to stress/threat stimuli is disturbed in these individuals (Blair, 2003a; Blair et al., submitted a). Interestingly, there have been recent suggestions that noradrenaline is involved in mediating the impact of aversive cues in human choice (Rogers et al., 2004). Moreover, recent pharmacological data imply that noradrenergic manipulations selectively impact on the processing of sad expressions (Harmer et al., 2001). Further support for this suggestion comes from studies linking NA abnormalities to antisocial behavior/conduct disorder (Raine, 1993; Rogeness et al., 1990a, b). In this regard it is interesting to note that noradrenergic function appears to be *increased* in a range of anxiety disorders (Charney et al., 1984); i.e., it is increased in populations that present with a heightened responsiveness to aversive cues, the opposite of the emotional impairment seen in psychopathy. Thus, one possibility is that genetic anomalies considered to be present in individuals with psychopathy disrupt the functioning of the noradrenergic system such that the impact of aversive stimuli is muted.

SUMMARY

Data indicating that individuals with psychopathy present with relatively little or no impairment for functions known to require the integrity of the amygdala, such as the formation of stimulus–reward associations and aspects of social cognition, qualify the amygdala dysfunction position. They suggest that the genetic anomalies, which we assume are the fundamental causes of psychopathy, do not globally disrupt the functioning of the amygdala but rather have a more selective effect, perhaps by disrupting the functioning of specific neurotransmitter(s) involved in specific aspects of amygdala functioning. We suggest that the noradrenergic response to stress/threat stimuli may be disturbed in individuals with psychopathy.

Dysfunction beyond the amygdala

The amygdala is connected to a variety of structures including the hippocampus, superior temporal sulcus, fusiform cortex, anterior cingulate, and orbital frontal cortex (see the first section of this chapter). It is possible that lack of afferent input from the amygdala might lead to disturbance in any of these structures. Additionally, or alternatively, if the genetic anomalies lead to a neurotransmitter disturbance, it is unlikely that the dysfunction will be confined to the amygdala. Of course, one must also be careful not to assume dysfunction in a neural region simply because it demonstrates less activation in the patient population than the comparison group. If one neural region is dysfunctional and responding weakly to a stimulus, any region reliant on input from the disturbed region will also show reduced activation. It has been suggested that individuals with psychopathy present with anterior cingulate dysfunction, for example (Kiehl et al., 2001). However, this was on the basis of reduced activation during an emotional memory task. Emotional memory is known to implicate the amygdala (Cahill, 2000), which also showed reduced activation in the individuals with psychopathy. We are unconvinced by current data that there is anterior cingulate dysfunction in psychopathy. Certainly, functions for which the anterior cingulate is necessary, such as responding to situations of response/task conflict as indexed by the Stroop task (MacLeod and MacDonald, 2000), are not impaired in individuals with psychopathy. However, we would not argue that individuals with psychopathy only present with a specific form of amygdala dysfunction. There are strong reasons to believe that individuals with psychopathy present with orbital/ventrolateral frontal cortex dysfunction also. Orbital/ventrolateral frontal cortex are involved in two functions that have received empirical attention with individuals with psychopathy: response reversal/extinction and response control.

Orbital/ventrolateral frontal cortex and response reversal

Response reversal involves changing a response to a stimulus as a function of a change in contingency; i.e., learning to withhold a response that is now punished though previously it had been rewarded (Rolls, 1997). The reversal is the crucial component here; the individual must reverse their response to a stimulus. Response reversal is thus not involved in the passive avoidance task (Newman and Kosson, 1986) where the individual simply learns to respond to some stimuli and withhold responses to others but never has to reverse their response to a stimulus. There is a considerable neuropsychological and neuro-imaging literature demonstrating that orbital frontal cortex is crucially involved in response reversal (Cools et al., 2002; Rahman et al., 1999; Rolls et al., 1994).

We suggested some of the computations necessary to implement response reversal in chapter 7 (see figure 7.2). Within the model, the known role of orbital frontal cortex in response reversal (Cools et al., 2002; Dias et al., 1996; Rolls et al., 1994) is seen as a function of the degree to which there is a mismatch between the expectation of reinforcement and the presence of reinforcement. This suggests that if there is dysfunction in orbital frontal cortex, response reversal will be detrimentally affected. Moreover, the greater the degree of dysfunction, the more difficult it will be for the individual to identify the contingency change.

Children with psychopathic tendencies and adults with psychopathy show comparably impaired performance on measures of amygdala functioning such as passive avoidance (Newman and Kosson, 1986; Newman et al., 1985), the processing of fearful expressions (Blair et al., 2001c), and aversive conditioning (Lykken, 1957; Raine et al., 1996). However, there is less clear evidence that children with psychopathic tendencies show comparably impaired performance on measures requiring orbital frontal cortex such as response reversal or extinction. Newman's card playing task (Newman et al., 1987) involves extinction; the participant learns to play the card for reward but then must extinguish this response as, proceeding through the pack of cards, the probability of reward decreases successively. Both children with psychopathic tendencies and adult psychopathic individuals do show marked impairment on this task (Fisher and Blair, 1998; Newman et al., 1987; O'Brien and Frick, 1996). However, the intradimensional/extradimensional (ID/ED) paradigm also includes response reversal; the participant must reverse their responding to the object that, when responded to, had previously elicited rewarded but now elicits punishment.

While adult psychopathic individuals show notable impairment in response reversal on this task (Mitchell et al., 2002), children with psychopathic tendencies do not (Blair et al., 2001a). So why do children with psychopathic tendencies fail one task involving response reversal but pass another?

A major difference between these two tasks is in the salience of the contingency change. In the card-playing task, the probability of reinforcement decreases by 10 percent over every ten trials. In the ID/ED task, the probability of reinforcement changes from 100 percent to 0 percent once the initial learning criterion has been achieved. This indicates that while both children with psychopathic tendencies and adult psychopathic individuals are impaired in the detection of contingency change, this impairment is markedly more pronounced in the adult psychopathic individuals. Moreover, this suggests that if we reduce the salience of the contingency change, we should see impairment in the children with psychopathic tendencies and that the degree of impairment will be a function of the salience of the contingency change.

We have recently tested this hypothesis using a probabilistic response reversal paradigm. In this task, participants were presented with pairs of stimuli. For each pair, one of the stimuli was rewarded more often than the other. The probability of reward was different across pairs (i.e., for pair A, stimulus 1 was rewarded 100 percent of the time, for pair B, stimulus 1 was rewarded 90 percent of the time etc.). Following a set number of trials, the contingency was reversed (i.e., for pair A, stimulus 2 was rewarded 100 percent of the time, for pair B, stimulus 2 was rewarded 90 percent of the time etc.). While the children with psychopathic tendencies showed no difficulty reversing their responses for salient contingency changes, they did show significant difficulty as the salience of the contingency change decreased (Budhani and Blair, in press). This result then provided support for our hypothesis that while both children with psychopathic tendencies and adult psychopathic individuals are impaired in the detection of contingency change, this impairment is markedly more pronounced in adults with psychopathy.

Ventrolateral frontal cortex and response control

Ventrolateral frontal cortex is crucially involved in resolving motor response conflict. If two or more motor responses are activated by stimuli, orbital frontal cortex resolves the conflict and allows one motor response to be initiated. We have discussed above situations where decision making is a function of expectations of reward/punishment and violations of these expectations. However, ventrolateral frontal cortex is also involved in resolving response competition in tasks where there are no clear expectations of reward/punishment. We refer to these tasks as response control tasks.

Two examples of response control tasks are the go/no-go task and the stop task. In the go/no-go task, the participant is told to respond to one set of stimuli but not to respond to another set; for example, the participant is told to press a button whenever any letter is on the screen other than an X. Imaging work has shown that if there are relatively few no-go stimuli compared to the number of go stimuli (i.e., there is a prepotent response to respond), ventrolateral frontal cortex is recruited and is involved in the resolution of the conflict between the prepotent respond response and a goal to withhold from responding on the basis of the task instructions (Casey et al., 2001). In the stop task, the participant is presented with a stimulus and instructed to respond to these stimuli as rapidly as possible unless a stop signal is presented, in which case they are to stop their response (Logan et al., 1984).

Response control tasks are interesting because, although they involve orbital and ventrolateral frontal cortex (Casey et al., 2001), they do not involve the computation of rewards/punishments or the detection of reinforcement contingency violations. Response control tasks thus allow a direct test of whether there is a non-emotion-based difficulty in the control of motor responding in individuals with psychopathy. There have been relatively few investigations of the ability of individuals to perform response control tasks (Kiehl et al., 2000; LaPierre et al., 1995; Roussy and Toupin, 2000). However, two out of three studies using the go/no-go task, did report impairment in individuals with psychopathy (LaPierre et al., 1995; Roussy and Toupin, 2000). The third study did not report any behavioral impairment but did find an atypical ERP response in the individuals with psychopathy to the no-go trials (Kiehl et al., 2000). The only study using the stop task also reported that the psychopathic individuals were less successful than comparison individuals in withholding their response following the stop signal (Roussy and Toupin, 2000).

Orbital frontal cortex, aversive conditioning, and instrumental learning

There have been repeated suggestions that psychopathy is due to dysfunction within either frontal cortex more generally or orbital frontal cortex in particular (Damasio, 1994; Damasio et al., 1990; Gorenstein and Newman, 1980; Raine, 1997, 2002a). There is reason to believe that there may be pathology in orbital frontal cortex in this population (LaPierre et al., 1995; Mitchell et al., 2002; Raine et al., 2000). This pathology results in impairment on measures of response reversal, extinction, and other forms of response change. Could such pathology account for the impairments seen in psychopathic individuals in measures of aversive conditioning and instrumental learning?

There are data that neurons in orbital frontal cortex respond differentially to stimuli during aversive conditioning and instrumental and passive avoidance learning (Garcia et al., 1999; Schoenbaum et al., 1999; Tremblay and Schultz, 1999). According to the model developed in figure 8.3 (see Blair, 2004), we believe that these are crucial when the individual has to choose between two or more behavioral responses. However, there is no reason to believe that these neurons are crucial for aversive conditioning and instrumental learning *per se*. If only one stimulus is present in the environment to respond to, orbital frontal cortex involvement should not be necessary. In line with this position, lesions of orbital frontal cortex do not impair aversive conditioning (Bechara et al., 1999; Quirk et al., 2000) or instrumental learning/passive avoidance (Schoenbaum et al., 2002). This strongly suggests that orbital frontal cortex, unlike the amygdala, is not necessary for either function. Thus, while there may be orbital frontal cortex pathology in adult psychopathic individuals, this cannot be the explanation of the results discussed above.

Orbital/ventrolateral frontal cortex and the development of psychopathy

Earlier, we discussed data from aversive conditioning and instrumental learning tasks which strongly indicate amygdala dysfunction in individuals with psychopathy. Crucially, amygdala, but not orbital frontal cortex, lesions result in impairment in both functions (Ambrogi Lorenzini et al., 1999; Bechara et al., 1999; Davis, 2000; Killcross et al., 1997; Quirk et al., 2000; Schoenbaum et al., 2002). However, the data from the response control tasks reviewed above would suggest that there are indications of orbital frontal cortex pathology in individuals with psychopathy that are not a consequence of amygdala dysfunction. Moreover, the findings with the response reversal paradigms suggest that the orbital frontal cortex dysfunction may be greater in adults with psychopathy relative to children with the disorder. Thus, while both adults and children with psychopathy are insensitive, relative to comparison individuals, to subtle changes in reinforcement contingency (Fisher and Blair, 1998; Newman et al., 1987; O'Brien and Frick, 1996), only adults with psychopathy are insensitive to obvious changes in reinforcement contingency (Blair et al., 2001a; Mitchell et al., 2002).

Given the evidence of amygdala dysfunction discussed above, there are several possibilities regarding the origins of the orbital frontal cortex pathology found in individuals with psychopathy. First, the orbital frontal cortex pathology could be developmentally independent of the amygdala pathology. For example, there might be genetic influences that affect the development of the amygdala and orbital frontal cortex independently of one another. Second, there are considerable interconnections between the amygdala and orbital frontal cortex (Amaral et al., 1992; Carmichael and Price, 1995). It is possible that a lack of afferent input from the amygdala to orbital frontal cortex could disrupt the development of orbital frontal cortex to an increasingly greater degree as development progresses. Third, individuals with psychopathy present with higher levels of drug abuse, dependence, and poly-drug use than comparison individuals (Hemphill et al., 1994; Smith and Newman, 1990). Alcohol- and drug-dependent individuals present with impaired performance on measures assessing the functioning of orbital frontal cortex (Bechara et al., 2001; Grant et al., 2000; Rogers and Robbins, 2001). It is thus also possible that the lifestyle chosen by individuals with psychopathy may be the cause of their orbital frontal cortex pathology.

It is important to note here that the orbital/ventrolateral frontal cortex dysfunction seen in individuals with psychopathy, as evidenced by their difficulty with response reversal paradigms, is likely to be related to their heightened levels of reactive aggression. We argued in chapter 7 that an individual unable to successfully perform response reversal is an individual at risk for frustration – the individual will not be able to easily modify their behavior in order to achieve their goals if the contingencies change in their environment. It is well known that frustration is a cue for aggression (Berkowitz, 1993). We believe that individuals with psychopathy present with heightened levels of reactive aggression because of their orbital/ventrolateral frontal cortex dysfunction.

Conclusions

In this chapter, we have developed a neurocognitive model of the development of psychopathy. At the core of the model is the suggestion of amygdala dysfunction in individuals with the disorder. This amygdala dysfunction gives rise to impairments in aversive conditioning, instrumental learning, and the processing of fearful and sad expressions. These impairments interfere with socialization such that the individual does not learn to avoid actions that cause harm to other individuals. If such an individual has a reason to offend, because their other opportunities for financial resources or respect are limited, they will be more likely to offend than healthy developing individuals.

In addition, there are also indications that individuals with psychopathy present with orbital frontal cortex dysfunction. One aspect of this impairment, impairment on reversal learning tasks, may be related to the amygdala pathology.

However, a second aspect of this impairment, impairment on response control tasks, cannot easily be related to amygdala pathology. This suggests that there is orbital frontal cortex pathology that is additional to the amygdala pathology. As yet, the degree to which the amygdala and orbital frontal cortex pathology have similar developmental origins remains unclear.

9

CONUNDRUMS AND CONCLUSIONS

In this book, we have provided a description of the current prominent models of psychopathy, the limitations of these models, and then two newer accounts that address these limitations. One of these concerned neurocognitive systems involved in the regulation of reactive aggression (chapter 7). The second concerned neurocognitive systems involved in emotional learning. The suggestion made was that if these are impaired at an early age, the individual will present with the emotional difficulties associated with psychopathy. These difficulties will interfere with socialization such that the individual will be at risk for the display of elevated levels of instrumental aggression. In this final chapter, we have two goals: first, to consider any further conundrums that these two models may face, and second, to draw some conclusions.

Remaining conundrums

In this section, we will consider three conundrums. These are: (1) the high co-morbidity of psychopathy with attention deficit hyperactivity disorder (ADHD) despite the differences in the known pathophysiology of these two disorders; (2) the fact that another disorder of social cognition, autism, has also been linked to amygdala dysfunction despite the gross differences in disorder; and (3) the potential presence of impairment in semantic memory systems in individuals with psychopathy. We will consider each of these conundrums in turn.

Attention deficit hyperactivity disorder

As described in chapter 2, ADHD is "a persistent pattern of inattention and/or hyperactivity – impulsivity that is more frequent and severe than is typically observed in individuals at a comparable level of development" (American Psychiatric Association, 1994). ADHD is a conundrum because while there is high comorbidity of ADHD with psychopathic tendencies (Babinski et al., 1999; Barry et al., 2000; Colledge and Blair, 2001; Lynam, 1996), the neurocognitive impairments seen in children with ADHD are, to a large extent, not found in individuals with psychopathy.

When considering this conundrum, we will first consider current accounts of ADHD. In particular, we will consider Barkley's (e.g., 1999) "behavioral inhibition" account before going on to suggest that ADHD might be better interpreted with reference to dysfunction in the "task demands" component of Cohen's model of executive functioning. We will note that there is clear evidence of executive function in individuals with ADHD and as clear evidence of an absence of executive dysfunction in psychopathy (at least with respect to specific executive functions mediated by medial and dorsolateral prefrontal cortex). We will then account for this conundrum by referring to the ventrolateral prefrontal cortex dysfunction seen in individuals with psychopathy. We will suggest that individuals with psychopathy presenting with this ventrolateral prefrontal cortex dysfunction will be at heightened risk of presenting with the impulsivity component of ADHD. We will also suggest that individuals with ADHD may, if this is associated with ventrolateral prefrontal cortex dysfunction, be at heightened risk for the display of reactive aggression.

Barkley has claimed that there is a central deficit in "behavioral inhibition" in individuals with ADHD (Barkley, 1999). He suggests that the deficit in behavioral inhibition diminishes the effective employment of four executive functions. He terms these non-verbal working memory, verbal working memory, the self-regulation of affect/motivation/arousal, and reconstitution. Our purpose here is not to provide a full critique of Barkley's position. However, it should be noted that according to Barkley's position, the impairment in behavioral inhibition should disrupt all four forms of executive function. Yet, while individuals with ADHD show executive dysfunction, not all executive functions are comparably disturbed. In particular, performance on measures of verbal working memory is not particularly compromised in individuals with ADHD (Chhabildas et al., 2001; Pennington and Ozonoff, 1996; Rapport et al., 2001).

A second difficulty with Barkley's position is that it is rather under-specified. The computational properties of the putative four executive systems and behavioral inhibition itself have not been detailed. However, more precise theoretical formulations of executive functioning have been offered by other researchers. In particular, the task context module model developed by Cohen and colleagues is of interest here (Cohen et al., 1990, 1992, 2000). This model has been used to explain performance on the Stroop task and the continuous performance test (Cohen et al., 1990, 1992); individuals with ADHD present with severe difficulties on both of these tasks (Barkley et al., 2001; Epstein et al., 2003; Pennington and Ozonoff, 1996). Before describing the model, we shall very briefly describe the Stroop task.

The classic word-color Stroop task (Stroop, 1935) is a familiar paradigm. Stroop observed that it took longer for participants to name the color of the ink in which a color word was written (so, for example, naming "blue" as the color of the stimulus word GREEN typed in blue ink) compared to naming the hue of color patches. It is this increased color naming latency that is referred to as the Stroop effect.

The task context module model of Stroop performance consists of two processing pathways, one for word reading and one for color naming. Stimuli are coded by feature-specific representations, and converge on an output layer with units corresponding to each response. Processing occurs via activation spreading between units along the pathways. Within each module, representations are mutually inhibitory (see figure 9.1) (Cohen et al., 1996, 2000). The strength of these pathways is determined by the degree of training that the model receives for a specific class of input. The model receives more extensive training on the word-reading task than the color-naming task following the assumption that humans have more extensive experience with the former than the latter. This asymmetry in training intensity leads to greater connection weights in the word-reading path compared to the color-naming path; i.e., following training, word reading becomes the prepotent response (represented in figure 9.1 by thicker lines from the word input units to the output responses). The task context module model also stipulates the existence of an executive feature, the context module. This contains units corresponding to each of the two task-relevant stimulus features. In conditions of response competition (i.e., naming the hue), the context module resolves the conflict by means of supporting the processing of the task-relevant information, so that it can out-compete the task-irrelevant information. Thus, the task context module model predicts that an individual's level of Stroop interference is not only a function of training on the respective domains but also the degree to which the context module is functioning efficiently.

More recent developments include the addition of a more fully specified control system, with a layer that responds to conflict (co-activation) of response units (Cohen et al., 1996, 2000); see figure 9.1. This drives a neuro-modulatory system that increases responsiveness of processing units globally (for instance,

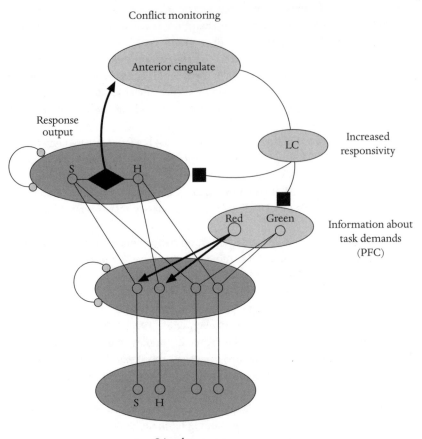

Figure 9.1 The task context module model of Cohen et al. (2000). Copyright © 2000 Nature Publishing Group. Reprinted by permission of the authors and Nature Publishing Group.

Components related to performance of the basic task have dark shading, and components related to control have light shading. Stimuli are coded by feature-specific representations, and converge on an output layer with units corresponding to each response. The task demand layer has units corresponding to each of the two task-relevant stimulus features. Representations within layers are mutually inhibitory (that is, they compete, as designated by looped connections with filled circles). Note that this model is homologous to well-studied models of other response competition tasks, such as the Stroop task, except that there is no asymmetry between task-relevant and -irrelevant dimensions of processing. This model also adds a more fully specified control system, including a layer that responds to conflict (co-activation) of response units (ACC). This drives a neuromodulatory system (locus coeruleus, LC) that increases responsivity of processing units globally (for instance by a change in gain, designated by connections with squares). This modulates selective attention by its influence on representations of specific task demands (PFC) as well as motor preparation by its influence on response units.

by a change in gain, designated by connections with squares). This modulates selective attention by its influence on representations of specific task demands, as well as motor preparation by its influence on response units.

An important aspect of Cohen's model is that it specifically predicts that dysfunction within the task demands module will lead to impairment, relative to populations without this dysfunction, on the naming the hue condition. According to the model, the activation of the hue-naming task demand representations increases activation of the hue-naming pathway, leading to improved performance. This task demands activation is relatively more important for hue naming compared to word reading, because the hue naming is a far weaker route (due to less hue-naming experience) than the word-reading route.

If we assume that ADHD is related to disturbance in the task demands module, we must predict therefore that individuals with ADHD will show impairment in the color-naming as well as color–word interference conditions. This prediction is in direct contradiction of an account based on behavioral inhibition. As there is no response competition in the color-naming condition, a behavioral inhibition position should not predict impairment in this condition. Repeated studies have shown that individuals with ADHD perform poorly relative to comparison children on both the color-naming and color–word interference conditions (Corbett and Stanczak, 1999; Leung and Connolly, 1996; Nigg et al., 2002; Reeve and Schandler, 2001); in other words, the predictions derived from the task demands module are supported while those derived from a behavioral inhibition account are not.

In short, we consider there to be clear evidence that ADHD is related to executive dysfunction. We would suggest that this dysfunction can be best characterized within Cohen's task context module model. In contrast to ADHD, we believe that there are no indications of executive dysfunction in this sense in individuals with psychopathy. Individuals with psychopathy show no impairment on classic measures of executive functioning such as the Wisconsin Card Sorting Task (LaPierre et al., 1995) or the ED-shift component of the ID/ED task (Mitchell et al., 2002). Individuals with ADHD show difficulty with both of these tasks (Pennington and Ozonoff, 1996; Williams et al., 2000). Individuals with psychopathy show no impairment, or even reduced interference (Newman et al., 1997), on Stroop, or Stroop-like, tasks (Blair et al., under revision; Smith et al., 1992). As described above, individuals with ADHD show striking difficulty with such tasks (Corbett and Stanczak, 1999; Leung and Connolly, 1996; Nigg et al., 2002; Pennington and Ozonoff, 1996; Reeve and Schandler, 2001). Moreover, at the anatomical level ADHD has been associated with dysfunction of right-sided prefrontal-striatal systems but not with amygdala dysfunction (Castellanos et al., 1996; Giedd et al., 2001). As we have argued, amygdala dysfunction is a crucial component of psychopathy. Yet despite these striking differences in pathology, ADHD is not only highly comorbid with conduct disorder (Biederman et al., 1991; Hinshaw, 1987; Taylor et al., 1986), it is highly comorbid with psychopathic tendencies also; over 75 percent in our own work (Colledge and Blair, 2001).

We now suggest a possible explanation for this apparent comorbidity conundrum. In chapter 8, we developed our neurocognitive account of psychopathy. This suggested that psychopathy is associated with amygdala dysfunction but also with dysfunction in some frontal regions, particularly ventrolateral prefrontal cortex (Brodmann's Area (BA) 47). BA 47 has been implicated in response reversal (as indexed by response reversal paradigms) and response control (as indexed by stop and go/no-go paradigms) tasks (Aron et al., 2003; Casey et al., 2001; Cools et al., 2002; Kringelbach and Rolls, 2003). Individuals with psychopathy show clear difficulties on response reversal (Blair et al., 2001a; Mitchell et al., 2002) and some evidence of difficulty with response control tasks (LaPierre et al., 1995; Roussy and Toupin, 2000). There have been suggestions that individuals with ADHD may present with difficulty on response reversal tasks (Itami and Uno, 2002). There are considerable data that individuals with ADHD present with difficulty on response control paradigms (Berlin and Bohlin, 2002; Castellanos et al., 2000; Langley et al., 2004; Murphy, 2002; Pennington and Ozonoff, 1996; Wodushek and Neumann, 2003).

We argued in chapter 8 that the pathology associated with psychopathy disrupts the functioning of BA 47. We argued that this disruption gives rise to the impairments on response reversal and response control tasks seen in individuals with psychopathic tendencies (Blair et al., 2001a; LaPierre et al., 1995; Mitchell et al., 2002; Roussy and Toupin, 2000). In chapter 8, we suggested that BA 47 dysfunction might be associated with the reactive aggression seen in individuals with psychopathic tendencies. We suggested that this dysfunction would dysregulate the modulation of brainstem systems mediating the basic response to threat, leading to an increase in the probability of reactive aggression. However, BA 47 is also involved in the regulation of on-line instrumental behavior; particularly with respect to changing this behavior following changes in contingency or task demands. Damage to BA 47 should therefore be associated with difficulties in behavioral regulation. We would argue that that this dysfunction may give rise to the hyperactivity seen in children with ADHD. Individuals with BA 47 dysfunction would therefore be expected to present with hyperactivity. It is the hyperactivity rather than the inattention component of ADHD that is associated with psychopathic tendencies (Colledge and Blair, 2001).

This suggestion is represented as a causal model in figure 9.2. In chapter 8, we suggested that a neurotransmitter abnormality, perhaps related to noradrenergic functioning, is responsible for the amygdala dysfunction seen in individuals with psychopathy. This may also compromise the functioning of BA 47 but an

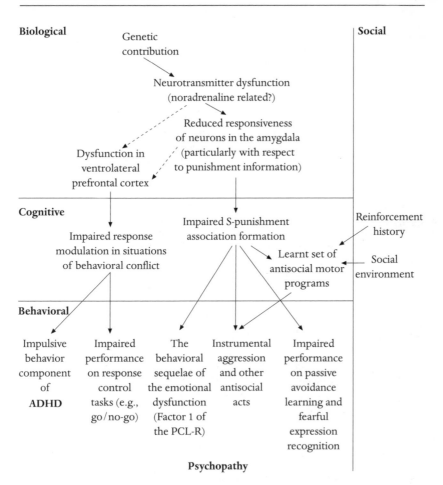

Biological　　Genetic
　　　　　　　　contribution

　　　　　　　　　Neurotransmitter dysfunction
　　　　　　　　　　(noradrenaline related?)

　　　　　　　　　　Reduced responsiveness
　　　　　　　　　　of neurons in the amygdala
Dysfunction in　　(particularly with respect
ventrolateral　　to punishment information)
prefrontal cortex

Cognitive

　　　　　　　　Impaired S-punishment
Impaired response　association formation
modulation in situations
of behavioral conflict　　　　Learnt set of
　　　　　　　　　　　　　antisocial motor
　　　　　　　　　　　　　programs

Social

Reinforcement
history

Social
environment

Behavioral

| Impulsive behavior component of **ADHD** | Impaired performance on response control tasks (e.g., go/no-go) | The behavioral sequelae of the emotional dysfunction (Factor 1 of the PCL-R) | Instrumental aggression and other antisocial acts | Impaired performance on passive avoidance learning and fearful expression recognition |

Psychopathy

Figure 9.2　A causal model of the development of psychopathy and its potential relationship with ADHD.

alternative conceptualization would be that the BA 47 dysfunction is a secondary consequence of reduced afferent input from the amygdala (both possibilities are represented in figure 9.2). BA 47 dysfunction gives rise to difficulties in response control and response reversal at the cognitive level. Consequences at the behavioral level would include increased probability of hyperactivity and reactive aggression (and impaired go/no-go and response reversal performance), respectively. In short, we might expect high comorbidity of at least a hyperactive form of ADHD with psychopathic tendencies because of the known pathology associated with psychopathic tendencies. However, we would not expect

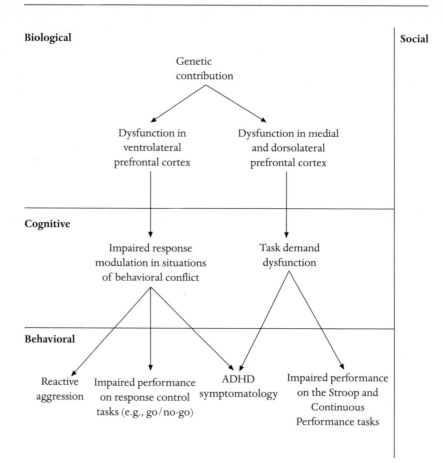

Figure 9.3   A causal model of the development of ADHD representing the hypothesized explanation for the increased risk of reactive aggression that may be seen in some patients with this disorder.

inattention problems in this population; individuals with psychopathy should not present with impaired performance on tasks such as Stroop, continuous performance, and the ED shift in the ID/ED task.

According to the position developed in figure 9.3, "pure" cases of ADHD (i.e., without comorbid psychopathic tendencies) might present with increased risk of reactive aggression in conjunction with their inattention and hyperactivity difficulties. This would occur if their pathology led to ventrolateral prefrontal cortex dysfunction. However, they would not present with the instrumental aggression seen in individuals with psychopathy. This is assumed to be dependent on amygdala dysfunction (see chapter 8). Amygdala dysfunction is not seen in individuals with ADHD (Castellanos et al., 1996; Giedd et al., 2001).

The case of autism

The second conundrum to consider is autism. The disorder of autism is described by DSM-IV) (American Psychiatric Association, 1994) as "the presence of markedly abnormal or impaired development in social interaction and communication and a markedly restricted repertoire of activities and interests" (p. 66). This disorder is a conundrum with respect to psychopathy not because autism is strikingly comorbid with psychopathy. It is not. Indeed, some of the features of autism, social withdrawal, are so diametrically different from the charming interaction styles of many individuals with psychopathy that comorbidity may almost be an impossibility. However, autism is, like psychopathy, a disorder of social cognition. Moreover, like psychopathy, autism has also been linked to impairments in amygdala functioning (Baron-Cohen et al., 2000).

There is evidence of structural abnormalities of the amygdala in individuals with autism. However, in contrast to the decrease in amygdala volume reported in individuals with psychopathy (Tiihonen et al., 2000), enlarged amygdala volumes have usually been described for adolescent and adult patients with autism (Abell et al., 1999; Howard et al., 2000; Sparks et al., 2002) – though there has been one study suggesting reduced amygdala volumes (Aylward et al., 1999) and another suggesting no group differences (Haznedar et al., 2000); for a review see Brambilla et al. (2003).

Functionally, the situation is complex but may allow a clarification of the conundrum. As discussed in chapter 8, the amygdala is involved in the formation of stimulus–punishment and stimulus–reward associations as well as some affect-laden components of social cognition. We will consider the ability to form stimulus–punishment associations first. The suggestion is that in individuals with psychopathy, sensitivity to punishment, and therefore the ability to form stimulus–punishment associations, is disproportionately impaired (Blair et al., submitted a). However, there is no reason to believe that this is the case in individuals with autism. Indeed, individuals with autism are at increased risk of presenting with anxiety (Gillott et al., 2001; Rumsey et al., 1985), rather than the decreased risk seen in individuals with psychopathy (Frick et al., 1999; Patrick, 1994; Verona et al., 2001). In short, while individuals with psychopathy are impaired for the formation of stimulus–punishment associations, individuals with autism are not.

What about the affect-laden components of social cognition? In chapter 8, we considered two tasks that measure affect-laden aspects of social cognition. These were the eyes task and the face trustworthiness judgment tasks (Adolphs et al., 2001; Baron-Cohen et al., 2001). Individuals with psychopathy show no indications of impaired performance on these tasks (Richell et al., 2003, in press). In contrast, patients with autism present with impairment on both tasks (Adolphs et al., 2001; Baron-Cohen et al., 2001).

In short, the impairments seen in individuals with autism are strikingly different from those seen in individuals with psychopathy. It is possible that both disorders are associated with amygdala dysfunction. We certainly believe a strong case can be made with respect to psychopathy (see chapter 8). With respect to autism, recent neuro-imaging work has demonstrated an amygdala response in variants of both the eyes (Baron-Cohen et al., 1999) and trustworthiness (Winston et al., 2002) tasks. Moreover, and crucially, patients with amygdala lesions are impaired when performing both the eyes and trustworthiness tasks (Adolphs et al., 2001; Stone et al., 2003). If both disorders are marked by amygdala dysfunction, it is important to note that the functional impairment found in both populations is notably different. Individuals with psychopathy present with impairment in the formation of stimulus – punishment associations but not the affect-laden components of social cognition. Individuals with autism present with impairment in the affect-laden components of social cognition but not the formation of stimulus – punishment associations.

Of course, it is possible that the impairments in the affect-laden components of social cognition seen in individuals with autism do not reflect amygdala dysfunction *per se*. It is possible that they are developmental consequences of impoverished face representations or on-line consequences of impaired face representations. Certainly, there are strong suggestions of impairments in individuals with autism in regions such as fusiform gyrus and superior temporal sulcus involved in face representation (Schultz et al., 2003). This issue will require further investigation.

The full range of impairment

The third conundrum is not really a conundrum. It is a statement of fact. The model that we have developed within this book cannot account for the full range of impairments seen in individuals with psychopathy. Specifically, there is one type of impairment seen in individuals with psychopathy that cannot be explained currently with reference to the integrated emotion systems model described in chapter 8. This is the impairments seen in individuals with psychopathy in semantic processing. We will briefly summarize the data.

There have been several indications that individuals with psychopathy present with impairment in some forms of semantic processing. For example, in the

Hare and Jutai (1988) study, participants had to match words to categories. If the category was the "abstract" semantic category of living things, individuals with psychopathy showed impairment if the word stimulus was presented to the right visual field (though not if it was presented to the left). Kiehl et al. (1999a) examined the influence of word concreteness on lexical decision. They found that the individuals with psychopathy made significantly more errors than comparison individuals stating that the abstract words were words. However, there were no group differences for concrete words. This work has been recently extended in a neuro-imaging paradigm with individuals with psychopathy and comparison individuals (Kiehl et al., 2004). Participants in this study performed lexical decision for abstract and concrete words. The individuals with psychopathy showed a reduced differentiation in their neural responses between abstract and concrete stimuli in the right anterior temporal gyrus and surrounding cortex.

The previous results, particularly those of Kiehl and colleagues, would indicate that individuals with psychopathy present with impairment for the processing of abstract words. However, other data might suggest a more general impairment in semantic/linguistic processing; specifically, two results by Newman and colleagues (Lorenz and Newman, 2002; Newman et al., 1997). In the Newman et al. (1997) study, participants were instructed to determine whether two pictures or two words were conceptually related. At the same time as the two target stimuli were presented, a distracter stimulus was also presented (a word if the judgment was of two pictures or a picture if the judgment was of two words). Whereas, healthy individuals and low anxious comparison individuals in this study were faster to state that two target stimuli are unrelated if the distracter stimulus was not conceptually related to either of the target stimuli, low anxious individuals with psychopathy were not; they showed no interference of the distracter stimulus on the processing of the target stimuli. Lorenz and Newman (2002) found that the facilitation of speed of word recognition in a lexical decision task by higher word frequency was shown significantly less in individuals with psychopathy than comparison individuals.

There are several ways that the Newman et al. (1997) study might be interpreted. We will consider three here. First, the semantic associations between words may be reduced in individuals with psychopathy. This does not appear likely, however. If the semantic associations between words are reduced in individuals with psychopathy, reduced semantic priming must be predicted. Yet individuals with psychopathy have been reported to present with intact semantic priming using two different types of paradigm (see chapter 4) (Brinkley et al., in press; Blair et al., in preparation). In short, the formation and processing of the semantic associations between words appears intact in individuals with psychopathy. Second, it is possible that the problem for the individuals with psychopathy in the Newman et al. (1997) study lay in the task demands to consider whether the images were conceptually related or not. It is possible that this task demand, to consider words by semantic category, led to the difficulty in the individuals with psychopathy. It is perhaps interesting to note in this respect that in the Hare and Jutai (1988) study, the individuals with psychopathy presented with impairment when asked to consider whether words matched a particular "abstract" semantic category. Finally, there is a third form of explanation. The first two explanations did not consider the Lorenz and Newman (2002) data suggesting reduced coding of word frequency information in individuals with psychopathy. This could indicate catastrophic differences between the properties of the language system in individuals with psychopathy and comparison individuals. However, this is unlikely in the context of findings indicating intact semantic priming (Brinkley et al., in press; Blair et al., in preparation). The third form of explanation then would make reference to the educational history of individuals with psychopathy. Children with psychopathic tendencies are more likely to truant than comparison children. Abstract concepts are more difficult to learn than concrete concepts and are learnt at later ages (Colunga and Smith, 2003; Nippold et al., 1997). It is possible that these apparent difficulties in linguistic processing reflect the poorer education of individuals with psychopathy. Currently, this conundrum remains.

Conclusions

In this last section, we will consider six final conclusions with respect to the development of psychopathy and other syndromes associated with antisocial behavior.

The diagnoses of CD and ASPD are severely limited

There is a clear test that any diagnosis should pass for it to be considered useful: specifically, does the diagnosis identify a specific pathology that can be treated in a particular way? Neither the diagnosis of conduct disorder (CD) nor that of antisocial personality disorder (ASPD) passes this test. Both identify highly heterogeneous populations that can be offered a wide variety of treatments, most of which are of questionable efficacy. In this book, we have considered six developmental routes to disorders where there would be heightened levels of antisocial behavior: the "maturity gap" induced syndrome of adolescent-limited CD (chapter 3), endogenous and exogenous routes to heightened responsiveness of the basic threat circuitry (chapter 7), endogenous and exogenous routes to reduced function of frontal systems involved in the regulation of the basic threat circuitry (chapter 7), and the amygdala-dysfunction-based emergence of the development of psychopathy (chapter 8). Clearly, the appropriate treatment of individuals who present with these disorders should be specific to the type of pathology. Currently, it is not.

In short, we would argue that the diagnoses of CD and ASPD must be improved. There is not one single syndrome but rather a series of dissociable syndromes, all of which are marked by different social/biological antecedents and all of which are likely to need specific treatment strategies.

The distinction between reactive and instrumental aggression must not be ignored

A related issue to the problem of grouping a variety of pathologies under the global labels CD or ASPD is the issue of considering all aggression to be of a similar nature. One major conclusion of this book is that a distinction must be made between reactive and instrumental aggression. We would argue that researchers investigating parameters relating to aggression ought to consider before they conduct their study whether they believe that the parameters they are interested in are related to either reactive or instrumental aggression. We would argue that studies investigating patients with diagnoses of CD or ASPD should, at the very least, consider whether they might split their population into individuals presenting with mostly reactive or reactive and instrumental aggression. As we have argued in this book, reactive and instrumental aggression are reliant on at least partially dissociable neural systems. Individuals presenting elevated levels of mostly reactive or reactive and instrumental aggression are going to require treatments targeted to their specific pathology.

While criticisms of the distinction between reactive and instrumental aggression have been made (Bushman and Anderson, 2001), and while it may be difficult to classify any particular aggressive episode, there is overwhelming data that there are two relatively separable populations of aggressive individuals: those who present with mostly reactive aggression and those who present with very high levels of instrumental aggression and also reactive aggression (Barratt et al., 1999; Connor, 2002; Crick and Dodge, 1996; Linnoila et al., 1983). Moreover, the discriminant validity of instrumental and reactive aggression on a factorial level has been demonstrated; while instrumental and reactive aggression are substantially correlated, a two-factor model fits the data better than a one-factor model (Poulin and Boivin, 2000).

As we have argued in chapters 7 and 8, the pathology related to reactive and instrumental aggression is at least partially separable. To provide effective treatment it is crucial to recognize this dissociation.

The antisocial behavior of most individuals does not have a biological basis

In this book, we have, for the most part, been considering brain-based pathologies associated with an increased risk of aggression. However, it should not be taken from this that there is a biologically based explanation to all antisocial behavior. There is not. While we would argue that there is a biological basis to the antisocial behavior of the 5 percent of criminals who commit a disproportionate percentage of crime (mostly individuals with psychopathy), we certainly would not argue that there is a biological basis to the antisocial behavior of most criminals. Indeed, in chapter 3, in the context of adolescent-limited CD, we considered a pathology where specific social phenomena potentially give rise to a motivational emphasis towards antisocial behavior.

Many disorders and developmental routes are associated with an increased risk of reactive aggression

Many psychiatric conditions are associated with an increased risk of aggression, including generalized anxiety disorder (GAD), post-traumatic stress disorder (PTSD), unipolar and bipolar depression, bipolar disorder in children, intermittent explosive disorder, borderline personality disorder (BPD), attention deficit and hyperactivity disorder, and psychopathy. In chapter 7, we outlined four developmental routes to a heightened risk of reactive aggression: endogenous and exogenous routes to heightened responsiveness of the basic threat circuitry and to reduced function of frontal systems involved in the regulation of the basic threat circuitry. As noted in chapter 7, some psychiatric conditions are likely to be related to heightened responsiveness of the basic threat circuitry (e.g., GAD and PTSD). Others are likely to be related to reduced function of frontal systems involved in the regulation of the basic threat circuitry (e.g., bipolar disorder in children and BPD).

No biologically based disorder other than psychopathy is associated with an increased risk of instrumental aggression

Currently, there are no reasons to believe that there are any biologically-based disorders associated with a heightened risk of instrumental antisocial behavior other than psychopathy. There are other disorders associated with a heightened risk of instrumental antisocial behavior (e.g., adolescent-limited CD) but they are not biologically based. In chapter 8, we developed an account of psychopathy. In essence, this account suggests that genetic anomalies give rise to a disorder where there is reduced responsiveness of the amygdala to aversive stimuli in particular. This specific form of reduced emotional responsiveness interferes with socialization such that the individual is more likely to learn to use anti-social behavior to achieve goals.

There is work to be done

We believe that the understanding of psychopathy has increased enormously in the past 10 years. It is now possible to consider the biological basis of the disorder and emerge with a coherent picture. Computational models of the functional impairments allow considerably greater specificity with regard to predictions than has been possible before. However, some crucial questions remain. While we are confident that there is a genetic basis to the emotional component of psychopathy, which genes are involved and what they are specifically affecting remains basically unknown. While we are confident that there is both amygdala and orbital frontal cortex pathology in individuals with psychopathy, is the orbital frontal cortex dysfunction caused by the same genetic anomalies that contribute to the amygdala dysfunction? Alternatively, is the orbital frontal cortex dysfunction a developmental consequence of the amygdala dysfunction (for example, due to reduced afferent input)? Alternatively, is the orbital frontal cortex dysfunction a consequence of the lifestyle of the individuals with psychopathy? Are other neural systems involved, for example the anterior cingulate? Functionally, is there a difference between the ability of individuals with psychopathy to process punishment- and reward-based information? If there is, why?

Finally, and perhaps the most important question of all, how can we use this increased knowledge to maximally improve the treatment of the disorders of antisocial behavior?

REFERENCES

Abell F., Krams M., Ashburner J., Passingham R., Friston K., Frackowiak R., Happe F., Frith C., Frith U. (1999). The neuroanatomy of autism: a voxel-based whole brain analysis of structural scans. *Neuroreport*, 10(8), 1647–1651.

Adolphs R. (2003). Is the human amygdala specialized for processing social information? *Annals of the New York Academy of Sciences*, 985, 326–340.

Adolphs R., Tranel D., Damasio A. R. (1998). The human amygdala in social judgment. *Nature*, 393, 470–474.

Adolphs R., Sears L., Piven J. (2001). Abnormal processing of social information from faces in autism. *Journal of Cognitive Neuroscience*, 13(2), 232–240.

Adolphs R., Baron-Cohen S., Tranel D. (2002). Impaired recognition of social emotions following amygdala damage. *Journal of Cognitive Neuroscience*, 2002; 14, 1264–1274.

Alexander M., Perachio A. A. (1973). The influence of target sex and dominance on evoked attack in Rhesus monkeys. *American Journal of Physical Anthropology*, 38(2), 543–547.

Amaral D. G. (2001). The amygdaloid complex and the neurobiology of social behaviour. Paper presented at the Society for Research in Child Development, Minneapolis.

Amaral D. G., Price J. L., Pitkanen A., Carmichael S. T. (1992). Anatomical organization of the primate amygdaloid complex. In J. P. Aggleton (ed.), *The Amygdala: Neurobiological aspects of emotion, memory, and mental dysfunction*, 1–66. New York: John Wiley & Sons.

Ambrogi Lorenzini C. G., Bucherelli C., Giachetti A., Mugnai L., Tassoni G. (1991). Effects of nucleus basolateralis amygdalae neurotoxic lesions on aversive conditioning in the rat. *Physiology and Behavior*, 49, 765–770.

Ambrogi Lorenzini C. G., Baldi E., Bucherelli C., Sacchetti B., Tassoni G. (1999). Neural topography and chronology of memory consolidation: a review of functional inactivation findings. *Neurobiology of Learning and Memory*, 71, 1–18.

American Psychiatric Association (1994). *Diagnostic and Statistical Manual of Mental Disorders*, 4th edn. Washington, DC: American Psychiatric Association.

Anderson A. K., Phelps E. A. (2001). Lesions of the human amygdala impair enhanced perception of emotionally salient events. *Nature*, 411, 305–309.

Anderson S. W., Bechara A., Damasio H., Tranel D., Damasio A. R. (1999). Impairment of social and moral behaviour related to early damage in human prefrontal cortex. *Nature Neuroscience*, 2, 1032–1037.

Angrilli A., Mauri A., Palomba D., Flor H., Birhaumer N., Sartori G., et al. (1996). Startle reflex and emotion modulation impairment after a right amygdala lesion. *Brain*, 119, 1991–2000.

Aniskiewicz A. S. (1979). Autonomic components of vicarious conditioning and psychopathy. *Journal of Clinical Psychology*, 35, 60–67.

Aron A. R., Fletcher P. C., Bullmore E. T., Sahakian B. J., Robbins T. W. (2003). Stop-signal inhibition disrupted by damage to right inferior frontal gyrus in humans. *Nature Neuroscience*, 6(2), 115–116.

Arsenio W. F., Fleiss K. (1996). Typical and behaviourally disruptive children's understanding of the emotion consequences of socio-moral events. *British Journal of Developmental Psychology*, 14, 173–186.

Asendorpf J. B., Nunner-Winkler G. (1992). Children's moral motive strength and temperamental inhibition reduce their immoral behaviour in real moral conflicts. *Child Development*, 63, 1223–1235.

Aylward E. H., Minshew N. J., Goldstein G., Honeycutt N. A., Augustine A. M., Yates K. O., Barta P. E., Pearlson G. D. (1999). MRI volumes of amygdala and hippocampus in non-mentally retarded autistic adolescents and adults. *Neurology*, 53(9), 2145–2150.

Babinski L. M., Hartsough C. S., Lambert N. M. (1999). Childhood conduct problems, hyperactivity-impulsivity, and inattention as predictors of adult criminal activity. *Journal of Child Psychology and Psychiatry and Allied Disciplines*, 40, 347–355.

Baddeley A., Della Sala S. (1998). Working memory and executive control. In A. C. Roberts, T. W. Robbins, L. Weiskrantz (eds), *The Prefrontal Cortex*, pp. 9–21. New York: Oxford University Press.

Baird A. A., Gruber S. A., Fein D. A., Maas L. C., Steingard R. J., Renshaw P. F., et al. Functional magnetic resonance imaging of facial affect recognition in children and adolescents. *Journal of the American Academy of Child and Adolescent Psychiatry*, 1999; 38, 195–199.

Bandler R. (1988). Brain mechanisms of aggression as revealed by electrical and chemical stimulation: suggestion of a central role for the midbrain periaqueductal gray region. In A. N. Epsein, A. R. Morrison (eds), *Progress in Psychobiology and Physiological Psychology*, vol. 14, pp. 135–233. San Diego, CA: Academic Press.

Bandura A., Rosenthal T. L. (1966). Viacarous classical conditioning as a function of arousal level. *Journal of Personality and Social Psychology*, 3, 54–62.

Barkley R. A. (1999). Theories of attention-deficit/hyperactivity disorder. In H. C. Quay, A. E. Hogan (eds), *Handbook of Disruptive Behavior Disorders*, pp. 295–316. New York: Kluwer Academic/Plenum.

Barkley R. A., Edwards G., Laneri M., Fletcher K., Metevia L. (2001). Executive functioning, temporal discounting, and sense of time in adolescents with attention deficit hyperactivity disorder (ADHD) and oppositional defiant disorder (ODD). *Journal of Abnormal Child Psychology*, 29(6), 541–556.

Baron-Cohen S., Wheelwright S., Joliffe T. (1997). Is there a "language of the eyes"? Evidence from normal adults, and adults with autism or Asperger syndrome. *Visual Cognition*, 4, 311–331.

Baron-Cohen S., Ring H. A., Wheelwright S., Bullmore E. T., Brammer M. J., Simmons A., et al. (1999). Social intelligence in the normal and autistic brain: an fMRI study. *European Journal of Neuroscience*, 11, 1891–1898.

Baron-Cohen S., Ring H. A., Bullmore E. T., Wheelwright S., Ashwin C., Williams S. C. (2000). The amygdala theory of autism. *Neuroscience and Biobehavioral Reviews*, 24, 355–364.

Baron-Cohen S., Wheelwright S., Hill J., Raste Y., Plumb I. (2001). The "Reading the Mind in the Eyes" test revised version: a study with normal adults, and adults with Asperger syndrome or high-functioning autism. *Journal of Child Psychology and Psychiatry*, 42(2), 241–251.

Barratt E. S. (1994). Impulsiveness and aggression. In J. Monahan, H. Steadman (eds), *Violence and Mental Disorders: Developments in risk assessment*, pp. 61–79. Chicago, IL: University of Chicago Press.

Barratt E. S., Stanford M. S., Kent T. A., Felthous A. (1997). Neuropsychological and cognitive psychophysiological substrates of impulsive aggression. *Biological Psychiatry*, 41, 1045–1061.

Barratt E. S., Stanford M. S., Dowdy L., Liebman M. J., Kent T. A. (1999). Impulsive and premeditated aggression: a factor analysis of self-reported acts. *Psychiatry Research*, 86, 163–173.

Barry C. T., Frick P. J., DeShazo T. M., McCoy M. G., Ellis M., Loney B. R. (2000). The importance of callous-unemotional traits for extending the concept of psychopathy to children. *Journal of Abnormal Psychology*, 109(2), 335–340.

Baumrind D. (1971). Current patterns of parental authority. *Developmental Psychology Monographs*, 4, 1–103.

Baumrind D. (1983). Rejoinder to Lewis's interpretation of parental firm control effects: are authoritative families really harmonious? *Psychological Bulletin*, 94, 132–142.

Baxter M. G., Murray E. A. (2002). The amygdala and reward. *Nature Reviews Neuroscience*, 3, 563–573.

Bechara A., Damasio A. R., Damasio H., Anderson S. W. (1994). Insensitivity to future consequences following damage to human prefrontal cortex. *Cognition*, 50, 7–15.

Bechara A., Damasio H., Damasio A. R., Lee G. P. (1999). Different contributions of the human amygdala and ventromedial prefrontal cortex to decision-making. *Journal of Neuroscience*, 19, 5473–5481.

Bechara A., Damasio H., Damasio A. R. (2000a). Emotion, decision making and the orbitofrontal cortex. *Cerebral Cortex*, 10, 295–307.

Bechara A., Tranel D., Damasio H. (2000b). Characterization of the decision-making deficit of patients with ventromedial prefrontal cortex lesions. *Brain*, 123(11), 2189–2202.

Bechara A., Dolan S., Denburg N., Hindes A., Anderson S. W., Nathan P. E. (2001). Decision-making deficits, linked to a dysfunctional ventromedial prefrontal cortex, revealed in alcohol and stimulant abusers. *Neuropsychologia*, 39, 376–389.

Begleiter H., Gross M. M., Kissin B. (1967). Evoked cortical responses to affective visual stimuli. *Psychophysiology*, 3, 336–344.

Bell C., Abrams J., Nutt D. (2001). Tryptophan depletion and its implications for psychiatry. *British Journal of Psychiatry*, 178, 399–405.

Berkowitz L. (1993). *Aggression: Its causes, consequences, and control*. Philadelphia, PA: Temple University Press.

Berlin L., Bohlin G. (2002). Response inhibition, hyperactivity, and conduct problems among preschool children. J Clin Child Adolesc Psychol, 31(2), 242–251.

Berthoz S., Armony J., Blair R. J. R., Dolan R. (2002). Neural correlates of violation of social norms and embarrassment. *Brain*, 125(8), 1696–1708.

Best M., Williams J. M., Coccaro E. F. (2002). Evidence for a dysfunctional prefrontal circuit in patients with an impulsive aggressive disorder. *Proceedings of the National Academy of Sciences U.S.A.*, 99, 8448–8453.

Biederman J., Newcorn J., Sprich S. (1991). Comorbidity of attention deficit hyperactivity disorder with conduct, depressive, anxiety, and other disorders. *American Journal of Psychiatry*, 148, 564–577.

Bjork J. M., Dougherty D. M., Moeller F. G., Swann A. C. (2000). Differential behavioral effects of plasma tryptophan depletion and loading in aggressive and nonaggressive men. *Neuropsychopharmacology*, 22, 357–369.

Blackburn R. (1988). On moral judgements and personality disorders: the myth of psychopathic personality revisited. *British Journal of Psychiatry*, 153, 505–512.

Blair H. T., Schafe G. E., Bauer E. P., Rodrigues S. M., LeDoux J. E. (2001). Synaptic plasticity in the lateral amygdala: a cellular hypothesis of fear conditioning. *Learning and Memory*, 8, 229–242.

Blair K. S., Leonard A., Morton J., Blair R. J. R. (submitted a) Differential stimulus – reward and stimulus – punishment learning in individuals with psychopathy.

Blair K. S., Leonard A., Morton J., Blair R. J. R. (submitted b) Primed up for positive, but not negative, words: affective priming in individuals with psychopathy.

Blair K. S., Richell R. A., Mitchell D. G. V., Leonard A., Morton J., Blair R. J. R. (submitted c) Primed up for positive, but not negative, words: affective priming in individuals with psychopathy.

Blair K. S., Mitchell D. G., Leonard A., Blair R. J. R. (in preparation). Impaired affective priming in psychopathic individuals.

Blair K. S., Newman C., Mitchell D. G., Richell R. A., Leonard A., Morton J., Blair R. J. R. (under revision). Differentiating among prefrontal substrates in psychopathy: neuropsychological test findings.

Blair R. J. R. (1995). A cognitive developmental approach to morality: investigating the psychopath. *Cognition*, 57, 1–29.

Blair R. J. R. (1997). Moral reasoning in the child with psychopathic tendencies. *Personality and Individual Differences*, 22, 731–739.

Blair R. J. R. (1999a). Psycho-physiological responsiveness to the distress of others in children with autism. *Personality and Individual Differences*, 26, 477–485.

Blair R. J. R. (1999b). Responsiveness to distress cues in the child with psychopathic tendencies. *Personality and Individual Differences*, 27, 135–145.

Blair R. J. R. (2001). Neuro-cognitive models of aggression, the antisocial personality disorders and psychopathy. *Journal of Neurology, Neurosurgery and Psychiatry*, 71, 727–731.

Blair R. J. R. (2002). A neuro-cognitive model of the psychopathic individual. In M. A. Ron, T. W. Robbins (eds), *Disorders of Brain and Mind*, vol. 2. Cambridge: Cambridge University Press.

Blair R. J. R. (2003a). Neurobiological basis of psychopathy. *British Journal of Psychiatry*, 182, 5–7.

Blair R. J. R. (2003b). Facial expressions, their communicatory functions and neuro-cognitive substrates. *Philosophical Transactions of the Royal Society of London B*, 358, 561–572.

Blair R. J. R. (2004). The roles of orbital frontal cortex in the modulation of antisocial behavior. *Brain and Cognition* (special issue on Development of Orbitofrontal Function), 55, 198–208.

Blair R. J. R., Cipolotti L. (2000). Impaired social response reversal: a case of "acquired sociopathy". *Brain*, 123, 1122–1141.

Blair R. J. R., Coles M. (2000). Expression recognition and behavioural problems in early adolescence. *Cognitive Development*, 15, 421–434.

Blair R. J. R., Morton J. (1995). Putting cognition into sociopathy. *Brain and Behavioral Science*, 18, 548.

Blair R. J. R., Jones L., Clark F., Smith M. (1995a). Is the psychopath "morally insane"? *Personality and Individual Differences*, 19, 741–752.

Blair R. J. R., Sellars C., Strickland I., Clark F., Williams A. O., Smith M., Jones L. (1995b). Emotion attributions in the psychopath. *Personality and Individual Differences*, 19, 431–437.

Blair R. J. R., Jones L., Clark F., Smith M. (1997). The psychopathic individual: a lack of responsiveness to distress cues? *Psychophysiology*, 34, 192–198.

Blair R. J. R., Morris J. S., Frith C. D., Perrett D. I., Dolan R. (1999). Dissociable neural responses to facial expressions of sadness and anger. *Brain*, 122, 883–893.

Blair R. J. R., Colledge E., Mitchell D. G. (2001a). Somatic markers and response reversal: is there orbitofrontal cortex dysfunction in boys with psychopathic tendencies? *Journal of Abnormal Child Psychology*, 29(6), 499–511.

Blair R. J. R., Colledge E., Murray L., Mitchell D. G. (2001b). A selective impairment in the processing of sad and fearful expressions in children with psychopathic tendencies. *Journal of Abnormal Child Psychology*, 29(6), 491–498.

Blair R. J. R., Monson J., Frederickson N. (2001c). Moral reasoning and conduct problems in children with emotional and behavioural difficulties. *Personality and Individual Differences*, 31, 799–811.

Blair R. J. R., Mitchell D. G., Richell R. A., Kelly S., Leonard A., Newman C., Scott S. K. (2002). Turning a deaf ear to fear: impaired recognition of vocal affect in psychopathic individuals. *Journal of Abnormal Psychology*, 111(4), 682–686.

Blair R. J. R., Mitchell D. G. V., Leonard A., Budhani S., Peschardt K. S., Newman C. (2004). Passive avoidance learning in individuals with psychopathy: modulation by reward but not by punishment. *Personality and Individual Differences*, 37, 1179–1192.

Blair R. J. R., Budhani S., Colledge E., Scott S. K. (in press). Deafness to fear in boys with psychopathic tendencies. *Journal of Child Psychology and Psychiatry*.

Blanchard R. J., Blanchard D. C., Takahashi L. K. (1977). Attack and defensive behaviour in the albino rat. *Animal Behavior*, 25, 197–224.

Blasi A. (1980). Bridging moral cognition and moral action: a critical review of the literature. *Psychological Bulletin*, 88, 1–45.

Blonigen D. M., Carlson R. F., Krueger R. F., Patrick C. J. (2003). A twin study of self-reported psychopathic personality traits. *Personality and Individual Differences*, 35, 179–197.

Blumstein A., Cohen J. (1987). Characterizing criminal careers. *Science*, 237, 985–991.

Bond A. J., Wingrove J., Critchlow D. G. (2001). Tryptophan depletion increases aggression in women during the premenstrual phase. *Psychopharmacology*, 156, 477–480.

Bowlby J. (1982). Attachment and loss: retrospect and prospect. *American Journal of Orthopsychiatry*, 52, 664–678.

Brake W. G., Sullivan R. M., Gratton A. (2000). Perinatal distress leads to lateralized medial prefrontal cortical dopamine hypofunction in adult rats. *Journal of Neuroscience*, 20, 5538–5543.

Brambilla P., Hardan A., di Nemi S. U., Perez J., Soares J. C., Barale F. (2003). Brain anatomy and development in autism: review of structural MRI studies. *Brain Research Bulletin*, 61(6), 557–569.

Breiter H. C., Etcoff N. L., Whalen P. J., Kennedy W. A., Rauch S. L., Buckner R. L., et al. (1996). Response and habituation of the human amygdala during visual processing of facial expression. *Neuron*, 17, 875–887.

Bremner J. D., Vermetten E. (2001). Stress and development: behavioral and biological consequences. *Development and Psychopathology*, 13, 473–489.

Bremner J. D., Randall P., Scott T. M., Capelli S., Delaney R., McCarthy G., Charney D. S. (1995). Deficits in short-term memory in adult survivors of childhood abuse. *Psychiatry Research*, 59, 97–107.

Brennan P. A., Raine A., Schulsinger F., Kirkegaard-Sorensen L., Knop J., Hutchings B., Rosenberg R., Mednick S. A. (1997). Psychophysiological protective factors for male subjects at high risk for criminal behavior. *American Journal of Psychiatry*, 154, 853–855.

Brinkley C. A., Schmitt W. A., Newman J. P. (in press). Semantic processing in psychopathic offenders. *Personality and Individual Differences*.

Brody G. H., Shaffer D. R. (1982). Contributions of parents and peers to children's moral socialisation. *Developmental Review*, 2, 31–75.

Brown G. L., Goodwin F. K., Ballenger J. C., Goyer P. F., Major L. F. (1979). Aggression in humans correlates with cerebrospinal fluid amine metabolites. *Psychiatry Research*, 1, 131–139.

Brownell H. H., Potter H. H., Michelow D. (1984). Sensitivity to lexical denotation and connotation in brain-damaged patients: a double dissociation? *Brain and Language*, 22, 253–265.

Brunner H. G., Nelen M., Breakefield X. O., Ropers H. H., van Oost B. A. (1993). Abnormal behavior associated with a point mutation in the structural gene for monoamine oxidase A. *Science*, 262, 578–580.

Budhani S., Blair R. J. R. (in press). Probabilistic response reversal in children with psychopathic tendencies. *Journal of Child Psychology and Psychiatry.*

Burdach K. F. (1819–1826). *Vom baue und Leben des Gehirns.* Leipzig: Dyk.

Burgess N., Maguire E. A., Spiers H. J., O'Keefe J. (2001). A temporoparietal and prefrontal network for retrieving the spatial context of lifelike events. *Neuroimage*, 14, 439–453.

Burgess P. W., Shallice T. (1996). Response suppression, initiation and strategy use following frontal lobe lesions. *Neuropsychologia*, 34, 263–272.

Burgess P. W., Wood R. L. (1990). Neuropsychology of behaviour disorders following brain injury. In R. L. Wood (ed.), *Neurobehavioural Sequelae of Traumatic Brain Injury*, pp. 110–133. London: Taylor & Francis.

Burns L. H., Everitt B. J., Robbins T. W. (1999). Effects of excitotoxic lesions of the basolateral amygdala on conditional discrimination learning with primary and conditioned reinforcement. *Behavioural Brain Research*, 100, 123–133.

Bushman B. J., Anderson C. A. (2001). Is it time to pull the plug on the hostile versus instrumental aggression dichotomy? *Psychological Review*, 108, 273–279.

Cahill L. (2000). Neurobiological mechanisms of emotionally influenced, long-term memory. *Progress in Brain Research*, 126, 29–37.

Calder A. J., Young A. W., Rowland D., Perrett D. I. (1996). Facial emotion recognition after bilateral amygdala damage: differentially severe impairment of fear. *Cognitive Neuropsychology*, 13, 699–745.

Cale E. M., Lilienfeld S. O. (2002). Sex differences in psychopathy and antisocial personality disorder. A review and integration. Clin Psychol Rev, 22(8), 1179–1207.

Campagna A. F., Harter S. (1975). Moral judgements in sociopathic and normal children. *Journal of Personality and Social Psychology*, 31, 199–205.

Camras L. A. (1977). Facial expressions used by children in a conflict situation. *Child Development*, 48, 1431–1435.

Carmichael S. T., Price J. L. (1995). Sensory and premotor connections of the orbital and medial prefrontal cortex of macaque monkeys. *Journal of Comparative Neurology*, 363, 642–664.

Casey B. J., Forman S. D., Franzen P., Berkowitz A., Braver T. S., Nystrom L. E., et al. (2001). Sensitivity of prefrontal cortex to changes in target probability: a functional MRI study. *Human Brain Mapping*, 13, 26–33.

Caspi A., Henry B., McGee R., Moffitt T., Silva P. (1995). Temperamental origins of child and adolescent behaviour problems: from age three to age fifteen. *Child Development*, 66, 55–68.

Castellanos F. X., Giedd J. N., Marsh W. L., Hamburger S. D., Vaituzis A. C., Dickstein D. P., Sarfatti S. E., Vauss Y. C., Snell J. W., Lange N., Kaysen D., Ritchie G. F., Rajapakse J. C., Rapoport J. L. (1996). Quantitative brain magnetic resonance imaging in attention-deficit hyperactivity disorder. *Archives of General Psychiatry*, 53, 607–616.

Castellanos F. X., Marvasti F. F., Ducharme J. L., Walter J. M., Israel M. E., Krain A., Pavlovsky C., Hommer D. W. (2000). Executive function oculomotor tasks in girls with ADHD. *Journal of the American Academy of Child and Adolescent Psychiatry*, 39(5), 644–650.

Cauffman E., Feldman S. S., Waterman J., Steiner H. (1998). Posttraumatic stress disorder among female juvenile offenders. *Journal of the American Academy of Child and Adolescent Psychiatry*, 37, 1209–1216.

Chaplin T. C., Rice M. E., Harris G. T. (1995). Salient victim suffering and the sexual responses of child molesters. *Journal of Consulting and Clinical Psychology*, 63, 249–255.

Charney D. S. (2003). Neuroanatomical circuits modulating fear and anxiety behaviors. *Acta Psychiatrica Scandinavica Supplement*, (417), 38–50.

Charney D. S., Heninger G. R., Breier A. (1984). Noradrenergic function in panic anxiety. Effects of yohimbine in healthy subjects and patients with agoraphobia and panic disorder. *Archives of General Psychiatry*, 41, 751–763.

Chhabildas N., Pennington B. F., Willcutt E. G. (2001). A comparison of the neuropsychological profiles of the DSM-IV subtypes of ADHD. *Journal of Abnormal Child Psychology*, 29(6), 529–540.

Christianson S. A. (1992). Emotional stress and eyewitness memory: a critical review. *Psychological Bulletin*, 112, 284–309.

Christianson S. A., Forth A. E., Hare R. D., Strachan C., Lidberg L., Thorell L. H. (1996). Remembering details of emotional events: a comparison between psychopathic and nonpsychopathic offenders. *Personality and Individual Differences*, 20, 437–443.

Church R. M. (1959). Emotional reactions of rats to the pain of others. *Journal of Comparative and Physiological Psychology*, 52, 132–134.

Cicone M., Wapner W., Gardner H. (1980). Sensitivity to emotional expressions and situations in organic patients. *Cortex*, 16, 145–158.

Cleare A. J., Bond, A. J. (2000). Experimental evidence that the aggressive effect of tryptophan depletion is mediated via the 5-HT1A receptor. *Psychopharmacology*, 147, 439–441.

Cleckley H. M. (1941). *The Mask of Sanity*, 4th edn. St Louis, MO: Mosby.

Cleckley H. M. (1976). *The Mask of Sanity*, 5th edn. St Louis, MO: Mosby.

Coccaro E. F. (1998). Impulsive aggression: a behavior in search of clinical definition. *Harvard Review of Psychiatry*, 5, 336–339.

Cohen J. D., Dunbar K., McClelland J. L. (1990). On the control of automatic processes: a parallel distributed processing account of the Stroop effect. *Psychological Review*, 97(3), 332–361.

Cohen J. D., Servan-Schreiber D., McClelland J. L. (1992). A parallel distributed processing approach to automaticity. *American Journal of Psychology*, 105(2), 239–269.

Cohen J. D., Braver T. S., O'Reilly R. C. (1996). A computational approach to prefrontal cortex, cognitive control and schizophrenia: recent developments and current challenges. *Philosophical Transactions of the Royal Society of London B*, 351, 1515–1527.

Cohen J. D., Botvinick M., Carter C. S. (2000). Anterior cingulate and prefrontal cortex: who's in control? *Nature Neuroscience*, 3(5), 421–423.

Coie J. D., Belding M., Underwood M. (1988a). Aggression and peer rejection in childhood. In B. Lahey, A. Kazdin (eds), *Advances in Clinical Child Psychology*. Cambridge: Cambridge University Press.

Coie J. D., Dodge K. A., Kupersmidt J. (1988b). Peer group behavior and social status. In S. R. Asher, J. D. Coie (eds), *Peer Rejection in Childhood*. Cambridge: Cambridge University Press.

Colby A., Kohlberg L. (1987). *The Measurement of Moral Judgment*. New York: Cambridge University Press.

Colledge E., Blair R. J. R. (2001). Relationship between attention-deficit-hyperactivity disorder and psychopathic tendencies in children. *Personality and Individual Differences*, 30, 1175–1187.

Colunga E., Smith L. B. (2003). The emergence of abstract ideas: evidence from networks and babies. *Philosophical Transactions of the Royal Society of London B*, 358(1435), 1205–1214.

Connor D. F. (2002). *Aggression and Anti-Social Behaviour in Children and Adolescents. Research and treatment*. New York: Guilford Press.

Cooke D. J., Michie C. (2001). Refining the construct of psychopathy: towards a hierarchical model. *Psychological Assessment*, 13, 171–188.

Cooke D. J., Kosson D. S., Michie C. (2001). Psychopathy and ethnicity: structural, item and test generalizability of the Psychopathy Checklist – Revised (PCL-R) in Caucasian and African American participants. *Psychological Assessment*, 13(4), 531–542.

Cools R., Clark L., Owen A. M., Robbins T. W. (2002). Defining the neural mechanisms of probabilistic reversal learning using event-related functional magnetic resonance imaging. *Journal of Neuroscience*, 22(11), 4563–4567.

Corbett B., Stanczak D. E. (1999). Neuropsychological performance of adults evidencing attention-deficit hyperactivity disorder. *Archives of Clinical Neuropsychology*, 14(4), 373–387.

Cornell D. G., Warren J., Hawk G., Stafford E., Oram G., Pine D. (1996). Psychopathy in instrumental and reactive violent offenders. *Journal of Consulting and Clinical Psychology*, 64, 783–790.

Corruble E., Ginestet D., Guelfi J. D. (1996). Comorbidity of personality disorders and unipolar major depression: a review. *Journal of Affective Disorders*, 37(2/3), 157–170.

Crick N. R., Dodge K. A. (1994). A review and reformulation of social information-processing mechanisms in children's social adjustment. *Psychological Bulletin*, 115, 74–101.

Crick N. R., Dodge K. A. (1996). Social information-processing mechanisms on reactive and proactive aggression. *Child Development*, 67, 993–1002.

Critchley H. D., Simmons A., Daly E. M., Russell A., van Amelsvoort T., Robertson D. M., Glover A., Murphy D. G. (2000). Prefrontal and medial temporal correlates of repetitive violence to self and others. *Biological Psychiatry*, 47(10), 928–934.

Damasio A. R. (1994). *Descartes' Error: Emotion, rationality and the human brain*. New York: Putnam.

Damasio A. R., Tranel D., Damasio H. C. (1990). Individuals with sociopathic behaviour caused by frontal damage fail to respond autonomically to social stimuli. *Behavioural Brain Research*, 41, 81–94.

Damasio A. R., Tranel D., Damasio H. C. (1991). Somatic markers and the guidance of behavior: theory and preliminary testing. In H. S. Levin, H. M. Eisenberg, A. L.

Benton (eds), *Frontal Lobe Function and Dysfunction*, pp. 217–229. New York: Oxford University Press.

Davis M. H. (1983). Measuring individual differences in empathy: evidence for a multi-dimensional approach. *Journal of Personality and Social Psychology*, 44(1), 113–126.

Davis M. H. (2000). The role of the amygdala in conditioned and unconditioned fear and anxiety. In J. P. Aggleton (ed.), *The Amygdala: A functional analysis*, pp. 289–310. Oxford: Oxford University Press.

Day R., Wong S. (1996). Anomalous perceptual asymmetries for negative emotional stimuli in the psychopath. *Journal of Abnormal Psychology*, 105, 648–652.

DeKlyen M., Speltz M. L., Greenberg M. T. (1998). Fathering and early onset conduct problems: positive and negative parenting, father – son attachment, and the marital context. *Clinical Child and Family Psychology Review*, 1, 3–21.

Desimone R., Duncan J. (1995). Neural mechanisms of selective visual attention. *Annual Review of Neuroscience*, 18, 193–222.

Dias R., Robbins T. W., Roberts A. C. (1996). Dissociation in prefrontal cortex of affective and attentional shifts. *Nature*, 380, 69–72.

Dickinson A. (1980). *Contemporary Animal Learning Theory*. Cambridge: Cambridge University Press.

Dickinson A., Dearing M. F. (1979). Appetitive-aversive interactions and inhibitory processes. In A. Dickinson, R. A. Boakes (eds), *Mechanisms of Learning and Motivation*, pp. 203–231. Hillsdale, NJ: Lawrence Erlbaum Associates.

Dodge K. A. (1980). Social cognition and children's aggressive behaviour. *Child Development*, 51, 162–170.

Dodge K. A. (1991). The structure and function of reactive and proactive aggression. In D. J. Pepler, K. H. Rubin (eds), *The Development and Treatment of Childhood Aggression*, pp. 201–218. Hillsdale, NJ: Lawrence Erlbaum Associates.

Dodge K. A., Coie J. D. (1987). Social information processing factors in reactive and proactive aggression in children's peer groups. *Journal of Personality and Social Psychology*, 53, 1146–1158.

Dodge K. A., Coie J. D., Brakke N. P. (1982). Behavior patterns of socially rejected and neglected preadolescents: the roles of social approach and aggression. *Journal of Abnormal Child Psychology*, 10, 389–409.

Dodge K. A., Pettit G. S., Bates J. E., Valente E. (1995). Social information-processing patterns partially mediate the effect of early physical abuse on later conduct problems. *Journal of Abnormal Psychology*, 104, 632–643.

Dolan M. C., Deakin J. F., Roberts N., Anderson I. M. (2002). Quantitative frontal and temporal structural MRI studies in personality-disordered offenders and control subjects. *Psychiatry Research*, 116(3), 133–149.

Dougherty D. D., Shin L. M., Alpert N. M., Pitman R. K., Orr S. P., Lasko M., Macklin M. L., Fischman A. J., Rauch S. L. (1999). Anger in healthy men: a PET study using script-driven imagery. *Biological Psychiatry*, 46(4), 466–472.

Drevets W. C. (2003). Neuroimaging abnormalities in the amygdala in mood disorders. *Annals of the New York Academy of Sciences*, 985, 420–444.

Drevets W. C., Lowry T., Gautier C., Perrett D. I., Kupfer D. J. (2000). Amygdalar blood flow responses to facially expressed sadness. *Biological Psychiatry*, 47, 160S.

Duncan J. (1998). Converging levels of analysis in the cognitive neuroscience of visual attention. *Philosophical Transactions of the Royal Society B*, 353, 1307–1317.

Duncan J., Humphreys G., Ward R. (1997). Competitive brain activity in visual attention. *Current Opinion in Neurobiology*, 7(2), 255–261.

Dunn J., Hughes C. (2001). "I got some swords and you're dead!": violent fantasy, antisocial behavior, friendship, and moral sensibility in young children. *Child Development*, 72(2), 491–505.

DuPaul G. J. (1991). Parent and teacher ratings of ADHD symptoms: psychometric properties in a community-based sample. *Journal of Clinical Child Psychology*, 20, 245–253.

Eisenberg N., Fabes R. A., Guthrie I. K., Murphy B. C., Maszk P., Holmgren R., Suh K. (1996). The relations of regulation and emotionality to problem behaviour in elementary school children. *Development and Psychopathology*, 8, 141–162.

Elliot F. A. (1978). Neurological aspects of antisocial behavior. In W. H. Reid (ed.), The psychopath. New York: Bruner/Mazel.

Epstein J. N., Erkanli A., Conners C. K., Klaric J., Costello J. E., Angold A. (2003). Relations between Continuous Performance Test performance measures and ADHD behaviors. *Journal of Abnormal Child Psychology*, 31(5), 543–554.

Everitt B. J., Cardinal R. N., Hall J., Parkinson J. A., Robbins T. W. (2000). Differential involvement of amygdala subsystems in appetitive conditioning and drug addiction. In J. P. Aggleton (ed.), *The Amygdala: A functional analysis*, pp. 289–301. Oxford: Oxford University Press.

Everitt B. J., Cardinal R. N., Parkinson J. A., Robbins T. W. (2003). Appetitive behavior: impact of amygdala-dependent mechanisms of emotional learning. *Annals of the New York Academy of Sciences*, 985, 233–250.

Eysenck H. J. (1964). *Crime and Personality*. London: Routledge & Kegan Paul.

Eysenck H. J., Gudjonsson G. H. (1989). *The Causes and Cures of Criminality*. London: Plenum Press.

Farrington D. P. (1983). Offending from 10 to 25 years of age. In S. A. Mednick (ed.), *Prospective Studies of Crime and Delinquency*. Boston, MA: Kluwer-Nijhoff.

Farrington D. P. (1986). Age and crime. In M. Tonry, N. Morris (eds), *Crime and Justice: An annual review of research*, vol. 7, pp. 189–250. Chicago, IL: University of Chicago Press.

Farrington D. P., Loeber R. (2000). Epidemiology of juvenile violence. *Child and Adolescent Psychiatric Clinics of North America*, 9, 733–748.

Fazel S., Danesh J. (2002). Serious mental disorder in 23,000 prisoners: a systematic review of 62 surveys. *Lancet*, 359(9306), 545–550.

Feshbach N. D. (1987). Parental empathy and child adjustment/maladjustment. In N. Eisenberg, J. Strayer (eds), *Empathy and its Development*. New York: Cambridge University Press.

File S. E., Deakin J. F. (1980). Chemical lesions of both dorsal and median raphe nuclei and changes in social and aggressive behaviour in rats. *Pharmacology, Biochemistry and Behavior*, 12, 855–859.

Fisher L., Blair R. J. R. (1998). Cognitive impairment and its relationship to psychopathic tendencies in children with emotional and behavioural difficulties. *Journal of Abnormal Child Psychology*, 26, 511–519.

Flor H., Birbaumer N., Hermann C., Ziegler S., Patrick C. J. (2002). Aversive Pavlovian conditioning in psychopaths: peripheral and central correlates. *Psychophysiology*, 39, 505–518.

Fodor E. M. (1973). Moral development and parent behaviour antecedents in adolescent psychopaths. *Journal of Genetic Psychology*, 122, 37–43.

Fonagy P. (2000). Attachment and borderline personality disorder. *Journal of the American Psychoanalytical Association*, 48, 1129–1146; discussion 1175–1187.

Forth A. E., Burke H. C. (1998). Psychopathy in adolescents: assessment, violence, and developmental precursors. In R. D. Hare (ed.), *Psychopathy: Theory, research and implications for society*, pp. 205–230. Dordrecht: Kluwer.

Forth A. E., Kosson D. S., Hare R. D. (2003). *The Psychopathy Checklist: Youth Version*. Toronto, Ontario: Multi-Health Systems.

Fowles D. C. (1988). Psychophysiology and psychopathy: a motivational approach. *Psychophysiology*, 25, 373–391.

Francis D. D., Meaney M. J. (1999). Maternal care and the development of stress responses. *Current Opinion in Neurobiology*, 9(1), 128–134.

Francis D. D., Caldji C., Champagne F., Plotsky P. M., Meaney M. J. (1999). The role of corticotropin-releasing factor – norepinephrine systems in mediating the effects of early experience on the development of behavioral and endocrine responses to stress. *Biological Psychiatry*, 46(9), 1153–1166.

Frick P. J., Hare R. D. (2001a). *The Antisocial Process Screening Device*. Toronto, Ontario: Multi-Health Systems.

Frick P. J., Hare R. D. (2001b). *Antisocial Process Screening Device (ASPD) Technical Manual*. Toronto, Ontario: Multi-Health Systems.

Frick P. J., O'Brien B. S., Wootton J. M., McBurnett K. (1994). Psychopathy and conduct problems in children. *Journal of Abnormal Psychology*, 103, 700–707.

Frick P. J., Lilienfeld S. O., Ellis M., Loney B., Silverthorn P. (1999). The association between anxiety and psychopathy dimensions in children. *Journal of Abnormal Child Psychology*, 27(5), 383–392.

Frith C. (2000). The role of dorsolateral prefrontal cortex in the selection of action, as revealed by functional imaging. In S. Monsell, J. Driver (eds), *Control of Cognitive Processes: Attention and performance*, vol. XVIII, pp. 549–567. Camridge, MA: MIT Press.

Fuster J. M. (1980). The prefrontal cortex. New York: Raven Press.

Garber J., Quiggle N. L., Panak W., Dodge K. A. (1991). Aggression and depression in children: comorbidity, specificity, and social cognitive procession. In D. Cicchetti, S. L. Toth (eds), *Internalizing and Externalizing Expressions of Dysfunction: Rochester symposium on developmental psychopathology*, vol. II. Hillsdale, N J: Lawrence Erlbaum Associates.

Garcia R., Vouimba R. M., Baudry M., Thompson R. F. (1999). The amygdala modulates prefrontal cortex activity relative to conditioned fear. *Nature*, 402, 294–296.

Gernsbacher M. A., Faust M. E. (1991). The mechanism of suppression: a component of general comprehension skill. *Journal of Experimental Psychology. Learning, Memory, and Cognition,* 17(2), 245–262.

Giedd J. N., Blumenthal J., Molloy E., Castellanos F. X. (2001). Brain imaging of attention deficit/hyperactivity disorder. *Annals of the New York Academy of Sciences,* 931, 33–49.

Gillott A., Furniss F., Walter A. (2001). Anxiety in high-functioning children with autism. *Autism,* 5(3), 277–286.

Goldsmith H. H., Gottesman I. I. (1996). Heritable variability and variable heritability in developmental psychopathology. In M. F. Lenzenweger, J. J. Haugaard (ed.), *Frontiers of Developmental Psychopathology,* pp. 5–43. Oxford: Oxford University Press.

Goodman G. S., Hirschman J. E., Hepps D., Rudy L. (1991). Children's memory for stressful events. *Merrill-Palmer Quarterly,* 37, 109–157.

Goodwin R. D., Hamilton S. P. (2003). Lifetime comorbidity of antisocial personality disorder and anxiety disorders among adults in the community. *Psychiatry Research,* 117(2), 159–166.

Gorenstein E. E. (1982). Frontal lobe functions in psychopaths. Journal of Abnormal Psychology, 91, 368–379.

Gorenstein E. E., Newman J. P. (1980). Disinhibitory psychopathology: a new perspective and a model for research. *Psychological Review,* 37, 301–315.

Gorrindo T., Blair R. J. R., Budhani S., Pine D. S., Leibenluft E. (in press). Probabilistic response reversal deficits in pediatric bipolar disorder. *American Journal of Psychiatry.*

Gouze K. R. (1987). Attention and social problem solving as correlates of aggression in preschool males. *Journal of Abnormal Child Psychology,* 15(2), 181–197.

Goyer P. F., Andreason P. J., Semple W. E., Clayton A. H., King A. C., Compton-Toth B. A., Schulz S. C., Cohen R. M. (1994). Positron-emission tomography and personality disorders. Neuropsychopharmacology, 10(1), 21–28.

Grafman J., Schwab K., Warden D., Pridgen B. S., Brown H. R. (1996). Frontal lobe injuries, violence, and aggression: a report of the Vietnam head injury study. *Neurology,* 46, 1231–1238.

Grann M., Langstrom N., Tengstrom A., Kullgren G. (1999). Psychopathy (P. C. L-R) predicts violent recidivism among criminal offenders with personality disorders in Sweden. *Law and Human Behavior,* 23, 205–217.

Grant S., Contoreggi C., London E. D. (2000). Drug abusers show impaired performance in a laboratory test of decision-making. *Neuropsychologia,* 38, 1180–1187.

Graves R., Landis T., Goodglass H. (1981). Laterality and sex differences for visual recognition of emotional and non-emotional words. *Neuropsychologia,* 19, 95–102.

Gray J. A. (1971). *The Psychology of Fear and Stress.* London: Weienfeld & Nicolson.

Gray J. A. (1982). *The Neuropsychology of Anxiety: an inquiry into the functions of the septo-hippocampal system.* Oxford: Oxford University Press.

Gray J. A. (1987). *The Psychology of Fear and Stress,* 2nd edn. Cambridge: Cambride University Press.

Gray J. A., McNaughton N. (1996). The neuropsychology of anxiety: reprise. *Nebraska Symposium on Motivation,* 43, 61–134.

Gregg T. R., Siegel A. (2001). Brain structures and neurotransmitters regulating aggression in cats: implications for human aggression. *Progress in Neuro-Psychopharmacology and Biological Psychiatry*, 25, 91–140.

Guy J. D., Majorski L. V., Wallace C. J., Guy M. P. (1983). The incidence of minor physical anomalies in adult male schizophrenics. *Schizophrenia Bulletin*, 9, 571–582.

Hamann S., Mao H. (2002). Positive and negative emotional verbal stimuli elicit activity in the left amygdala. *Neuroreport*, 13, 15–19.

Hare R. D. (1965). Temporal gradient of fear arousal in psychopaths. *Journal of Abnormal Psychology*, 70, 442–445.

Hare R. D. (1970). *Psychopathy: Theory and Research*. New York: John Wiley & Sons.

Hare R. D. (1980). A research scale for the assessment of psychopathy in criminal populations. *Personality and Individual Differences*, 1, 111–119.

Hare R. D. (1982). Psychopathy and physiological activity during anticipation of an aversive stimulus in a distraction paradigm. *Psychophysiology*, 19, 266–271.

Hare R. D. (1984). Performance of psychopaths in cognitive tasks related to frontal lobe function. *Journal of Abnormal Psychology*, 93, 133–140.

Hare R. D. (1991). *The Hare Psychopathy Checklist – Revised*. Toronto, Ontario: Multi-Health Systems.

Hare R. D. (1996). Psychopathy: a clinical construct whose time has come. *Criminal Justice and Behavior*, 23, 25–54.

Hare R. D. (1998). Psychopathy, affect, and behavior. In D. J. Cooke, A. E. Forth, R. D. Hare (eds), *Psychopathy: Theory, research and implications for society*, pp. 105–137. Dordrecht: Kluwer, 81–105.

Hare R. D. (2003). *The Hare Psychopathy Checklist – Revised (PCL-R)*, 2nd edn. Toronto, Ontario: Multi-Health Systems.

Hare R. D., Jutai J. W. (1988). Psychopathy and cerebral asymmetry in semantic processing. *Personality and Individual Differences*, 9(2), 329–337.

Hare R. D., McPherson L. M. (1984). Psychopathy and perceptual assymetry during verbal dichotic listening. Journal of Abnormal Psychology, 93, 141–149.

Hare R. D., Quinn M. J. (1971). Psychopathy and autonomic conditioning. *Journal of Abnormal Psychology*, 77, 223–235.

Hare R. D., Frazelle J., Cox D. N. (1978). Psychopathy and physiological responses to threat of an aversive stimulus. *Psychophysiology*, 15, 165–172.

Hare R. D., McPherson L. M., Forth A. E. (1988a). Male psychopaths and their criminal careers. *Journal of Consulting and Clinical Psychology*, 56(5), 710–714.

Hare R. D., Williamson S. E., Harpur T. J. (1988b). Psychopathy and language. In T. E. Moffitt, A. M. Sarnoff (eds), *Biological Contributions to Crime Causation*, NATO Advanced Science Series D: Behavior and Social Sciences, pp. 68–92. Dordrecht: Martinus Nishoff.

Hare R. D., Harpur T. J., Hakstian A. R., Forth A. E., Hart S. D. (1990). The Revised Psychopathy Checklist: reliability and factor structure. *Psychological Assessment*, 2, 338–341.

Hare R. D., Clark D., Grann M., Thornton D. (2000). Psychopathy and the predictive validity of the P. C. L-R: an international perspective. *Behavioral Sciences and the Law*, 18, 623–645.

Harmer C. J., Perrett D. I., Cowen P. J., Goodwin G. M. (2001). Administration of the beta-adrenoceptor blocker propranolol impairs the processing of facial expressions of sadness. *Psychopharmacology (Berl)*, 154, 383–389.

Harpur T. J., Hare R. D. (1994). Assessment of psychopathy as a function of age. *Journal of Abnormal Psychology*, 103, 604–609.

Harpur T. J., Hakstian A. R., Hare R. D. (1988). The factor structure of the Psychopathy Checklist. *Journal of Consulting and Clinical Psychology*, 56, 741–747.

Harpur T. J., Hare R. D., Hakstian A. R. (1989). Two-factor conceptualization of psychopathy: construct validity and assessment implications. *Journal of Consulting and Clinical Psychology*, 1, 6–17.

Hart C. H., Ladd G. W., Burleson B. (1990). Children's expectations of the outcomes of social strategies: relations with sociometric status and maternal disciplinary styles. *Child Development*, 61, 127–137.

Hart S. D., Hare R. D. (1996). Psychopathy and antisocial personality disorder. *Current Opinion in Psychiatry*, 9, 129–132.

Hart S. D., Kropp P. R., Hare R. D. (1988). Performance of male psychopaths following conditional release from prison. *Journal of Consulting and Clinical Psychology*, 56, 227–232.

Haznedar M. M., Buchsbaum M. S., Wei T. C., Hof P. R., Cartwright C., Bienstock C. A., Hollander E. (2000). Limbic circuitry in patients with autism spectrum disorders studied with positron emission tomography and magnetic resonance imaging. *American Journal of Psychiatry*, 157(12), 1994–2001.

Hebb D. O. (1949). *The Organization of Behavior*. New York: John Wiley & Sons.

Hecaen H., Albert M. L. (1978). Human Neuropsychology. New York: Wiley.

Heim C., Owens M. J., Plotsky P. M., Nemeroff C. B. (1997). Persistent changes in corticotropin-releasing factor systems due to early life stress: relationship to the pathophysiology of major depression and post-traumatic stress disorder. *Psychopharmacology Bulletin*, 33, 1851–192.

Hemphill J. F., Hart S. D., Hare R. D. (1994). Psychopathy and substance use. *Journal of Personality Disorders*, 8, 169–180.

Hemphill J. F., Hare R. D., Wong S. (1998). Psychopathy and recidivism: a review. *Legal and Criminological Psychology*, 3, 139–170.

Herpertz S. C., Werth U., Lukas G., Qunaibi M., Schuerkens A., Kunert H. J., Freese R., Flesch M., Mueller-Isberner R., Osterheider M., Sass H. (2001). Emotion in criminal offenders with psychopathy and borderline personality disorder. *Archives of General Psychiatry*, 58(8), 737–745.

Hettema J. M., Neale M. C., Kendler K. S. (2001). A review and meta-analysis of the genetic epidemiology of anxiety disorders. *American Journal of Psychiatry*, 158, 1568–1578.

Hinshaw S. P. (1987). On the distinction between attentional deficits/hyperactivity and conduct problems/aggression in child psychopathology. *Psychological Bulletin*, 101, 443–463.

Hinshaw S. P., Lahey B. B., Hart E. L. (1993). Issues of taxonomy and comorbidity in the development of conduct disorder. *Development and Psychopathology*, 5, 31–49.

Hirschi T., Gottfredson M. (1983). Age and explanation of crime. *American Journal of Sociology*, 89, 552–584.

Hobson J., Shine J. (1998). Measurement of psychopathy in a UK prison population referred for long-term psychotherapy. *British Journal of Criminology*, 38, 504–515.

Hobson R. P. (1993). *Autism and the Development of Mind*. Hove, East Sussex: Lawrence Erlbaum Associates.

Hodgins S., Kratzer L., McNeil T. F. (2001). Obstetric complications, parenting, and risk of criminal behavior. *Archives of General Psychiatry*, 58, 746–752.

Hodgins S., Kratzer L., McNeil T. F. (2002). Obstetrical complications, parenting practices and risk of criminal behaviour among persons who develop major mental disorders. *Acta Psychiatrica Scandinavica*, 105, 179–188.

Hoffman M. L. (1984). Empathy, its limitations, and its role in a comprehensive moral theory. In W. Kurtines (ed.), *Morality, Moral Development, and Moral Behavior*, pp. 283–302. New York: John Wiley & Sons.

Hoffman M. L. (1988). Moral development. In M. Bornstein, M. Lamb (eds), *Developmental Psychology: An advanced textbook*, pp. 497–548. Hillsdale, NJ: Lawrence Erlbaum Associates.

Hoffman M. L. (1994). Discipline and internalisation. *Developmental Psychology*, 30, 26–28.

Hoffman M. L., Saltzstein H. D. (1967). Parent discipline and the child's moral development. *Journal of Personality and Social Psychology*, 5, 45–57.

Hollingshead A. B., Redlich F. C. (1958). *Social Class and Mental Illness: A community study*. New York: John Wiley & Sons.

House T. H., Milligan W. L. (1976). Autonomic responses to modeled distress in prison psychopaths. *Journal of Personality and Social Psychology*, 34, 556–560.

Howard M. A., Cowell P. E., Boucher J., Broks P., Mayes A., Farrant A., Roberts N. (2000). Convergent neuroanatomical and behavioural evidence of an amygdala hypothesis of autism. *Neuroreport*, 11(13), 1931–1935.

Howland E. W., Kosson D. S., Patterson C. M., Newman J. P. (1993). Altering a dominant response: performance of psychopaths and low-socialization college students on a cued reaction time task. *Journal of Abnormal Psychology*, 102(3), 379–387.

Hughes C., Dunn J. (2000). Hedonism or empathy? Hard-to-manage children's moral awareness and links with cognitive and maternal characteristics. *British Journal of Developmental Psychology*, 18, 227–245.

Itami S., Uno H. (2002). Orbitofrontal cortex dysfunction in attention-deficit hyperactivity disorder revealed by reversal and extinction tasks. *Neuroreport*, 13(18), 2453–2457.

Jackson H. J., Whiteside H. L., Bates G. W., Bell R., Rudd R. P., Edwards J. (1991). Diagnosing personality disorders in psychiatric inpatients. *Acta Psychiatrica Scandinavica*, 83(3), 206–213.

Jacobson L., Sapolsky R. (1991). The role of the hippocampus in feedback regulation of the hypothalamic-pituitary-adrenocortical axis. *Endocrine Reviews*, 12, 118–134.

Johnson W., McGue M., Gaist D., Vaupel J. W., Christensen K. (2002). Frequency and heritability of depression symptomatology in the second half of life: evidence from Danish twins over 45. *Psychological Medicine*, 32, 1175–1185.

Johnston J. B. Further contributions to the study of the evolution of the forebrain. *Journal of Comparative Neurology* 1923; 35, 337–481.

Jonides J., Yantis S. (1988). Uniqueness of abrupt visual onset in capturing attention. *Perception and Psychophysics*, 43, 346–354.

Jurkovic G. J., Prentice P. M. (1977). Relation of moral and cognitive development to dimensions of juvenile delinquency. *Journal of Abnormal Psychology*, 86, 414–420.

Jutai J. W., Hare R. D. (1983). Psychopathy and selective attention during performance of a complex perceptual-motor task. *Psychophysiology*, 20, 146–151.

Jutai J. W., Hare R. D., Connolly J. F. (1987). Psychopathy and event related brain potentials (ERPs) associated with attention to speech stimuli. *Personality and Individual Differences*, 8, 175–184.

Kagan J., Snidman N. (1999). Early childhood predictors of adult anxiety disorders. *Biological Psychiatry*, 46, 1536–1541.

Kandel E., Freed D. (1989). Frontal lobe dysfunction and antisocial behavior: a review. *Journal of Clinical Psychology*, 45, 404–413.

Kesler-West M. L., Andersen A. H., Smith C. D., Avison M. J., Davis C. E., Kryscio R. J., Blonder L. X. (2001). Neural substrates of facial emotion processing using fMRI. *Cognitive Brain Research*, 11(2), 213–226.

Kiehl K. A., Hare R. D., McDonald J. J., Brink J. (1999a). Semantic and affective processing in psychopaths: an event-related potential (ERP) study. *Psychophysiology*, 36, 765–774.

Kiehl K. A., Hare R. D., Liddle P. F., McDonald J. J. (1999b). Reduced P300 responses in criminal psychopaths during a visual oddball task. *Biological Psychiatry*, 45(11), 1498–1507.

Kiehl K. A., Smith A. M., Hare R. D., Liddle P. F. (2000). An event-related potential investigation of response inhibition in schizophrenia and psychopathy. *Biological Psychiatry*, 48, 210–221.

Kiehl K. A., Smith A. M., Hare R. D., Mendrek A., Forster B. B., Brink J., Liddle P. F. (2001). Limbic abnormalities in affective processing by criminal psychopaths as revealed by functional magnetic resonance imaging. *Biological Psychiatry*, 50, 677–684.

Kiehl K. A., Smith A. M., Mendrek A., Forster B. B., Hare R. D., Liddle P. F. (2004). Temporal lobe abnormalities in semantic processing by criminal psychopaths as revealed by functional magnetic resonance imaging. Psychiatry Research: Neuroimaging, 130, 27–42.

Killcross S., Robbins T. W., Everitt B. J. (1997). Different types of fear-conditioned behaviour mediated by separate nuclei within amygdala. *Nature*, 388, 377–380.

King S. M. (1999). Escape-related behaviours in an unstable, elevated and exposed environment. II. Long-term sensitization after repetitive electrical stimulation of the rodent midbrain defence system. *Behavioural Brain Research*, 98, 127–142.

Kochanska G. (1993). Toward a synthesis of parental socialization and child temperament in early development of conscience. *Child Development*, 64, 325–347.

Kochanska G. (1997). Multiple pathways to conscience for children with different temperaments: from toddlerhood to age 5. *Developmental Psychology*, 33, 228–240.

Kochanska G., De Vet K., Goldman M., Murray K., Putman P. (1994). Maternal reports of conscience development and temperament in young children. *Child Development*, 65, 852–868.

Kohlberg L. (1969). Stage and sequence: the cognitive-developmental approach to socialization. In D. A. Goslin (ed.), *Handbook of Socialization Theory and Research*. Chicago, IL: Rand McNally.

Kohlberg L., Kramer R. (1969). Continuities and disconuities in childhood and adult moral development. *Human Development*, 12, 93–120.

Kohlberg L., Levine C., Hewer A. (1983). *Moral Stages: A current formulation and a response to critics*. Basel: Karger.

Kosson D. S. (1996). Psychopathy and dual-task performance under focusing conditions. *Journal of Abnormal Psychology*, 105(3), 391–400.

Kosson D. S. (1998). Divided visual attention in psychopathic and nonpsychopathic offenders. *Personality and Individual Differences*, 24, 373–391.

Kosson D. S., Newman J. P. (1986). Psychopathy and the allocation of attentional capacity in a divided-attention situation. *Journal of Abnormal Psychology*, 95, 257–263.

Kosson D. S., Smith S. S., Newman J. P. (1990). Evaluating the construct validity of the psychopathy construct in blacks: a preliminary investigation. *Journal of Abnormal Psychology*, 99, 250–259.

Kosson D. S., Cyterski T. D., Steuerwald B. L., Neumann C. S., Walker-Matthews S. (2002a). The reliability and validity of the psychopathy checklist: youth version (PCL:YV) in nonincarcerated adolescent males. *Psychological Assessment*, 14, 97–109.

Kosson D. S., Suchy Y., Mayer A. R., Libby J. (2002b). Facial affect recognition in criminal psychopaths. *Emotion*, 2(4), 398–411.

Kringelbach M. L., Rolls E. T. (2003). Neural correlates of rapid reversal learning in a simple model of human social interaction. *Neuroimage*, 20(2), 1371–1383.

Krueger R. F., Schmutte P. S., Caspi A., Moffitt T. E., Campbell K., Silva P. A. (1994). Personality traits are linked to crime among men and women: evidence from a birth cohort. *Journal of Abnormal Psychology*, 103(2), 328–338.

Laakso M. P., Gunning-Dixon F., Vaurio O., Repo-Tiihonen E., Soininen H., Tiihonen J. (2002). Prefrontal volumes in habitually violent subjects with antisocial personality disorder and type 2 alcoholism. *Psychiatry Research*, 114(2), 95–102.

Lahey B. B., Loeber R., Hart E. L., Frick P. J., Applegate B., Zhang Q., Green S. M., Russo M. F. (1995). Four-year longitudinal study of conduct disorder in boys: patterns and predictors of persistence. *Journal of Abnormal Psychology*, 104, 83–93.

Lahey B. B., Loeber R., Quay H. C., Applegate B., Shaffer D., Waldman I., Hart E. L., McBurnett K., Frick P. J., Jensen P. S., Dulcan M. K., Canino G., Bird H. R. (1998). Validity of DSM-IV subtypes of conduct disorder based on age of onset. *Journal of the American Academy of Child and Adolescent Psychiatry*, 37(4), 435–442.

Lang P. J., Bradley M. M., Cuthbert B. N. (1990). Emotion, attention, and the startle reflex. *Psychological Review*, 97, 377–398.

Langley K., Marshall L., Van Den Bree M., Thomas H., Owen M., O'Donovan M., Thapar A. (2004). Association of the dopamine D(4) receptor gene 7-repeat allele with neuropsychological test performance of children with ADHD. *American Journal of Psychiatry*, 161(1), 133–138.

LaPierre D., Braun C. M. J., Hodgins S. (1995). Ventral frontal deficits in psychopathy: neuropsychological test findings. *Neuropsychologia*, 33, 139–151.

Laucht M., Esser G., Baving L., Gerhold M., Hoesch I., Ihle W., Steigleider P., Stock B., Stoehr R. M., Weindrich D., Schmidt M. H. (2000). Behavioral sequelae of perinatal insults and early family adversity at 8 years of age. *Journal of the American Academy of Child and Adolescent Psychiatry*, 39, 1229–1237.

Lavie N. (1995). Perceptual load as a necessary condition for selective attention. *Journal of Experimental Psychology: Human Perception and Performance*, 21(3), 451–468.

LeDoux J. E. (1998). *The Emotional Brain*. New York: Weidenfeld & Nicolson.

LeDoux J. E. (2000). The amygdala and emotion: a view through fear. In J. P. Aggleton (ed.), *The Amygdala: A functional analysis*, pp. 289–310. Oxford: Oxford University Press.

Lee M., Prentice N. M. (1988). Interrelations of empathy, cognition, and moral reasoning with dimensions of juvenile delinquency. *Journal of Abnormal Child Psychology*, 16, 127–139.

Lee R., Coccaro E. (2001). The neuropsychopharmacology of criminality and aggression. *Canadian Journal of Psychiatry*, 46, 35–44.

Leibenluft E., Blair R. J., Charney D. S., Pine D. S. (2003). Irritability in pediatric mania and other childhood psychopathology. *Annals of the New York Academy of Sciences*, 1008, 201–218.

Leung P. W. L., Connolly K. J. (1996). Distractibility in hyperactive and conduct disordered children. *Journal of Child Psychology and Psychiatry*, 37, 305–312.

Levenston G. K., Patrick C. J., Bradley M. M., Lang P. J. (2000). The psychopath as observer: emotion and attention in picture processing. *Journal of Abnormal Psychology*, 109, 373–386.

Levine S., Wiener S. G., Coe C. L. (1993). Temporal and social factors influencing behavioral and hormonal responses to separation in mother and infant squirrel monkeys. *Psychoneuroendocrinology*, 18, 297–306.

Lichter J. B., Barr C. L., Kennedy J. L., Van Tol H. H., Kidd K. K., Livak K. J. (1993). A hypervariable segment in the human dopamine receptor D4 (DRD4) gene. *Human Molecular Genetics*, 2, 767–773.

Lilienfeld S. O., Andrews B. P. (1996). Development and preliminary validation of a self-report measure of psychopathic personality traits in noncriminal populations. *Journal of Personality Assessment*, 66, 488–524.

Linnoila M., Virkkunen M., Scheinin M., Nuutila A., Rimon R., Goodwin F. K. (1983). Low cerebrospinal fluid 5-hydroxy indoleacetic acid concentration differentiates impulsive from nonimpulsive violent behavior. *Life Sciences*, 33, 2609–2614.

Liu D., Diorio J., Tannenbaum B., Caldji C., Francis D., Freedman A., Sharma S., Pearson D., Plotsky P. M., Meaney M. J. (1997). Maternal care, hippocampal glucocorticoid receptors, and hypothalamic-pituitary-adrenal responses to stress. *Science*, 277, 1659–1662.

Liu D., Caldji C., Sharma S., Plotsky P. M., Meaney M. J. (2000). Influence of neonatal rearing conditions on stress-induced adrenocorticotropin responses and norepinepherine release in the hypothalamic paraventricular nucleus. *Journal of Neuroendocrinology*, 12(1), 5–12.

Loeber R. (1991). Antisocial behavior: more enduring than changeable? *Journal of the American Academy of Child and Adolescent Psychiatry*, 30(3), 393–397.

Loeber R., Stouthamer-Loeber M., Van Kammen D. P., Farrington D. P. (1989). Development of a new measure of self-reported antisocial behavior for young children: prevalence and reliability. In M. Klein (ed.), Cross-National Research in Self-Reported Crime and Delinquency. Boston, MA: Kluwer-Nijhoff.

Loeber R., Farrington D. P., Stouthamer-Loeber M., Van-Kammen W. B. (1998). Antisocial behavior and mental health problems: explanatory factors in childhood and adolescence. Mahwah, NJ: Lawrence Erlbaum Associates.

Logan G. D., Cowan W. B., Davis K. A. (1984). On the ability to inhibit simple and choice reaction time responses: a model and a method. *Journal of Experimental Psychology: Human Perception and Performance*, 10, 276–291.

Lorenz A. R., Newman J. P. (2002). Deficient response modulation and emotion processing in low-anxious caucasian psychopathic offenders: results from a lexical decision task. *Emotion*, 2(2), 91–104.

Lovelace L., Gannon L. (1999). Psychopathy and depression: mutually exclusive constructs? *Journal of Behavior Therapy and Experimental Psychiatry*, 30(3), 169–176.

Luria A. (1966). Higher cortical functions in man. New York: Basic Books.

Lykken D. T. (1957). A study of anxiety in the sociopathic personality. *Journal of Abnormal and Social Psychology*, 55, 6–10.

Lykken D. T. (1995). *The Antisocial Personalities*. Hillsdale, NJ: Lawrence Erlbaum Associates.

Lynam D. R. (1996). Early identification of chronic offenders: who is the fledgling psychopath? *Psychological Bulletin*, 120(2), 209–224.

Lyons-Ruth K. (1996). Attachment relationships among children with aggressive behavior problems: the role of disorganized early attachment patterns. *Journal of Consulting and Clinical Psychology*, 64, 64–73.

Lyons-Ruth K., Alpern L., Repacholi B. (1993). Disorganized infant attachment classification and maternal psychosocial problems as predictors of hostile-aggressive behavior in the preschool classroom. *Child Development*, 64, 572–585.

MacLeod C. M., MacDonald P. A. (2000). Interdimensional interference in the Stroop effect: uncovering the cognitive and neural anatomy of attention. *Trends in Cognitive Science*, 4, 383–391.

Malkova L., Gaffan D., Murray E. A. (1997). Excitotoxic lesions of the amygdala fail to produce impairment in visual learning of auditory scondary reinforcement but interfere with reinforcer devlauation effects in rhesus monkeys. *Journal of Neuroscience*, 17, 6011–6020.

Manuck S. B., Flory J. D., McCaffery J. M., Matthews K. A., Mann J. J., Muldoon M. F. (1998). Aggression, impulsivity, and central nervous system serotonergic responsivity in a nonpatient sample. *Neuropsychopharmacology*, 19, 287–299.

Marshall L. A., Cooke D. J. (1999). The childhood experiences of psychopaths: a retrospective study of familial and societal factors. *Journal of Personality Disorders*, 13, 211–225.

Masserman J. H., Wechkin S., Terris W. (1964). "Altruistic" behavior in rhesus monkeys. *American Journal of Psychiatry*, 121(6), 584–585.

McClure E. B., Pope K., Hoberman A. J., Pine D. S., Leibenluft E. (2003). Facial expression recognition in adolescents with mood and anxiety disorders. *American Journal of Psychiatry*, 160, 1172–1174.

McEwen B. S., Angulo J., Cameron H., Chao H. M., Daniels D., Gannon M. N., Gould E., Mendelson S., Sakai R., Spencer R., et al. (1992a). Paradoxical effects of adrenal steroids on the brain: protection versus degeneration. *Biological Psychiatry*, 31, 177–199.

McEwen B. S., Gould E. A., Sakai R. R. (1992b). The vulnerability of the hippocampus to protective and destructive effects of glucocorticoids in relation to stress. *British Journal of Psychiatry*, 160(suppl. 15), 18–24.

McNaughton N., Gray J. A. (2000). Anxiolytic action on the behavioural inhibition system implies multiple types of arousal contribute to anxiety. Journal of Affective Disorders, 61(3), 161–176.

Mealey L. (1995). The sociobiology of sociopathy: an integrated evolutionary model. *Behavioral and Brain Sciences*, 18, 523–599.

Mednick S. A., Kandel E. S. (1988). Congenital determinants of violence. *Bulletin of the American Academy of Psychiatry Law*, 16, 101–109.

Mitchell D. G. V., Colledge E., Leonard A., Blair R. J. R. (2002). Risky decisions and response reversal: is there evidence of orbitofrontal cortex dysfunction in psychopathic individuals? *Neuropsychologia*, 40, 2013–2022.

Mitchell D. G. V., Richell R. A., Leonard A., Blair R. J. R. (under revision). Emotion at the expense of cognition: psychopathic individuals outperform controls on an operant response task. *Journal of Abnormal Psychology*.

Moffitt T. E. (1993a). Adolescence-limited and life-course-persistent antisocial behavior: a developmental taxonomy. *Psychological Review*, 100, 674–701.

Moffitt T. E. (1993b). The neuropsychology of conduct disorder. *Development and Psychopathology*, 5, 135–152.

Moffitt T. E., Caspi A., Harrington H., Milne B. J. (2002). Males on the life-course-persistent and adolescence-limited antisocial pathways: follow-up at age 26 years. *Developmental Psychopathology*, 14, 179–207.

Molto J., Poy R., Torrubia R. (2000). Standardization of the Hare Psychopathy Checklist – Revised in a Spanish prison sample. *Journal of Personality Disorders*, 14, 84–96.

Moran P. (1999). Antisocial personality disorder: an epidemiological perspective. London: Royal College of Psychiatrists.

Morgan A. B., Lilienfield S. O. (2000). A meta-analytic review of the relation between antisocial behavior and neuropsychological measures of executive function. *Clinical Psychology Review*, 20, 113–136.

Morgan C. A., 3rd, Grillon C., Southwick S. M., Davis M., Charney D. S. (1996). Exaggerated acoustic startle reflex in Gulf War veterans with posttraumatic stress disorder. *American Journal of Psychiatry*, 153(1), 64–68.

Morgan C. A., 3rd, Grillon C., Lubin H., Southwick S. M. (1997). Startle reflex abnormalities in women with sexual assault-related posttraumatic stress disorder. *American Journal of Psychiatry*, 154(8), 1076–1080.

Morris J. S., Frith C. D., Perrett D. I., Rowland D., Young A. W., Calder A. J., et al. (1996). A differential response in the human amygdala to fearful and happy facial expressions. *Nature*, 383, 812–815.

Morton J., Frith U. (1993). Causal modelling: a structural approach to developmental psychopathology. In D. Cicchetti, D. H. Cohen (eds), *Manual of Developmental Psychopathology*. New York: John Wiley & Sons.

Muller J. L., Sommer M., Wagner V., Lange K., Taschler H., Roder C. H., Schuierer G., Klein H. E., Hajak G. (2003). Abnormalities in emotion processing within cortical and subcortical regions in criminal psychopaths: evidence from a functional magnetic resonance imaging study using pictures with emotional content. *Biological Psychiatry*, 54(2), 152–162.

Murphy P. (2002). Inhibitory control in adults with attention-deficit/hyperactivity disorder. *Journal of Attention Disorders*, 6(1), 1–4.

Newman J. P. (1998). Psychopathic behaviour: an information processing perspective. In D. J. Cooke, A. E. Forth, R. D. Hare (eds), *Psychopathy: Theory, research and implications for society*, pp. 81–104. Dordrecht: Kluwer.

Newman J. P., Kosson D. S. (1986). Passive avoidance learning in psychopathic and nonpsychopathic offenders. *Journal of Abnormal Psychology*, 95, 252–256.

Newman J. P., Schmitt W. A. (1998). Passive avoidance in psychopathic offenders: a replication and extension. *Journal of Abnormal Psychology*, 107, 527–532.

Newman J. P., Widom C. S., Nathan S. (1985). Passive avoidance in syndromes of disinhibition: psychopathy and extraversion. *Journal of Personality and Social Psychology*, 48, 1316–1327.

Newman J. P., Patterson C. M., Kosson D. S. (1987). Response perseveration in psychopaths. *Journal of Abnormal Psychology*, 96, 145–148.

Newman J. P., Patterson C. M., Howland E. W., Nichols S. L. (1990). Passive avoidance in psychopaths: the effects of reward. *Personality and Individual Differences*, 11, 1101–1114.

Newman J. P., Schmitt W. A., Voss W. D. (1997). The impact of motivationally neutral cues on psychopathic individuals: assessing the generality of the response modulation hypothesis. *Journal of Abnormal Psychology*, 106, 563–575.

Nigg J. T., Blaskey L. G., Huang-Pollock C. L., Rappley M. D. (2002). Neuropsychological executive functions and DSM-IV ADHD subtypes. *Journal of the American Academy of Child and Adolescent Psychiatry*, 41(1), 59–66.

Nippold M. A., Uhden L. D., Schwarz I. E. (1997). Proverb explanation through the lifespan: a developmental study of adolescents and adults. *Journal of Speech, Language, and Hearing Research*, 40(2), 245–253.

Nisenbaum L. K., Zigmond M. J., Sved A. F., Abercrombie E. D. (1991). Prior exposure to chronic stress results in enhanced synthesis and release of hippocampal norepinephrine in response to a novel stressor. *Journal of Neuroscience*, 11(5), 1478–1484.

Nucci L. P. (1981). Conceptions of personal issues: a domain distinct from moral or societal concepts. *Child Development*, 52, 114–121.

Nucci L. P., Herman S. (1982). Behavioral disordered children's conceptions of moral, conventional, and personal issues. *Journal of Abnormal Child Psychology*, 10, 411–425.

Nucci L. P., Nucci M. (1982). Children's social interactions in the context of moral and conventional transgressions. *Child Development*, 53, 403–412.

Nucci L., Turiel E., Encarnacion-Gawrych G. E. (1983). Social interactions and social concepts: analysis of morality and convention in the Virgin Islands. *Journal of Cross-Cultural Psychology*, 14, 469–487.

O'Brien B. S., Frick P. J. (1996). Reward dominance: associations with anxiety, conduct problems, and psychopathy in children. *Journal of Abnormal Child Psychology*, 24, 223–240.

O'Keefe J. (1991). The hippocampal cognitive map and navigational strategies. In J. Paillard (ed.), *Brain and Space*, pp. 273–295. Oxford: Oxford University Press.

Ogloff J. R., Wong S. (1990). Electrodermal and cardiovascular evidence of a coping response in psychopaths. *Criminal Justice and Behaviour*, 17, 231–245.

Panksepp J. (1998). *Affective Neuroscience: The foundations of human and animal emotions*. New York: Oxford University Press.

Pastor M. C., Molto J., Vila J., Lang P. J. (2003). Startle reflex modulation, affective ratings and autonomic reactivity in incarcerated Spanish psychopaths. *Psychophysiology*, 40, 934–938.

Patrick C. J. (1994). Emotion and psychopathy: startling new insights. *Psychophysiology*, 31, 319–330.

Patrick C. J., Bradley M. M., Lang P. J. (1993). Emotion in the criminal psychopath: startle reflex modulation. *Journal of Abnormal Psychology*, 102, 82–92.

Patrick C. J., Cuthbert B. N., Lang P. J. (1994). Emotion in the criminal psychopath: Fear image processing. *Journal of Abnormal Psychology*, 103, 523–534.

Patterson C. M., Newman J. P. (1993). Reflectivity and learning from aversive events: toward a psychological mechanism for the syndromes of disinhibition. *Psychological Review*, 100: 716–736.

Pennington B. F., Bennetto L. (1993). Main effects or transaction in the neuropsychology of conduct disorder? Commentary on "The neuropsychology of conduct disorder". *Development and Psychopathology*, 5, 153–164.

Pennington B. F., Ozonoff S. (1996). Executive functions and developmental psychopathology. *Journal of Child Psychology and Psychiatry*, 37, 51–87.

Perry D. G., Perry L. C. (1974). Denial of suffering in the victim as a stimulus to violence in aggressive boys. *Child Development*, 45, 55–62.

Perry D. G., Perry L. C., Rasmussen P. (1986). Cognitive social learning mediators of aggression. *Child Development*, 57, 700–711.

Petrides M. (1982). Motor conditional associative-learning after selective prefrontal lesions in the monkey. *Behavioural Brain Research*, 5, 407–413.

Petrides M. (1985). Deficits on conditional associative-learning tasks after frontal- and temporal-lobe lesions in man. *Neuropsychologia*, 23, 601–614.

Pham T. H. (1998). Psychometric evaluation of Hare's Psychopathy Checklist – Revised amongst a population of incarcerated Belgian prisoners. *L'Encephale*, 24, 435–441.

Phelps E. A., O'Connor K. J., Gatenby J. C., Gore J. C., Grillon C., Davis M. (2001). Activation of the left amygdala to a cognitive representation of fear. *Nature Neuroscience*, 4, 437–441.

Phillips M. L., Young A. W., Senior C., Brammer M., Andrews C., Calder A. J., et al. (1997). A specified neural substrate for perceiving facial expressions of disgust. *Nature*, 389, 495–498.

Phillips M. L., Young A. W., Scott S. K., Calder A. J., Andrew C., Giampietro V., et al. (1998). Neural responses to facial and vocal expressions of fear and disgust. *Proceedings of the Royal Society of London B*, 265, 1809–1817.

Pichot P. (1978). Psychopathic behavior: a historical review. In R. D. Hare, D. S. Schalling (eds), *Psychopathic Behavior: Approaches to research*. Chichester: John Wiley & Sons.

Pickens C. L., Saddoris M. P., Setlow B., Gallagher M., Holland P. C., Schoenbaum G. (2003). Different roles for orbitofrontal cortex and basolateral amygdala in a reinforcer devaluation task. *Journal of Neuroscience*, 23, 11078–11084.

Pine D. S., Shaffer D., Schonfeld I. S., Davies M. (1997). Minor physical anomalies: modifiers of environmental risks for psychiatric impairment? *Journal of the American Academy of Child and Adolescent Psychiatry*, 36, 395–403.

Pine D. S., Cohen E., Cohen P., Brook J. S. (2000). Social phobia and the persistence of conduct problems. *Journal of Child Psychology and Psychiatry*, 41(5), 657–665.

Piquero A., Tibbetts S. (1999). The impact of pre/perinatal disturbances and disadvantaged familial environment in predicting criminal offending. *Studies on Crime and Crime Prevention*, 8, 52–70.

Plotsky P. M., Meaney M. J. (1993). Early, postnatal experience alters hypothalamic corticotropin-releasing factor (CRF) mRNA, median eminence CRF content and stress-induced release in adult rats. *Brain Research. Molecular Brain Research*, 18, 195–200.

Poulin F., Boivin M. (2000). Reactive and proactive aggression: evidence of a two-factor model. *Psychological Assessment*, 12, 115–122.

Prather M. D., Lavenex P., Mauldin-Jourdain M. L., Mason W. A., Capitanio J. P., Mendoza S. P., Amaral D. G. (2001). Increased social fear and decreased fear of objects in monkeys with neonatal amygdala lesions. *Neuroscience*, 106(4), 653–658.

Price J. L. (2003). Comparative aspects of amygdala connectivity. *Annals of the New York Academy of Sciences*, 2003; 985, 50–58.

Quiggle N. L., Garber J., Panak W. F., Dodge K. A. (1992). Social information processing in aggressive and depressed children. *Child Development*, 63, 1305–1320.

Quirk G. J., Russo G. K., Barron J. L., Lebron K. (2000). The role of ventromedial prefrontal cortex in the recovery of extinguished fear. *Journal of Neuroscience*, 20, 6225–6231.

Rahman S., Sahakian B. J., Hodges J. R., Rogers R. D., Robbins T. W. (1999). Specific cognitive deficits in mild frontal variant frontotemporal dementia. *Brain*, 122, 1469–1493.

Raine A. (1993). *The Psychopathology of Crime: Criminal behavior as a clinical disorder*. San Diego, CA: Academic Press.

Raine A. (1997). *The Psychopathology of Crime*. New Yory: Academic Press.

Raine A. (2002a). Annotation: the role of prefrontal deficits, low autonomic arousal, and early health factors in the development of antisocial and aggressive behavior in children. *Journal of Child Psychology and Psychiatry*, 43, 417–434.

Raine A. (2002b). Biosocial studies of antisocial and violent behavior in children and adults: a review. *Journal of Abnormal Child Psychology*, 30, 311–326.

Raine A., Venables P. H. (1988). Enhanced P3 evoked potentials and longer recovery times in psychopaths. *Psychophysiology*, 25, 30–38.

Raine A., O'Brien M., Smiley N., Scerbo A., Chan C. J. (1990). Reduced lateralization in verbal dichotic listening in adolescent psychopaths. *Journal of Abnormal Psychology*, 99(3), 272–277.

Raine A., Brennan P., Mednick S. A. (1994a). Birth complications combined with early maternal rejection at age 1 year predispose to violent crime at age 18 years. *Archives of General Psychiatry*, 51, 984–988.

Raine A., Buchsbaum M. S., Stanley J., Lottenberg S., Abel L., Stoddard J. (1994b). Selective reductions in prefrontal glucose metabolism in murderers. *Biological Psychiatry*, 15, 365–373.

Raine A., Venables P. H., Williams M. (1996). Better autonomic conditioning and faster electrodermal half-recovery time at age 15 years as possible protective factors against crime at age 29 years. *Developmental Psychology*, 32, 624–630.

Raine A., Buchsbaum M. S., LaCasse L. (1997). Brain abnormalities in murderers indicated by positron emission tomography. *Biological Psychiatry*, 42, 495–508.

Raine A., Meloy J. R., Birhle S., Stoddard J., LaCasse L., Buchsbaum M. S. (1998a). Reduced prefrontal and increased subcortical brain functioning assessed using positron emission tomography in predatory and affective murderers. *Behaviour Science and Law*, 16, 319–332.

Raine A., Phil D., Stoddard J., Bihrle S., Buchsbaum M. (1998b). Prefrontal glucose deficits in murderers lacking psychosocial deprivation. *Neuropsychiatry, Neuropsychology, and Behavioral Neurology*, 11(1), 1–7.

Raine A., Lencz T., Bihrle S., LaCasse L., Colletti P. (2000). Reduced prefrontal gray matter volume and reduced autonomic activity in antisocial personality disorder. *Archives of General Psychiatry*, 57, 119–127.

Ramboz S., Saudou F., Amara D. A., Belzung C., Segu L., Misslin R., Buhot M. C., Hen R. (1996). 5-HT1B receptor knock out – behavioral consequences. *Behavioural Brain Research*, 73, 305–312.

Rapport L. J., Van Voorhis A., Tzelepis A., Friedman S. R. (2001). Executive functioning in adult attention-deficit hyperactivity disorder. *Clinical Neuropsychology*, 15(4), 479–491.

Rees G., Frith C. D., Lavie N. (1997). Modulating irrelevant motion perception by varying attentional load in an unrelated task. *Science*, 278(5343), 1616–1619.

Reeve W. V., Schandler S. L. (2001). Frontal lobe functioning in adolescents with attention deficit hyperactivity disorder. *Adolescence*, 36(144), 749–765.

Rhee S. H., Waldman I. D. (2002). Genetic and environmental influences on antisocial behavior: a meta-analysis of twin and adoption studies. *Psychological Bulletin*, 128, 490–529.

Rice G. E. (1965). Aiding responses in rats: not in guinea pigs. In *Proceedings of the Annual Convention of the American Psychological Association*, pp. 105–106.

Rice G. E., Gainer P. (1962). "Altruism" in the albino rat. *Journal of Comparative and Physiological Psychology*, 55(1), 123–125.

Richell R. A., Mitchell D. G., Newman C., Leonard A., Baron-Cohen S., Blair R. J. (2003). Theory of mind and psychopathy: can psychopathic individuals read the "language of the eyes"? *Neuropsychologia*, 41, 523–526.

Richell R. A., Mitchell D. G. V., Peschardt K. S., Winston J. S., Leonard A., Dolan R. J., et al. (in press). Trust and distrust: the perception of trustworthiness of faces in psychopathic and non-psychopathic offenders. *Personality and Individual Differences*.

Roberts A. C., Robbins T. W., Weiskrantz L. (1998). *The Prefrontal Cortex: Executive and cognitive functions*. Oxford: Oxford University Press.

Robins L. N. (1966). *Deviant Children Grow Up*. Baltimore, MD: Williams & Wilkins.

Robins L. N., Tipp J., Pryzbeck T. (1991). Antisocial personality. In L. N. Robins, D. A. Regier (eds), *Psychiatric Disorders in North America*. New York: Free Press.

Robinson G., Blair J., Cipolotti L. (1998). Dynamic aphasia: an inability to select between competing verbal responses? *Brain*, 121, 77–89.

Rogeness G. A., Cepeda C., Macedo C. A., Fischer C., Harris W. R. (1990a). Differences in heart rate and blood pressure in children with conduct disorder, major depression, and separation anxiety. *Psychiatry Research*, 33, 199–206.

Rogeness G. A., Javors M. A., Mass J. W., Macedo C. A. (1990b). Catecholamines and diagnoses in children. *Journal of the American Academy of Child and Adolescent Psychiatry*, 29, 234–241.

Rogers R. D., Robbins T. W. (2001). Investigating the neurocognitive deficits associated with chronic drug misuse. *Current Opinions in Neurobiology*, 11, 250–257.

Rogers R. D., Lancaster M., Wakeley J., Bhagwagar Z. (2004). Effects of beta-adrenoceptor blockade on components of human decision-making. *Psychopharmacology*, 172, 157–164.

Roland E., Idsoe T. (1995). Aggression and bullying. *Aggressive Behavior*, 27, 446–462.

Rolls E. T. (1997). The orbitofrontal cortex. *Philosophical Transactions of the Royal Society B*, 351, 1433–1443.

Rolls E. T. (2000). The orbitofrontal cortex and reward. *Cerebral Cortex*, 10, 284–294.

Rolls E. T., Hornak J., Wade D., McGrath J. (1994). Emotion-related learning in patients with social and emotional changes associated with frontal lobe damage. *Journal of Neurology, Neurosurgery, and Psychiatry*, 57, 1518–1524.

Roth R. M., Flashman L. A., Saykin A. J., McAllister T. W., Vidaver R. (2004). Apathy in schizophrenia: reduced frontal lobe volume and neuropsychological deficits. *American Journal of Psychiatry*, 161(1), 157–159.

Rothbart M., Ahadi S., Hershey K. L. (1994). Temperament an social behaviour in children. *Merrill-Palmer Quarterly*, 40, 21–39.

Roussy S., Toupin J. (2000). Behavioral inhibition deficits in juvenile psychopaths. *Aggressive Behavior*, 26, 413–424.

Rumsey J. M., Rapoport J. L., Sceery W. R. (1985). Autistic children as adults: psychiatric, social, and behavioral outcomes. *Journal of the American Academy of Child Psychiatry*, 24(4), 465–473.

Russo M. F., Beidel D. C. (1993). Co-morbidity of childhood anxiety and externlizing disorders: prevalence, associated characteristics, and validation issues. *Clinical Psychology Review*, 14, 199–221.

Salekin R. T., Rogers R., Sewell W. (1997). Construct validity of psychopathy in a female offender sample: a multitrait-multimethod evaluation. *Journal of Abnormal Psychology*, 106(4), 576–585.

Salekin R. T., Rogers R., Ustad K. L., Sewell K. W. (1998). Psychopathy and recidivism among female inmates. *Law and Human Behavior*, 22, 109–128.

Saltaris C. (2002). Psychopathy in juvenile offenders: can temperament and attachment be considered as robust developmental precursors? *Clinical Psychology Review*, 22, 729–752.

Samuels J. F., Nestadt G., Romanoski A. J., Folstein M. F., McHugh P. R. (1994). DSM-III personality disorders in the community. *American Journal of Psychiatry*, 151(7), 1055–1062.

Scerbo A., Raine A., O'Brien M., Chan C. J., Rhee C., Smiley N. (1990). Reward dominance and passive avoidance learning in adolescent psychopaths. *Journal of Abnormal Child Psychology*, 18(4), 451–463.

Schmauk P. J. (1970). Punishment, arousal, and avoidance learning in psychopaths. *Journal of Abnormal Psychology*, 76, 325–335.

Schmitt W. A., Newman J. P. (1999). Are all psychopathic individuals low-anxious? *Journal of Abnormal Psychology*, 108, 353–358.

Schneider F., Gur R. C., Gur R. E., Muenz L. R. (1994). Standardized mood induction with happy and sad facial expression. *Psychiatry Research*, 51, 19–31.

Schneider F., Weiss U., Kessler C., Muller-Gartner H. W., Posse S., Salloum J. B., Grodd W., Himmelmann F., Gaebel W., Birbaumer N. (1999). Subcortical correlates of differential classical conditioning of aversive emotional reactions in social phobia. *Biological Psychiatry*, 45(7), 863–871.

Schneider F., Habel U., Kessler C., Posse S., Grodd W., Muller-Gartner H. W. (2000). Functional imaging of conditioned aversive emotional responses in antisocial personality disorder. *Neuropsychobiology*, 42(4), 192–201.

Schoenbaum G., Chiba A. A., Gallagher M. (1999). Neural encoding in orbitofrontal cortex and basolateral amygdala during olfactory discrimination learning. *Journal of Neuroscience*, 19, 1876–1884.

Schoenbaum G., Nugent S. L., Saddoris M. P., Setlow B. (2002). Orbitofrontal lesions in rats impair reversal but not aquisition of go, no-go odor discriminations. *Neuroreport*, 13, 885–890.

Schultz R. T., Grelotti D. J., Klin A., Kleinman J., Van der Gaag C., Marois R., Skudlarski P. (2003). The role of the fusiform face area in social cognition: implications for the pathobiology of autism. *Philosophical Transactions of the Royal Society of London B*, 358(1430), 415–427.

Serin R. C., Amos N. L. (1995). The role of psychopathy in the assessment of dangerousness. *International Journal of Law and Psychiatry*, 18, 231–238.

Shaikh M. B., De Lanerolle N. C., Siegel A. (1997). Serotonin 5-HT1A and 5-HT2/1C receptors in the midbrain periaqueductal gray differentially modulate defensive rage behavior elicited from the medial hypothalamus of the cat. *Brain Research*, 765, 198–207.

Shallice T., Burgess P. W., Frith C. D. (1991). Can the neuropsychological case-study approach be applied to schizophrenia? *Psychological Medicine*, 21, 661–673.

Shih J. C., Chen K., Ridd M. J. (1999). Monoamine oxidase: from genes to behavior. *Annual Review of Neuroscience*, 22, 197–217.

Shweder R. A., Mahapatra M., Miller J. G. (1987). Culture and moral development. In J. Kagan, S. Lamb (eds), *The Emergence of Morality in Young Children*, pp. 1–83. Chicago, IL: University of Chicago Press.

Silva J. A., Derecho D. V., Leong G. B., Weinstock R., Ferrari M. M. (2001). A classification of psychological factors leading to violent behavior in posttraumatic stress disorder. *Journal of Forensic Science*, 46(2), 309–316.

Silverthorn P., Frick P. J. (1999). Developmental pathways to antisocial behavior: the delayed-onset pathway in girls. *Developmental Psychopathology*, 11(1), 101–126.

Smetana J. G. (1981). Preschool children's conceptions of moral and social rules. *Child Development*, 52, 1333–1336.

Smetana J. G. (1985). Preschool children's conceptions of transgressions: the effects of varying moral and conventional domain-related attributes. *Developmental Psychology*, 21, 18–29.

Smetana J. G. (1993). Understanding of social rules. In M. Bennett (ed.), *The Child as Psychologist: An introduction to the development of social cognition*, pp. 111–141. New York: Harvester Wheatsheaf.

Smetana J. G., Braeges J. L. (1990). The development of toddlers' moral and conventional judgments. *Merrill-Palmer Quarterly*, 36, 329–346.

Smith S. S., Newman J. P. (1990). Alcohol and drug abuse-dependence disorders in psychopathic and nonpsychopathic criminal offenders. *Journal of Abnormal Psychology*, 99, 430–439.

Smith S. S., Arnett P. A., Newman J. P. (1992). Neuropsychological differentiation of psychopathic and nonpsychopathic criminal offenders. *Personality and Individual Differences*, 13(11), 1233–1243.

Soderstrom H., Tullberg M., Wikkelso C., Ekholm S., Forsman A. (2000). Reduced regional cerebral blood flow in non-psychotic violent offenders. *Psychiatry Research*, 98(1), 29–41.

Soderstrom H., Hultin L., Tullberg M., Wikkelso C., Ekholm S., Forsman A. (2002). Reduced frontotemporal perfusion in psychopathic personality. *Psychiatry Research*, 114(2), 81–94.

Song M., Smetana J. G., Kim S. Y. (1987). Korean children's conceptions of moral and conventional transgressions. *Developmental Psychology*, 23, 577–582.

Sparks B. F., Friedman S. D., Shaw D. W., Aylward E. H., Echelard D., Artru A. A., Maravilla K. R., Giedd J. N., Munson J., Dawson G., Dager S. R. (2002). Brain structural abnormalities in young children with autism spectrum disorder. *Neurology*, 59(2), 184–192.

Sprengelmeyer R., Rausch M., Eysel U. T., Przuntek H. (1998). Neural structures associated with the recognition of facial basic emotions. *Proceedings of the Royal Society of London B*, 265, 1927–1931.

Stanton M. E., Gutierrez Y. R., Levine S. (1988). Maternal deprivation potentiates pituitary-adrenal stress responses in infant rats. *Behavioral Neuroscience*, 102, 692–700.

Steiner H., Garcia I. G., Matthews Z. (1997). Posttraumatic stress disorder in incarcerated juvenile delinquents. *Journal of the American Academy of Child and Adolescent Psychiatry*, 36, 357–365.

Stevens D., Charman T., Blair R. J. R. (2001). Recognition of emotion in facial expressions and vocal tones in children with psychopathic tendencies. *Journal of Genetic Psychology*, 162(2), 201–211.

Stoddart T., Turiel E. (1985). Children's concepts of cross-gender activities. *Child Development*, 56, 1241–1252.

Stone V. E., Baron-Cohen S., Calder A., Keane J., Young A. (2003). Acquired theory of mind impairments in individuals with bilateral amygdala lesions. *Neuropsychologia*, 41, 209–220.

Strauss E. (1983). Perception of emotional words. *Neuropsychologia*, 21, 99–103.

Stroop J. R. (1935). Studies of interference in serial verbal reactions. *Journal of Experimental Psychology*, 18, 643–662.

Stuss D. T., Benson D. F. (1986). *The Frontal Lobes*. New York: Raven Press.

Sutker P. B. (1970). Vicarious conditioning and sociopathy. *Journal of Abnormal Psychology*, 76, 380–386.

Swann A. C. (2003). Neuroreceptor mechanisms of aggression and its treatment. *Journal of Clinical Psychiatry*, 64(Suppl 4), 26–35.

Swanson M. C., Bland R. C., Newman S. C. (1994). Antisocial personality disorders. *Acta Psychiatrica Scandinavica*, 376, 63–70.

Tanaka M., Yoshida M., Emoto H., Ishii H. (2000). Noradrenaline systems in the hypothalamus, amygdala and locus coeruleus are involved in the provocation of anxiety: basic studies. *European Journal of Pharmacology*, 405(1–3), 397–406.

Taylor E. A., Schachar R., Thorley G., Wieselberg M. (1986). Conduct disorder and hyperactivity: I. Separation of hyperactivity and antisocial conduct in British child psychiatric patients. *British Journal of Psychiatry*, 149, 760–767.

Thornquist M. H., Zuckerman M. (1995). Psychopathy, passive-avoidance learning and basic dimensions of personality. *Personality and Individual Differences*, 19(4), 525–534.

Tiihonen J., Hodgins S., Vaurio O., Laakso M., Repo E., Soininen H., Aronen H. J., Nieminen P., Savolainen L. (2000). Amygdaloid volume loss in psychopathy. *Society for Neuroscience Abstracts*, 2017.

Tomasson K., Vaglum P. (2000). Antisocial addicts: the importance of additional axis I disorders for the 28-month outcome. *European Psychiatry*, 15(8), 443–449.

Tomb I., Hauser M., Deldin P., Caramazza A. (2002). Do somatic markers mediate decisions on the gambling task? *Nature Neuroscience*, 5(11), 1103–1104; author reply 1104.

Tranel D., Damasio H. (1994). Neuroanatomical correlates of electrodermal skin conductance responses. *Psychophysiology*, 31, 427–438.

Trasler G. B. (1973). Criminal behaviour. In H. J. Eysenck (ed.), *Handbook of Abnormal Psychology*. London: Pitman.

Trasler G. B. (1978). Relations between psychopathy and persistent criminality – methodological and theoretical issues. In R. D. Hare, D. S. Schalling (eds), *Psychopathic Behaviour: Approaches to research*. Chichester: John Wiley & Sons.

Tremblay L., Schultz W. (1999). Relative reward preference in primate orbitofrontal cortex. *Nature*, 398, 704–708.

Trevethan S., Walker L. J. (1989). Hypothetical versus real-life moral reasoning among psychopathic and delinquent youth. *Development and Psychopathology*, 1, 91–103.

Triesman A. M., Gormican S. (1988). Feature analysis in early vision: evidence from search asymmetries. *Psychological Review*, 95, 15–48.

Turiel E. (1983). *The Development of Social Knowledge: Morality and convention*. Cambridge: Cambridge University Press.

Turiel E., Killen M., Helwig C. C. (1987). Morality: its structure, functions, and vagaries. In S. Lamb (ed.), *The Emergence of Morality in Young Children*, pp. 155–245. Chicago, IL: University of Chicago Press.

Tversky A., Kahneman D. (1981). The framing of decisions and the psychology of choice. *Science*, 211, 453–458.

Usher M., Cohen J. D. (1999). Short-term memory and selection processes in a frontal-lobe model. In D. Heinke, G. W. Humphries, A. Olsen (eds), *Connectionist models in Cognitive Neuroscience*, pp. 78–91. London: Springer-Verlag.

Vandenbergh D. J., Persico A. M., Hawkins A. L., Griffin C. A., Li X., Jabs E. W., et al. (1992). Human dopamine transporter gene (DAT1) maps to chromosome 5p15. 3 and displays a VNTR. *Genomics*, 14, 1104–1106.

Veit R., Flor H., Erb M., Hermann C., Lotze M., Grodd W., Birbaumer N. (2002). Brain circuits involved in emotional learning in antisocial behavior and social phobia in humans. *Neuroscience Letters*, 328(3), 233–236.

Verona E., Patrick C. J., Joiner T. E. (2001). Psychopathy, antisocial personality, and suicide risk. *Journal of Abnormal Psychology*, 110(3), 462–470.

Verona E., Curtin J. J., Patrick C. J., Bradley M. M., Lang P. J. (2004). Psychopathy and physiological response to emotionally evocative sounds. *Journal of Abnormal Psychology*, 113, 99–108.

Viding E., Blair R. J. R., Moffitt T. E., Plomin R. (submitted). Psychopathic syndrome indexes strong genetic risk for antisocial behaviour in 7-year-olds. *Journal of Child Psychology and Psychiatry*.

Virkkunen M., De Jong J., Bartko J., Linnoila M. (1989). Psychobiological concomitants of history of suicide attempts among violent offenders and impulsive fire setters. *Archives of General Psychiatry*, 46, 604–606.

Vitaro F., Gendreau P. L., Tremblay R. E., Oligny P. (1998). Reactive and proactive aggression differentially predict later conduct problems. *Journal of Child Psychology and Psychiatry*, 39, 377–385.

Vitaro F., Brendgen M., Tremblay R. E. (2002). Reactively and proactively aggressive children: antecedent and subsequent characteristics. *Journal of Child Psychology and Psychiatry*, 43, 495–505.

Vitiello B., Stoff D. M. (1997). Subtypes of aggression and their relevance to child psychiatry. *Journal of the American Academy of Child and Adolescent Psychiatry*, 36, 307–315.

Volavka J. (1995). *Neurobiology of Violence*. Washington, DC: American Psychiatric Press.

Volkow N. D., Tancredi L. (1987). Neural substrates of violent behaviour. A preliminary study with positron emission tomography. *British Journal of Psychiatry*, 151, 668–673.

Volkow N. D., Tancredi L. R., Grant C., Gillespie H., Valentine A., Mullan N., Wang G. J., Hollister L. (1995). Brain glucose metabolism in violent psychiatric patients: a preliminary study. *Psychiatry Research*, 61(4), 243–253.

Vuilleumier P., Armony J. L., Driver J., Dolan R. J. (2001). Effects of attention and emotion on face processing in the human brain: an event-related fMRI study. *Neuron*, 30, 829–841.

Vuilleumier P., Armony J. L., Driver J., Dolan R. J. (2003). Distinct spatial frequency sensitivities for processing faces and emotional expressions. *Nature Neuroscience, 6*, 624–631.

Vyas A., Mitra R., Shankaranarayana Rao B. S., Chattarji S. (2002). Chronic stress induces contrasting patterns of dendritic remodeling in hippocampal and amygdaloid neurons. *Journal of Neuroscience, 22*, 6810–6818.

Walsh E., Buchanan A., Fahy T. (2002). Violence and schizophrenia: examining the evidence. *British Journal of Psychiatry, 180*, 490–495.

Widom C. S. (1992). *The Cycle of Violence*. Washington, DC: US Department of Justice, Office of Justice Programs, National Institute of Justice.

Williams D., Stott C. M., Goodyer I. M., Sahakian B. J. (2000). Specific language impairment with or without hyperactivity: neuropsychological evidence for frontostriatal dysfunction. *Developmental Medicine and Child Neurology, 42*(6), 368–375.

Williamson S., Hare R. D., Wong S. (1987). Violence: criminal psychopaths and their victims. *Canadian Journal of Behavioral Science, 19*, 454–462.

Williamson S., Harpur T. J., Hare R. D. (1991). Abnormal processing of affective words by psychopaths. *Psychophysiology, 28*, 260–273.

Winston J. S., Strange B. A., O'Doherty J., Dolan R. J. (2002). Automatic and intentional brain responses during evaluation of trustworthiness of faces. *Nature Neuroscience, 5*, 277–283.

Wodushe T. R., Neumann C. S. (2003). Inhibitory capacity in adults with symptoms of attention deficit/hyperactivity disorder (ADHD). *Archives of Clinical Neuropsychology, 18*(3), 317–330.

Wolfgang M. E., Figlio R. M., Sellin T. (1972). *Delinquency in a Birth Cohort*. Chicago, IL: Chicago University Press.

Wolfgang M. E., Thornberry T. P., Figlio R. M. (1987). *From Boy to Man, From Delinquency to Crime*. Chicago, IL: Chicago University Press.

Wong M., Fenwick P., Fenton G., Lumsden J., Maisey M., Stevens J. (1997). Repetitive and non-repetitive violent offending behaviour in male patients in a maximum security mental hospital – clinical and neuroimaging findings. *Medicine, Science and Law, 37*(2), 150–160.

Wootton J. M., Frick P. J., Shelton K. K., Silverthorn P. (1997). Ineffective parenting and childhood conduct problems: the moderating role of callous – unemotional traits. *Journal of Consulting and Clinical Psychology, 65*, 292–300.

Zoccolillo M. (1992). Co-occurrence of conduct disorder and its adult outcomes with depressive and anxiety disorders: a review. *Journal of the American Academy of Child and Adolescent Psychiatry, 31*(3), 547–556.

SUBJECT INDEX

AUTHOR INDEX